Herbert J. Walberg
Andrew T. Kopan
Editors

RETHINKING
URBAN
EDUCATION

Jossey-Bass Inc., Publishers
San Francisco • Washington • London • 1972

RETHINKING URBAN EDUCATION
A Sourcebook of Contemporary Issues
     Herbert J. Walberg and Andrew T. Kopan, Editors

Copyright © 1972 by Jossey-Bass, Inc., Publishers

Published and copyrighted in Great Britain by
Jossey-Bass, Inc., Publishers
3, Henrietta Street
London W.C.2

Library of Congress Catalogue Card Number LC 72-83962

International Standard Book Number ISBN 0-87589-140-3

Manufactured in the United States of America

JACKET DESIGN BY WILLI BAUM

FIRST EDITION

Code 7225

Preface

During the first thirty years of this century William James, John Dewey, and other pragmatic philosophers, discontented with the traditional wisdom of schoolmen, argued for a scientific grounding of educational policy in psychology. Their writing shows a sensitive, integrative grasp of both the scientific and humanistic foundations of education. At the same time, E. L. Thorndike began developing scientific methods for the psychological study of the educational process. During the second third of the century other scholars interested in education drew increasingly upon the human sciences—first psychology, then sociology, later economics and political science, and finally systems analysis. The humanistic foundations, history, and philosophy of education, though still taught to education students, suffered a decline; their content seemed dreary and unrelated to contemporary problems; and scholars in these areas, unlike James and Dewey, lost touch with the accumulating developments in the human sciences related to education. Scientists were also losing touch with one another's work. Within psychology, for example, specialty areas, journals, and societies proliferated; a behaviorist would have difficulty reading an article on psychometrics, let alone a sociological treatise on educational stratification.

45050

It may no longer be possible for a scholar to master all fields of inquiry that have important bearings on the study of education, but it is important for him to understand the development of educational research from a variety of disciplinary perspectives. One way of attempting to promote such understanding is exemplified in *Rethinking Urban Education:* Scholars advancing knowledge within their own specialty have written chapters that focus on a single contemporary problem. Having the original chapters in one volume enables the reader to analyze the methods of inquiry within each discipline as well as to see the substantive and practical implications that can be drawn. We hope that by viewing the complexity of the problem from the many perspectives represented in this volume, the educational scholar can enrich his own research and the practitioner can improve urban education.

Following the historical emergence of disciplines that have successively and cumulatively influenced education in this century, *Rethinking Urban Education* is organized in six parts: Psychological Perspectives, Evaluation Perspectives, Sociological Perspectives, Systems Perspectives, Historical Perspectives, and Philosophical Perspectives. In Parts One and Two, the authors outline the progress made since the early work of Thorndike on the psychology of school subjects and the evaluation of learning. Parts Three and Four examine the sociology of urban education and the interacting political and economic forces that determine its policy and operation. Parts Five and Six treat the historical and philosophical foundations of education; these parts reveal how the human sciences are beginning to influence humanistic scholarship in education and in turn how humanistic scholarship can throw critical light on scientific inquiry. Finally, Part Seven, Concluding Perspectives, presents an assessment of the present crisis in urban education, identifying factors that have contributed to it and suggesting remedies to ameliorate it. This part concludes with a biography of the person in whose honor these chapters have been written, Robert J. Havighurst.

In spite of the diversity of issues raised and implications drawn by the chapter authors, one grand theme seems to pervade nearly all the chapters—adaptation to cultural and individual differences. As a social psychologist of great wisdom once noted, each person is like all persons in some respects, like some persons in some respects, and like no other person in some respects. The authors, despite their various scientific, humanistic, and practical perspectives, are saying there can be no universal system, no one best school, no perfect teacher because each ethnic and social group—indeed, each individual—presents the urban educator with a unique challenge.

Rethinking Urban Education developed from an idea that originated with the University of Chicago chapter of Phi Delta Kappa, a national professional fraternity for men in education, during the autumn of 1970. It was intended as a tribute to a distinguished Phi Delta Kappa member, who despite his many activities found time to serve the chapter and the fraternity in various capacities. The 1970–1971 lecture series of the chapter was built around the theme "Rethinking Urban Education," an area in which Professor Havighurst has excelled.

Educational scholars and practitioners were invited to the campus to address the academic community on the theory and practice of urban education. Specific issues were discussed under three broad categories: urban educational innovations, evaluation of urban education, and society and urban education. Several of these original papers are included in *Rethinking Urban Education*.

The program was climaxed by the presentation of the Educator of the Year award to Professor Havighurst at the annual dinner on May 22, 1971, at the Center for Continuing Education at the university. At this event he also received a citation from the office of the superintendent of public instruction of Illinois in recognition of his educational contributions to the state.

The program and the preparation of *Rethinking Urban Education* were made possible, in part, by the award of project funds to the chapter by District V of Phi Delta Kappa. Grateful acknowledgment for the procurement of these funds is made to Lowell C. Rose and H. A. O'Connor of Phi Delta Kappa headquarters. Acknowledgment is made of the DePaul University colloquium "Crisis in Urban Education," held in Chicago on November 13, 1970, in which several of the chapters in this volume were first presented. Appreciation is also extended to the Urban Educational Research Program of the University of Illinois at Chicago Circle for helping to support the preparation of this volume. All proceeds from this volume will accrue to the University of Chicago chapter of Phi Delta Kappa for the establishment of fellowship programs in honor of Professor Havighurst.

We were fortunate in being able to attract a distinguished group of contributors, whose wisdom has added significant dimensions to *Rethinking Urban Education*. We express deep appreciation for their participation. The editors also express gratitude to the participants in the 1970–1971 lectureship program: Nathaniel Blackman, Jr., principal, Chicago High School of Metropolitan Studies; Thomas Wilson, director Education Division, Urban Research Corporation of Chicago; Professors Allison Davis, John R. Ginther, and Robert L. McCaul of the University of Chicago; Professors Maurice Eash and Robert M. Rippey of the University of Illinois at Chicago Circle; Professors Barney M. Berlin of Loyola University and Hans A. Schieser of DePaul University; Superintendents Henry C. Springs, Jr., William Rohan, and Otho M. Robinson, along with Principal Myron B. Kuropas, all of the Chicago public schools. Appreciation is extended to the University of Chicago chapter of Phi Delta Kappa and its officers and members of the special committee, whose efforts made the program a reality: Thomas C. Lelon, Thomas J. Slocum, Hugh W. Crarey, Edward Levine, Philip R. Garrett, and Ettore Grimaldi.

Any undertaking of this nature obviously requires some division of labor. Each author prepared the particular chapter that bears his name. The editors assumed responsibility for integrating manuscripts into the overall format of the book as well as editing the chapters, and any errors committed in the revision process are solely ours.

Finally, we convey our thanks to the most significant persons in our lives—Alice Kopan and Madoka Walberg—our best critics, most devoted supporters, and colleagues in every endeavor.

Chicago
September 1972

Herbert J. Walberg
Andrew T. Kopan

Contents

Contributors

ARMIN BECK, *professor of education, University of Illinois at Chicago Circle*

BRUNO BETTELHEIM, *Stella M. Rowley Distinguished Service Professor of Education, University of Chicago*

JAMES H. BLOCK, *professor of education, University of California, Santa Barbara*

FRANCIS S. CHASE, *professor emeritus and educational consultant, University of Chicago*

VICTOR G. CICIRELLI, *professor of human development, Department of Child Development and Family Life, Purdue University*

CARL A. CLARK, *professor and chairman, Department of Psychology, Chicago State University*

DAVID K. COHEN, *professor of education and director, Center for Educational Policy Research, Harvard University*

JAMES S. COLEMAN, *professor of social relations, Johns Hopkins University*

RUSSELL C. DOLL, *professor of education, University of Missouri—Kansas City*

MAURICE J. EASH, *director, Office of Evaluation Research, College of Education, University of Illinois at Chicago Circle*

ANDREW M. GREELEY, *director, Center for the Study of American Pluralism, National Opinion Research Center, University of Chicago*

ROBERT J. HAVIGHURST, *professor of education and human development, University of Chicago*

CYRIL O. HOULE, *professor of education, University of Chicago*

ANDREW T. KOPAN, *professor and chairman, Department of Educational Foundations, School of Education, DePaul University*

LLOYD J. LEAVERTON, *director, Psycholinguistics Project, Chicago Board of Education*

DANIEL U. LEVINE, *professor of education, University of Missouri—Kansas City*

ROBERT L. McCAUL, *professor of education, University of Chicago*

S. M. MILLER, *professor of sociology and education, New York University*

VAN CLEVE MORRIS, *dean, College of Education, University of Illinois at Chicago Circle*

JAMES T. NAPOLITAN, *doctoral candidate in psychology, University of Illinois at Chicago Circle*

ROBERT RIPPEY, *professor, University of Illinois at Chicago Circle*

NANCY H. ST. JOHN, *fellow, Radcliffe Institute, Harvard University*

HANS A. SCHIESER, *professor of education, DePaul University*

BRUNO STEIN, *professor of economics, New York University*

SUSAN S. STODOLSKY, *professor, Department of Education and Committee on Human Development, University of Chicago*

DAVID TYACK, *professor of education and history, Stanford University*

HERBERT J. WALBERG, *research professor of urban education, University of Illinois at Chicago Circle*

WARD WELDON, *professor, University of Illinois at Chicago Circle*

EDWARD WYNNE, *professor, College of Education, University of Illinois at Chicago Circle*

Rethinking
Urban Education

A Sourcebook of
Contemporary Issues

*Published by Jossey-Bass,
in collaboration with
Phi Delta Kappa*

*In honor of Robert J. Havighurst,
University of Chicago*

PART I

Psychological Perspectives

෧෧෧ ෧෧෧ ෧෧෧ ෧෧෧ ෧෧෧ ෧෧෧ ෧෧෧ ෧෧෧

What is the psychology of the urban teacher? How can he use rewards and structure in his classroom to promote maximum growth in his students? What are the distinctive characteristics of urban children? How can education be adapted to meet cultural differences? Such questions as these are raised in the following chapters.

Bettelheim, in the first selection, distinguishes socialization from book learning. The school, he insists, must provide compensatory socialization for underprivileged children, and the teacher must recognize that shouting and disturbance are efforts to contribute and the expressions of a need for adult attention. Despite his good intentions, the teacher often finds it difficult to transcend his own middle-class values; to understand his students, he must first understand his own feelings.

Doll summarizes recent criticism of urban teachers: their lack of skills and appropriate materials, their cultural naïveté, their alienation. The discrepancy between what they see as the appropriate

1

"teacher" role and what they actually do brings about their sense of failure in highly problem-oriented schools. However, according to Doll, it is not the teachers but "societal and institutional deficiencies [that] have created situations in which the best of teachers fail." Therefore, programs aimed at assisting teachers should somehow increase these teachers' feelings of success—partly through strengthening their self-concepts. Alternative schools, better curricula, and more effective school organization are also required.

Clark, a reinforcement theorist, points to the punitive character of the urban classroom and suggests a highly specific way to improve teaching—by increasing and distributing rewards to all children for accomplishments. He describes a series of experimental studies in which verbal praise had powerful effects on achievement and on attitudes toward learning. Rewards, or "secondary reinforcement" as psychologists put it, make parents as well as teachers more effective in helping the inner-city child. Thus, the home and classroom can amplify one another.

Cicirelli describes three types of educational models for the disadvantaged. *Deficit models* hold that the urban child comes to school lacking environmental, nutritional, or genetic prerequisites. *School-disparity models* hold that the child is not inferior but culturally different and that institutional prejudice prevents him from learning. *Deactualization models* are humanistic and hold that experience is unique and cannot be objectively evaluated. All three models seem to be converging on the notion of individualized instruction.

Leaverton asks how language arts can be taught to the culturally different child. Some research has shown that the standard "elaborated" language code enables children to cogitate effectively and to solve complex problems; therefore, it is sometimes contended, children have a distinct disadvantage if they do not know, or are not taught, standard English. Others, however, believe that the imposition of standard English on the urban child destroys his self-concept. Leaverton's research illustrates a third position, the combination of standard and nonstandard forms in a single effective reading series.

CHAPTER 1

Middle-Class Teacher and Lower-Class Child

Bruno Bettelheim

$\textcircled{3}\textcircled{3}\textcircled{3}\textcircled{3}\textcircled{3}\textcircled{3}\textcircled{3}\textcircled{3}$

A few years ago I met with several groups of grade school teachers, in an effort to help them with their tasks in schools populated mainly by lower-class black children. Each group numbered some twenty teachers at the beginning of the ten-week session; about fifteen at the end. Most of the teachers were female. The meetings were very informal and were restricted to class-

This chapter is based on one segment of a series of studies (coordinated by Professor Morris Janowitz, Division of Social Sciences, University of Chicago) dealing with the application of social science concepts to youth problems. These studies were sponsored by training grant No. 62216 from the Office of Juvenile Delinquency and Youth Development, Welfare Administration, U.S. Department of Health, Education, and Welfare, in cooperation with the President's Committee on Juvenile Delinquency and Youth Crime.

room teachers only, though once or twice the local district superintendent attended.

Teachers ranged from beginners with only one or two years in the field to very experienced teachers. By chance, about equal numbers of white and black teachers were present in each group. As far as attitudes to the culturally deprived black children they teach were concerned, there was little difference between white and black teachers; nor was there any difference in their ability to analyze problems affecting these children or in their eagerness to deal with these problems constructively.

There was, however, a marked difference in the reactions of white and a few black teachers to what the meetings forced them to realize about themselves. During the first few sessions of each group, whenever a white teacher brought up some difficulties she had encountered with her black pupils, some black teachers in more or less veiled form would accuse the white teacher of creating her own difficulties because she did not accept children who were black. As the meetings proceeded, however, it became ever more apparent that the inner attitudes of both white and black teachers toward their pupils were quite similar; the real problem then became obvious. It was the clash between the teacher's middle-class attitudes and those of her lower-class pupils; it was her rejection of their lower-class behavior and had nothing to do with their or her color. As this realization was forced on them by what transpired at the meetings, those few black teachers who were most militant in believing they saw bias among the white teachers stopped attending. Their number was never more than three or four. The rest of the teachers attended regularly; and each group asked for a continuation when the series of ten meetings came to an end. In two groups this could be arranged, and we then met some five additional times.

At the first meeting of each group I tried briefly to say what such meetings can and what they cannot do. I could not possibly tell a teacher what to do or how to handle a particular child in a particular school situation. Instead, my purpose was to help her develop a certain way of thinking about these children and the problems she encounters with them; a method of analyzing problems; in short, an approach that might be called clinical. This I would try to teach by helping her think through any situation she was confronted with in her daily teaching experience and which she cared to discuss.

Instead of presenting a résumé of what transpired in these meetings, I shall use some abbreviated examples to illustrate what we talked about. From this the reader may form his own conclusions about what such a clinical approach can contribute to improving the education of underprivileged children in our big-city schools.

One recurrent problem was the teacher's anxiety that if she were to take time away from the teaching of subject matter, she would be falling down on her job. Despite the most elaborate lip service to the fact that these children need socialization more than anything else, and though convinced that it is the school's task to socialize them, these teachers became anxious and resistant whenever it came to letting the momentary learning task ride for a while to attend to the emotional or social needs of these children. It took several meetings and discussions of this problem in its various guises before the teachers could begin to act in line with their stated convictions. An example may illustrate.

One teacher said, "If you have just one person that is causing trouble, how can you consistently take time away from the rest?" I asked her to give an example. "Well," she said, "I have one boy in my class and he's a show-off. He likes a lot of attention and I found at first that by talking to him and giving him a lot of attention, I could quiet him down. But the rest of the class was suffering because I was giving this boy so much attention, so I stopped doing it." How did she know that they were suffering? "Well," she said, "I was taking time out from teaching." "True," I said, "but didn't they learn anything from it? Didn't they learn, for example, how to deal with a show-off, which might be useful knowledge later on in life?" The teacher allowed that this might be possible but was still troubled that it did not seem fair.

I remarked that this problem had come up again and again— that we call certain things "teaching" and other things not; that if they were to make a list of what they feel is most important for these children, "socialized behavior" would be very high on the list. Nevertheless, it seemed that teaching socialized behavior to this show-off could not be very high on her list because she insisted that she could not take time away from her subject-matter teaching to do it.

Three weeks later the same problem came up in different form. "I wrote some problems down," a teacher began, "and it's a long list. These are problems I have a hard time remembering when I'm here because they're so little, but they're so pervasive and so galling. First, there are the children who don't answer when they're called on, but when others are called on, they answer. And then the children who shout out and it's usually the wrong answer. It's very irritating."

"Why is it so galling?" I asked. "Well," she said, "first of all it's usually the wrong answer—though I'm always so gratified with a right answer that I forget to be angry that the right person didn't give it." "So it's really not the shouting out so much that annoys you?" I said. "Probably not," she agreed, "but it's very galling when it's all wrong."

I then asked her for an example of a question she had asked and the wrong answers she got. "Well, for instance," she said, "I point to the word *the* on the board and one shouts out 'my,' something like that." Her reaction was that the children had not learned the word, that they were thoughtless and inattentive.

I now asked her to speculate why anyone would shout out "my" when the word she asked for was *the*. "Because they don't know it. Sometimes they just want to answer anything." "That's about it," said another teacher; a third teacher thought that the children were just dying for attention and so would holler out anything at all.

"What is wrong with that?" I asked. "There isn't one teacher for every child," I was told; "that's what's wrong with it. The teacher just can't tolerate kids shouting out constantly and having the room in a turmoil. Because one thing leads to another, and the first thing you know, they're all talking, and then they're all walking around after that, and it's just bedlam."

By now, though, previous meetings began to pay off and another teacher said: "I kind of like it, within limits, this kind of response in my classroom; that everybody's jumping in, even if I have a noisy classroom. If I kind of listen, I find it's possible to distinguish who says what, so this isn't one of the things that bothers me."

"How about when they don't know it and still shout?" asked the first teacher, the one who raised the problem. And the second teacher replied, "I think this is good, and I'll tell you why: they're contributing, they're part of it, and this is what they want. The answer I recognize is the right answer. But even the children that don't know get the chance of contributing."

Still another teacher said she wished she could get this kind of enthusiasm. "To me, this is an enthusiasm for learning, even if it's the wrong thing. By the time you get them older, they've been told in the lower grades, 'That's not the right answer, keep your mouth shut and keep still,' and then things are bad. I have them in the higher grades and I wish I could just sometimes get them to say anything. But by then they've been so beaten down in the lower grades about 'Keep still, fold your hands' that you don't get any response from them at all."

I now suggested that we try to understand what goes on in the minds of the children while the teacher is writing *the* on the board.

"How many of you know the Greek alphabet?" I asked. "In parts," said the first teacher. "Now let's suppose," I said, "that you know the Greek alphabet, partly. Suppose somebody writes something on the blackboard in Greek letters. Try to visualize and try to feel this situation. You're trying to read it, but you don't quite know the letters. What are you going to feel? What will your reaction be; what will you feel about yourself? We're all very well able to be quiet. We're not going to shout out, and we're not going to shout out the wrong answer. We might even be afraid to say the right answer if we're not sure. But what are you going to think as you look up there, trying to figure it out?"

Teachers began to answer: "Why should I learn it?" "What's in it for me?" "I'd feel I don't know this and I have to go home and study it."

"That's right," I said. "Many of us would feel this, or else 'Why have I forgotten it; what's wrong with me?' But most of us would think, 'My God, what's that, what can that be?' All of these are rather uncomfortable feelings. Have these children learned to deal with their uncomfortable feelings; have we really taught them that? All of us have learned it. We all contain such moderate discomfort. But the children can't. Children in general, when they're uncomfortable, begin to holler and yell. I'm afraid that you overlook the discomfort you project the children into when you put something on the blackboard that they cannot read."

From all of this some psychological understanding was gained of what might be going on in these children, but it did not solve the problem yet. So I asked the teachers, "What did this child who shouted out 'my' want to learn?" One teacher replied, "I don't get what you said. What do you mean, 'What did he want to learn?' " "Well," I asked, "where was his interest?" And the teacher said, "With himself."

"Of course," I said, "because he shouted 'my.' " Now let's think for a moment about what's more important to a kid: to have a boat or to know that there is a boat somewhere?" To which they answered in chorus, "To have a boat that is mine."

"So actually," I said, "this boy gave us a very important clue about how to teach these children; namely, that we have got to personalize the whole thing. While they are not ready yet for abstract learning, they may be ready for personalized learning. In his own fashion he told us how he ought to be taught, if we just listened to him."

"Well, I always thought that *my* should be taught first in a lesson and *the* later," said another teacher. "It was always my feeling that *my* makes more sense to them right now." I agreed entirely. "It's another example," I said, "of how our teaching is geared to the middle-class child. I can't rewrite the curriculum or your textbooks. But I can help you understand what motivates this boy who says, 'I can learn only if a thing is very personal to me,' who by implication tells us: 'I might be interested in *my* boat, but I'm not interested in *the* boat.' All these weeks you have complained here that these children cannot distinguish very clearly between what is theirs and what is other people's—quite a difficult thing to learn. You complain about all the pencils they take and the paper they waste. Then we agreed that they feel 'What's yours is mine,' though they know that 'What's mine isn't yours.' All I'm trying to suggest is that here, in the simplest reading error, we are right smack against exactly the same problem."

This was a lengthy example, but I took time for it because it deals with the question "What is more important than to teach read-ing to these children?" and also with the difference between what is mine and what is not. My next example deals explicitly with this second problem.

"We have a teacher," I was told, "who's working with a particular group of lower-class children and we all admired her tremendously for how much she's been able to do with them, how empathetic she was and how well things were going. Then two of those children were picked up for purse snatching. When they came back, the teacher, who had an excellent relationship with them, said, 'If you needed money, why did you have to steal? You know I always have money in my desk.' The following day her desk was cleaned out of money."

"Well, she asked for it," I said, and the teacher nodded. "That's just the problem," she said. "None of us realized this. When the money was stolen, we were all stunned."

But things were more complicated than that. "The teacher meant very well." I said. "I'm sure she was ready to give these kids some money if they needed it. The trouble is, she didn't look at it the way it looked to the child. As good a person as she is, she didn't take the trouble to understand how differently these children view the world. Only recently have the sociologists and anthropologists begun to recognize something they call 'the culture of poverty.' In our example it might be better to call it 'the morals of poverty.' Within this culture of poverty, it is perfectly all right to take things if you can grab them, but never from the in-group. If you take from the in-group, then you're really a low-down scoundrel. On the other hand, if you take from the out-group and get away with it, you're smart."

"Like Robin Hood?" said the teacher. "If you like," I said. "Now these children snatched purses because they wanted money. It never occurred to them to take money from a good friend. If anything, they might have shared their loot with him. They considered this teacher a good friend, but lo and behold, she tells them they should take it from her, their close friend. That is, she tells them to do something which, in terms of their morality, is the worst thing a human being can do. So when this teacher says 'I expect you to come and take from me,' it means that she, whom they trusted, thinks they're bad persons. This makes her a stranger, if not an enemy. And if she has such a miserable opinion of us, we're going to teach her a lesson. In my opinion, this teacher's desk was cleaned out as a punishment."

"But did she really say they should take it from her?" asked a teacher. "No," I said. "She didn't ask them to take it. She just said something that to them meant: 'I think you haven't even enough knowledge of what's right and wrong to know that you don't take from a friend.' As you can see, an essential part of the culture of poverty is that you share with your friends and take from strangers."

This example shows that these teachers really want to be helpful to the culturally deprived child but that, despite their best intentions, they get bogged down when they cannot transcend their own value system to meet that of the children. What these teachers need is the clinician's help in going beyond their own middle-class mores, a task they find difficult at best, despite their conscious desires. Even more, they need help with their feeling of obligation to push the subject matter. And this grows worse with all the public clamor that everyone needs more education. Subject to this pressure, and sidetracked by it, they push academics at the expense of those emotional problems which, when not handled, prevent learning altogether. Perhaps a final example may illustrate.

"I have a little girl," said one teacher, "who has been troubling me. She alternates between extremely aggressive and extremely dependent behavior. She'll understand an assignment, but she'll ask me specifically to help her with it, and I do, because I feel that if this is going to get her interested in doing work, then fine. So I'll sit down and help her with an assignment even though it's obvious that she doesn't need the help. Sometimes she'll accept this help, and sometimes she'll just get angry instead. And if I'm not looking at her for five minutes, she'll get angry and she'll make a nasty comment."

"Like what?" I asked. "Well, she makes allusions to my race all the time." "What does she say?" I asked. " 'Oh, you ugly old white woman,' or something like that. Or she'll try to hit me, or something like that."

"And what do you do when she says you're an ugly white woman?" "Well," said the teacher, "I think I just probably make an ugly face when she says that." I was insistent and wanted to know what was the teacher's reaction. So she said, "I think I try to get her to sit down, or something like that, and actually ignore the problem. I never take her comments personally."

"Now this is something that's hard for me to believe," I said; "somebody tells you that you have an ugly white face, and you don't take it personally. How *do* you take it if you don't take it personally?"

"I mean I'm not insulted by the comments, really," she said. "But why not?" I wondered. "I have been a student of human emotions by now for more years than I care to remember, and people are always trying to teach me new things, but I'm an old dog and I don't learn new tricks any more. One of the new tricks people are trying to teach me is that if somebody tells somebody 'You have an ugly white face,' they don't take it personally. You can pretend not to be offended, but that's all. Because if that's really so, then the blacks haven't a thing to complain about. If all the remarks made about them don't hurt, then what's all the screaming about? But I think they have a right to scream, because I believe these remarks hurt."

"Well, let me put it this way," said the teacher; "she says enough good things to offset the bad things." "All right," I replied, "so your husband says many good things to you and just one bad one, that the dinner is awful. And that doesn't bother you because he said some nice things two days ago? Good things don't compensate for bad; they still hurt. And if somebody tells you 'I hate your ugly white face,' I don't see how you can help but be hurt. If you are not hurt, then you don't take the child seriously, and this is what I'm driving at. If we don't take their invectives, their nasty remarks, seriously, that means that we really don't take *them* seriously. It implies, 'You're irresponsible, no good, of no account,' because if they're of any account, then we must take seriously what they say."

"But don't children sometimes say something just for the shock value?" asked a teacher. "Of course," I said, "but if someone says something to shock you and you don't get shocked, then he's terribly deflated." "But if they continually do this kind of thing, you have to be shocked each time they say it," she insisted. "That's right," I said. "I'm shocked each time they do it. And the more shocked I am, the sooner they stop. If you pay no attention, they're driven to keep up or try harder all year long. But if when she says, 'You have an ugly white face,' you say 'Gee, I'm sorry you don't like my face; I like yours,' I think the kid would get some feeling. Because she says it to make you angry, or hurt you. And if you're not hurt, then she's a nincompoop.

"If, on the other hand, she can hurt you, then she might think, 'Do I really want to hurt my teacher?' and that's what we're striving for. Because then she might realize that sometimes she wants to, but most of the time she really doesn't want to hurt your feelings. Only, if it doesn't hurt your feelings, then she might as well keep it up."

What it comes down to, as I told them, is that we must have very clearly in our minds what are the educational goals we have for these children. Is it our goal that they learn what we think are the important things in life: not to show off, not to steal, not to hit people over the head; to be able to wait, to stand some small frustration, and still go on with the task? Or is it our goal that they learn to read and write, no matter what?

CHAPTER 2

Urban Teachers' Problems

Russell C. Doll

In the late 1950s it became clear that urban schools were not successfully educating low-income children, particularly children of minority groups recently arrived in our big cities. Assessments of the situation identified a complex of problems—among them, the need to improve the quality of classroom teaching for low-income youngsters. A theme common to the varied attempts (by governmental agencies and almost every kind of educational institution) at improving the quality of classroom teaching was that the problem lay, basically, within the classroom, centered on the teacher's competence and attitude. Criticism of the teacher, both hostile and sympathetic, has fallen within three categories, none of them mutually exclusive.

In the first category are those who complained that teachers lack technical skills and appropriate materials. Most teachers, according to this view, are basically competent people who do not know the learning styles of low-income children and are attempting to teach in an inappropriate manner, using inappropriate materials and methods.

This view has led to the development of different teaching techniques and the utilization and development of more appropriate kinds of materials. The improvement of the teacher as professional and technician was seen as a major step forward in improving the teacher's ability and willingness to function in an effective manner.

A second category includes those who held that the middle-class teacher is either intentionally or unintentionally callous toward the low-income pupil. The teacher enters the classroom with preconceived ideas of what is proper in behavior, language, and dress and, in most instances, feels that the children are deficient in meeting the expectations of correctness.

The model of teacher training based on "affective awareness" held that the teacher needs an opportunity to "understand" the child through an "understanding" of his culture. In addition, the teacher needs to look into his own psyche and dig out the roots of prejudice. He needs to realize that the child's self-concept and self-image are affected, often negatively, by the wider society and by the biased expectations of the school. The child's lowered self-concept then leads to patterns of failure.

Sensitivity to the child and an understanding of the child's total life space were seen as prerequisites to instructional success. The teacher was given help in understanding the sociopsychological background related to low-income life. Teachers searched their souls during the summers while they toured ghetto neighborhoods and became "sensitive."

Yet another group of critics saw the teacher as one who has lost the faith, a person suffering from a failure of will. Instead of being true to the teaching spirit of commitment and dedication, he has given up in the face of a difficult situation, abandoning the low-income children in their hour of need. Evangelists for the teacher of the "hard to teach" rode the circuits of the central city schools. Articles exhorting teachers to regain and retain the spirit of commitment showered down from the monastic universities. Apostles of teaching would then turn water to wine; would make the deaf hear, the blind see, and the dumb sing.

Although the assistance given the teacher undoubtedly did help him to be more proficient than he would have been had no help been given, on the whole classroom teaching and teachers' attitudes have improved very little in our highly problem-oriented schools. It seems as if teachers do not, or cannot, function as expected by the planners, university people, school districts, and public. In light of this, one might reasonably ask whether the planners, university people, school districts, and public have an adequate grasp of the full range of teachers' problems. Perhaps the aid given the teachers, as reflected in the above three categories, addresses only a part of the problem of why teachers seem to be functioning inadequately. Further, perhaps a great part of the problem cannot be remedied through segmental approaches such as workshops or institutes, books or movies, improvement of skills, urgings to be professional and to develop affective awareness.

Premises Guiding Improvement

It is thought that when the right formula for developing *professional skills* and *affective understanding* is found, then improvement of education in low-income areas will follow.

According to this "professional-affective" view, the teacher operates in a vacuum, seemingly unaffected by frustrations and threats to self-concept. Consequently, he can easily be changed from an "average human being" to an "efficient professional," responding to stress and failure in an entirely rational, objective, and professional fashion. Further, once he understands why the situation is as it is, he will be satisfied to function well in a technical capacity even though he has little evidence that technique and personal knowledge are producing results; even though, over long periods of time, he finds himself rejected as both professional and human being.

This view also implies that teachers can function within current school structures and organizational patterns. It divorces the teacher from the effects of school organization and implies that failure to make changes and to improve education in problem schools is a personal failure of the teacher.

This premise of professional inadequacy has guided teachers' pre-service and in-service training, which concentrates on developing teaching skills and techniques and an understanding of the child. The training—as well as the professional publications, with their entire emphasis upon development of increased technical skill and subject-matter mastery—has tended to develop certain self-expectations and role expectations. The teacher expects and is expected to be successful as a professional within the following categories (Brembeck, 1971): success in teaching tasks, success in nurturant tasks, success in cognitive training, success in affective training, and success in acculturating training. In differing degrees and with variance by category, the above are internalized by most teachers as their professional expectations. They hold a role expectation in which behaviors directly related to teaching are considered to be the appropriate kinds of behavior. They hold a professional expectation in which the visible academic growth of the child is considered to be the mark of a successful teacher (Wehling and Charters, 1961). The more they feel they meet the role expectation the greater satisfaction they find in teaching. The greater the satisfaction the more likely the teacher will work harder and not leave the situation. If the role expectations are not met there is greater possibility for dissatisfaction, and the more likely it is that the teacher will retreat from teaching and will transfer to another school.

Highly Problem-Oriented Schools

The opportunity to fulfill professional expectations and role expectations is lessened in schools categorized in recent studies as "highly problem oriented" (Doll, 1969, 1970, 1971; Havighurst, 1964; Havighurst and Levine, 1970). A highly problem-oriented school is one category of a four-school typology. The other three types are highly academically oriented, average academically oriented, and low academic or partially problem-oriented schools. Placement of the schools in one of the four categories was based on interview data focusing on the relationships between teachers and students, teachers and teachers, students and students, principal and teachers, and so on. Because the schools were not categorized on the basis of out-of-school factors such as geographical area of school or income level of residents, it was possible to find different types of schools in areas where all the schools would have been thought to be similar. This method of placement also allowed for an evaluation of teacher attitudes and degree of satisfaction. The sample was drawn from schools with a grading pattern of K–8, and the teachers were from grades 5–8. Ten areas of school life, identified from pilot interviews, formed the basis of later in-depth interviews of school staffs. While the initial categorizations were clinical in nature, a later objective verification was made. For purposes of this paper we will call the highly academically oriented schools A type; average academically oriented, B type; partially problem oriented, C type; and highly problem oriented, D type.

Teachers were asked, among other things, to talk about what they did in their classrooms, how they felt about the school, and whether or not what they were doing coincided with what they thought they should be doing. There were significant differences between teachers in the different types of schools in regard to satisfaction, willingness to continue in the situation, withdrawal to out-of-school sources for reward, and feelings about themselves as professionals and human beings. The differences seemed to center on perceived ability to function in the professional-affective roles, succeeding in their professional expectations and role expectations. A few selected quotes give an indication of the kinds of conflict experienced by teachers in the highly problem oriented or D schools.

> *I never would have come if I had known what the school situation was. There are dangers that I face all the time but I shouldn't have to. Why do I have to take away knives? Why do I have to break up fights?* I always thought that I was a teacher, but I'm no teacher; I'm a bouncer and a policeman with the assignment of dangerous duty.
>
> *An overriding part of our school day, practically all of it,* is just spent on an emphasis on control. It is very rarely that you get to do any great amount of teaching. If I do at least a half hour or an hour of good teaching . . . I go home satisfied. *As it is I go home very disturbed, frustrated, and with a sense of defeat nearly every day.*
>
> *One thing about this situation that really depresses you is that* you can't get any tangible evidence of what you're doing. You don't get any rewards *from the children. You can motivate your head off and only see tiny results. Oh, these may be adequate for the situation, but they're just not enough to keep a person in this type of situation.*

From interview data, it was evident that teachers had internalized role expectations of a highly professional-affective nature. When teachers in the D schools were not able to function as they thought "teachers" should function, they felt guilty and personally thwarted. Experiencing rejection and feelings of personal and professional deficiency, they wished to withdraw from the situation. Teachers in the A and B schools, however, expressed great satisfaction in their jobs and a willingness to stay in the school. They saw themselves as engaging in proper "teacher" behaviors, fulfilling their role and professional expectations, receiving rewards and being able to relate well to the children.

Teachers in the D schools, then, did not see themselves functioning as professionals, able to utilize the skills and affective awareness they possessed. Their roles became, in their eyes, something other than what they should have been and what teacher training, publications, and workshops had taught them to expect. Their role expectations were shattered when their role behaviors became those of policeman and disciplinarian, clerk and truant officer, parent and adviser. Teachers in the D schools felt that they could not utilize their teaching skills because of the necessity to control behavior. Most felt that their school was difficult, not necessarily because of academic deficiency but because of the combination of academic deficiency *and* behavioral difficulties.

Teachers in the D schools were faced with an overwhelming amount of work stemming from the school disorganization and the social disorganization outside of the school. Truancy and tardiness forms, parental conferences, parental visits because of student difficulties, memos to the principal, forms needed for governmental assistance —all took up an inordinate amount of time. Furthermore, the teachers (to some extent in all of the schools but most intensely and most frequently in the D schools) had to spend large amounts of time arbitrating children's quarrels, comforting of disturbed and unhappy children, and counseling of "maladjusted" children.

Teachers recognized the discrepancy between what they had internalized as proper teacher behavior and the behaviors in which they were engaged. This discrepancy was intensified by their inability to fulfill their professional expectations related to student achievement. Not only were they unable to *act* as teachers; they were unable to succeed in *teaching*.

The conflict in role is exacerbated by the need to expend great amounts of physical and emotional energies and not receive any personal or professional reward. If the expenditure of physical and emotional energies was related to instructional tasks such as planning, teaching, and evaluation, teachers probably would be more effective and more satisfied, since they would be receiving some sense of role fulfillment. However, when these expenditures of energies are related to clerical or extra duties, controlling behavior, socializing children, then teachers are less effective and less satisfied.

Teachers in the A and B schools received satisfaction and rewards, not only because their pupils were achieving academically but also because they themselves were engaged in behaviors harmonious with their expectations. In the D schools teachers were not receiving rewards through student achievement or through successful affective relationships. In fact, "understanding" the children's problems in D schools seemed to decrease rather than increase teachers' effectiveness. Much of the drain of emotional energy in the D schools was caused partly by the teachers' realization of the depth of the children's problems and of their own powerlessness to alleviate these problems.

Another factor that lessened the potential for success in the affective role was the inherent contradiction within the student-teacher contacts. Teachers felt that they should encourage their students to look upon them as "friends." Students were to feel free to approach teachers with their problems. But teachers were also faced with the necessity of rewarding or punishing through grades. The teacher-friend became teacher-professional, and the child felt "betrayed." Similarly, teachers were often forced into controlling behaviors. For most of the teachers and children the contradiction in the teacher-friend vs. policeman-disciplinarian role was difficult to cope with. The frustrating thing was that the students who teachers felt most needed "understanding" were those who forced the teacher into "betrayal" by actions necessitating a policeman-disciplinarian response.

For the average teacher the necessity of having to cope in a D school, with its general atmosphere of conflict and hostility, is too much. The rewards of successful coping are too few and the inner reserves of strength too meager for functioning as the experts exhort and as the model of a "successful" teacher is portrayed—the model of the teacher as professional.

New Approaches to Assisting Teachers

If any significant institutional assistance is to be given teachers, the assistance must not be segmental in nature and must meet professional and human needs of the teacher. The premises guiding programs of teacher assistance should not start with the narrowly conceived premise of professional inadequacy. Instead, they should recognize that societal and institutional deficiencies have created situations in which the best of teachers fail. What needs to be done is to implement programs to strengthen teachers' self-concepts, increase feelings of success, provide some degree of fate control, and work toward a strengthening of "self" through increasing the potential for rewarding experiences.

Four approaches might be explored: (1) an attempt to modify certain aspects of teachers' professional and role expectations; (2) an attempt to provide alternative kinds of schooling, or deschooling, experiences and to match teachers' professional and role expectations to the schooling experiences; (3) drastic curriculum revision to support the change of expectations and to develop curriculum fitting the alternative kinds of schooling or deschooling; (4) the creation of different organizational structures, which take into account all aspects of a school's social system and which allow for flexibility in the development of curriculum and support for the changing expectations needed for different kinds of schooling or deschooling.

Modification of expectations. As pointed out earlier, most attempts to modify teachers' expectations have concentrated exclusively on reinforcing the professional-affective role. These rigid expectations need to be modified so that the human as well as the professional aspects of teaching are included.

The teacher, then, *will* lose his temper; he *will* dislike some children; he might even push or smack a child. He cannot expect himself to be a successful, full-time therapist or social worker; he cannot expect to be successful in all things academic, or beautiful in all his personal relations. He understands the need to have days in which he "coasts" with the class. He will not be scintillating for five hours a day, five days a week, every semester for every subject period and with every personal relation in the classroom or on the playground or on hall or lunchroom duty. He will simply do *all within his power* to assist the child with his problems, *all within his power* to help the child academically. And he will stop flagellation when he does not succeed, especially when the failure to succeed may be the fault of situations beyond his control.

Besides a concentration on reinforcing the professional-affective role, we need in our training programs and workshops (1) to broaden the teacher's awareness to include an understanding of his own feelings; (2) to develop strategies to cope with academic and affective failures; (3) to redefine success, in certain situations, and to reevaluate teacher strengths, abilities, and potentials for success; (4) to develop reward structures based on other than academic criteria.

Alternative school and deschooling experiences. Simply modifying expectations will not lead to significant educational change or instructional improvement. It might increase the potential for teacher satisfaction, but it will not change the conditions that lead to the initial dissatisfactions. Alternative kinds of "schooling" must be developed which would attempt to match teachers' professional and role expectations to pupils' expectations and needs. David Hunt's (1971) excellent but overlooked work shows rather conclusively that students with different socioemotional makeups need different kinds of educational settings. There is evidence that the same holds true for teachers (Edgar and Clear, 1970; Goldberg, 1971). Expecting all teachers and students to function identically in identical settings is unrealistic. When teachers say in desperation, "About half my class shouldn't be in school," there is a tendency to react with horror at the callousness and lack of understanding. But what the teachers are actually saying, in their desperation, is "Half of my students need a different kind of learning experience. I am not qualified by temperament or expectations to provide that kind of experience. Yet, my other kids *can* benefit from my teaching because *we agree* on how it should take place. We would do well together and the others would be happier elsewhere with someone else."

Alternative structures for schooling would get students and teachers out of situations that are detrimental to both and into learning situations where both can feel comfortable and successful. "Alternative structures" means some schools that are graded and with self-contained classrooms, some nongraded and with modular kinds of scheduling; some schools that are street-corner academies, store-front schools, schools without walls, schools modeled after Harlem Prep; some based on the ideas of Ivan Illich, Paul Goodman, and other "de-schoolers."

Curriculum revision. There would need to be curriculum revision for both "traditional" and "alternative" structures. These revisions should aim at allowing for wide variance in curriculum sequence and scope and for flexibility in the teacher's expectations. This flexibility should take in the students' expectations as well. A curriculum model that seems to encompass these requirements is Wilson's (1971) "open-access curriculum." This flexible curriculum can be adapted to many different educational structures. Further, some of Wilson's proposals deal directly with the overlooked problems of role expectation. Among his proposals are the following (pp. 17–18):

> (1) *Compute as part of the teacher's normal load (beyond conventional teaching) the functions of a counseling, clinical, technological, and professional planning nature; concurrently remove from the teacher (for assignment to paraprofessionals, trainees, or aides) functions related to clerical services, security of the school plant and resources, and general record keeping. (2) Differentiate teacher roles in such a way that each teacher on a given team has a unique, nonduplicating task to perform; consider, in the process, teacher life styles (e.g., values, preferences, and interpersonal relations patterns) along with academic specialties. Build into each such a team of capability for planning and self-supervision rather than imposing such controls from above. (3) Orient all learning toward curiosity and/or a search for "the new consensus"; minimize, correspondingly, evaluative measures that implicitly assume or demand academic closure.*

Different organizational patterns. Even given alternative structures and a revised curriculum, new intraschool structures are still needed (1) to maintain and facilitate teacher involvement in planning; (2) to allow opportunities to "back up" if roles need redefining and programs need altering; (3) to provide opportunities for mutually supportive planning and program implementation; and (4) to integrate all in-school and out-of-school components into the school's social system in a supportive fashion. New organizational patterns would give teachers greater resources to choose from, opportunities for developing alternative intraschool structures, opportunities for some degree of "fate control," a voice in administrative decisions, and an opportunity to make bureaucratic organizations more responsive to immediate needs and problems.

One of the most promising models for achieving these ends is the "aggregate" model offered by Janowitz (1970). An organizational pattern which most closely resembles the "aggregate" approach, and which is already in operation, is the multi-unit school (Klausmeier et al., 1970; Nussel et al., 1971). Janowitz argues that past and current attempts to help the teacher have been "segmental" and have carried in them latent dysfunctional elements because they never addressed themselves to the full range of teachers' problems and never mobilized assistance on a "systems" basis. These "segmental" approaches have failed because there was no "aggregate" change, touching all parts of the social system. The multi-unit organization is not the mandatory arrangement for implementing the "aggregate" model. It does, however, provide the most suitable arrangement, to date, for needed flexibility when roles become modified, when approaches such as the open-access curriculum are contemplated, and when support needs to be mobilized for teacher and pupil. Further, a multi-unit arrangement can fit requirements needed for the functioning of the alternative structures mentioned earlier. Evidence is accumulating that this particular approach, or an approach that incorporates a "systems" idea, helps to sustain change and has built-in mutually supportive mechanisms in which curriculum and expectations can be defined and redefined (Bigelow, 1970; Levine and Doll, 1971).

References

BIGELOW, R. C. The Effect of Organizational Development on Classroom Climate. (Rev. ed.) Eugene, Oregon: University of Oregon, Center for the Advanced Study of Educational Administration, Project No. 3001, 1970.

BREMBECK, C. Social Foundations of Education. (2nd ed.) New York: John Wiley & Sons, 1971.

DOLL, R. C. "Types of Elementary Schools in a Big City." Doctoral dissertation, University of Chicago, 1969.

DOLL, R. C. *Variations among Inner-City Elementary Schools: An Investigation into the Nature and Causes of Their Differences.* Kansas City: Center for the Study of Metropolitan Problems in Education, 1970.

DOLL, R. C. "Toward a Typology of Big City Elementary Schools." Paper presented at the meeting of the American Studies Association, Chicago, February 1971.

EDGAR, D. E., AND CLEAR, D. K. "Training Change Agents in the Public School Context." Paper presented at the American Educational Research Association, Minneapolis, March 1970.

GOLDBERG, I. I. *Build Me a Mountain: Youth and Poverty and the Creation of New Settings.* Cambridge: MIT Press, 1971.

HAVIGHURST, R. J., AND LEVINE, D. U. *Education in Metropolitan Areas.* Boston: Allyn and Bacon, 1970.

HAVIGHURST, R. J. *The Public Schools of Chicago.* Chicago: Board of Education of the City of Chicago, 1964.

HUNT, D. *Matching Models in Education: The Coordination of Teaching Methods with Student Characteristics.* Ontario, Canada: Ontario Institute for Studies in Education, 1971.

JANOWITZ, M. *Institution Building in Urban Education.* New York: Russell Sage Foundation, 1970.

KLAUSMEIER, H. J., et al. *Individually Guided Instruction in the Multiunit Elementary School: Guidelines for Implementation.* Madison: Wisconsin Research and Development Center for Cognitive Learning, 1970.

LEVINE, D. U., AND DOLL, R. C. *Systems Renewal in the Louisville Public Schools: Lessons on the Frontier of Urban Educational Reform in a Big City School District.* Kansas City: Experienced Teacher Fellowship Program and Center for the Study of Metropolitan Problems in Education, 1971.

NUSSEL, E., et al. *The Ohio Model and the Multi-unit School.* Toledo, Ohio: University of Toledo, 1971.

WEHLING, L. J., AND CHARTERS, W. W. "Dimensions of Teacher Beliefs about the Teaching Process." *American Educational Research Journal,* 1961, 7, 127–135.

WILSON, C. L. *The Open Access Curriculum.* Boston: Allyn and Bacon, 1971.

CHAPTER 3

Making School Rewarding

Carl A. Clark

෧෧෧෧෧෧෧෧෧෧෧෧෧෧෧

A pressing problem of urban education is the difficulty in reconciling the child to his education in the "inner-city" school. An inner-city school, as we shall define it, is one in which children are predominantly or totally members of a minority group, in most cases of a black subculture; in contrast, the curricula and teachers are largely representative of a middle-class subculture. The annual income of the community supplying the school is in the lowest quartile, and a high percentage of families are on public aid. Many are migrants from areas having lower-quality segregated schools. Most live in overcrowded houses in poor condition, or in high-rises, the so-called "vertical slums." Obviously, there is a serious problem in getting the child, the community, and the school together in the educational process. And just as obviously, this problem is far from being solved.

One of the symptoms of the problem is the reluctance of many inner-city children to go to school. These schools have a very high absence and truancy rate. In one inner-city high school, the average number of days absent per pupil in a semester was fourteen. A survey of the attitudes and habits of students in this school (Clark and Groves, 1969) showed that students with high absence rates had generally unfavorable attitudes toward school and teachers, as well as low grades.

The inner-city child not only tends to dislike school; he has a tendency to self-dissatisfaction as well. Havighurst (1970) has noted this tendency and has emphasized the need of the minority-subculture child to increase his ego strength. That one source of the self-dissatis-faction—as well as the dislike of school—may be the unrewarding aspects of school is suggested by self-esteem studies now being conducted by Clark and Daly (1971). Low grades and poor relationship with teachers were significantly related to low self-esteem scores.

Primarily, these children react unfavorably to the scholastic process in the inner-city schools because the schools do not provide successful and rewarding experiences, because the curriculum lacks congruence with their immediate out-of-school life or their life in the future. Curriculum changes are considered by other writers in this book. Our concern here is, with a given curriculum, how to make school a more rewarding place for inner-city schoolchildren.

A basic problem with rewards, whatever the type, is that they usually are unequally distributed; only part of a group will get the high grades, the teacher's praise, or the peer approval. The ones who are performing better will receive more rewards, but they are also perform-ing better *because* they are being rewarded more. The low-achieving student is in part low-achieving because he is being rewarded less. His responses are becoming extinguished because they are not being re-warded and also because many of them, often being unsatisfactory, are punished. It can be said with some truth, then, that one explanation for low achievers is that they have been *taught* to be low achievers. One might carry this reasoning even further to say that some of these children have low IQs because from early childhood "bright" responses are rewarded and "dull" or "dumb" responses punished—and a child who is not early rewarded for the kinds of things that will later affect his score on IQ tests will do poorly on such tests.

Rewards and Achievement

A way to break down this academic and intellectual segregation is to break down the segregation of reward distribution; that is, to reward the low achiever as much as, or perhaps more than, the high achiever. A child who makes a sincere response that is wrong could be rewarded—not for making a wrong response but for making a response. Such a child might then increase his frequency of responses. Then there could be more rewarding for his right responses than wrong, and he might gradually make more and more right responses— become a higher achiever.

A number of studies (Hurlock, 1924; Mech, 1953; Thompson and Hunnicutt, 1944) have shown the beneficial effects of praise on school achievement. Therefore, since the effectiveness of rewards for learning in the classroom seems at least fairly well established, the use of rewards in inner-city classrooms on a systematic basis needs to be carefully considered. The inner-city schools have a disproportionately large number of pupils who are classified as "slow learners" and "mentally retarded." These students in particular need to be reached— and many others also, to prevent them from falling into such classifications. Will a highly stepped-up and distributed reward procedure in classrooms significantly raise the rate of achievement for inner-city children who have been having difficulty with their schoolwork?

An answer to this question was sought in a study by Clark and Walberg (1968). In this study, 110 minority schoolchildren, from one to four years behind in their schoolwork and considered potential dropouts, were randomly assigned to experimental and control conditions for after-school classes in reading. The study was so conducted that both the experimental and control classes considered themselves an experimental group—and, in fact, both groups were given the same procedures. These procedures involved the use of tally cards numbered consecutively beginning with one. Whenever the teacher praised a child, the teacher asked the child to circle the lowest uncircled number. Thus the last number circled indicated the number of times the child was praised. After the nine classes (five "experimental" and five "control") had accustomed themselves to the procedure through six class sessions, the experimental teachers were asked to double or triple their reward output for each child, while the control teachers were asked to "keep up the good work." At the end of the semester the pupils were given a reading test, on which the experimental pupils did much better (statistically significant) than the control.

This study demonstrated that a massive degree of rewarding is feasible with slow-learning inner-city schoolchildren and that it is effective in producing achievements. The rewards used were praise, and the reward value of accumulating the circles. It is important to note that the rewards were immediate—not the long-term reward of a grade at the end of a semester.

One type of reward that seems to have been avoided with slow-learning, "mentally retarded" inner-city schoolchildren is the reward of winning in a competitive event. It is often assumed that these children have met with so much discouragement and defeat in their academic endeavors that any sort of scholastic competition should be shunned. After all, most of them have been losers in the competition for grades in the regular classroom. Such a viewpoint—even if valid—is unfortunate, since competitive drives are very strong in our culture in general and in the inner-city subculture. In the study just cited, many of the children were avidly competing to see who could get the most circles, so that winning or nearly winning in this competition was one of the reward variables. Another study (Harris, 1958) concentrated directly on the reward of winning in a scholastic competitive event, a competitive spell-down. In each of five special classrooms for the mentally retarded, five students were organized at random into a spell-down group; five others, assigned to a control group, studied the same words and took the same tests but otherwise were taught as usual. The result was that the competitive group gained significantly more than the control, the gains being over twice as great.

Rewarding and Attitudes

Perhaps at least as important as the achievements of the inner-city child in school are the attitudes he develops—toward himself, toward school and teachers and parents, and toward his future. What effect will a high degree of rewarding have on these attitudes? The effect upon the child's level of aspiration was studied by Brown (1964). In her study the subjects were sixty-four children who lived in a low-rent public housing community with a median annual income (including public assistance) of $2,920. Forty-three per cent of the residents received welfare assistance. These children were in two fourth-grade classes. Their average age was 9.4, and the average IQ was 95.2. In each classroom sixteen boys and sixteen girls participated, a random half of the boys being assigned to a high-praise group and half to a low-praise group; the same for the girls.

Five dependent variables were used: a vocational level-of-aspiration test, a word-making task, and a dart-throwing task, the latter two having both an achievement score and an aspiration (or predicted achievement) score. These tests were given at the beginning of the experiment and at the end.

In the word-making task the child was to see how many words he could make in two minutes from the letters of a word in a booklet, proceeding a page at a time. As the two minutes for a page ended, the experimenter said "Stop," and the child was asked to put the score on the line provided, and also to indicate how many words he thought he could score on a following page. The sum of all the word-making scores constituted his achievement score, and the sum of all the predictions constituted his prediction or "aspiration" score. Similarly, with dart throwing, after a score was obtained, the subject was asked to estimate the score he would get next.

The independent variable, *praise,* was administered to the pupils by the teachers in the regular classroom-teaching process. Over a five-week period the randomly selected experimental children were praised for their responses, for the neatness of their work, for their attentiveness, for favorable social behavior; and encouraging words were written on their papers. The control children received the normal amount of praise. The teachers kept a tally of praise given to each child, the experimental children receiving about four times as much praise as the low-praise group.

At the end of the period, the five criterion scores were again obtained. The results showed significantly larger gains for the high-praise group on all measures except dart throwing, where the obtained scores were higher but not significantly so. The *predicted* dart-throwing scores were, however, significantly higher for the high-praise group. There were no significant differences between boys and girls on any of the measures with respect to praise, except that boys' aspirations in dart throwing were more affected by praise than were girls'.

This study indicates that increased amounts of praise to "culturally disadvantaged" children significantly affect aspirations as well as achievement.

Will rewards also affect a student's attitudes toward teachers and school, and even toward parents? An experiment was undertaken by Clark and Walberg (1969) to assess the effect of parental rewarding on the attitude of their children toward teachers. A teacher-rating scale (developed by Dr. B. D. Wright of Chicago University) was administered to children (aged six to thirteen), and the parents of these children were asked to take part in a program in which they would give their children regular quiz sessions on their schoolwork. Some forty parents volunteered, and twenty of these were selected at random. Twice a week these parents were sent a list of questions, related to their children's schoolwork, which they were to ask the children. The children were immediately given the correct answers (printed on the question sheets) after they had responded, thus receiving many reinforcements during the school term.

At the end of the term, all children in the classes were given the teacher-rating scale again; the over-all result was a lower average score, indicating a less favorable attitude toward teachers at the end of the semester. This decline in teacher regard with progression of the school year seems to be a usual finding in teacher attitude studies. The pupils of participating parents, however, had a large (statistically significant) gain. The pupils of volunteering parents who were not selected (by chance) showed a loss in attitude similar to that of the entire group.

There is also some indication that children who are more highly rewarded by teachers tend to develop more favorable attitudes toward their parents. At the beginning of the term, the pupils in the previous study rated their parents on a scale similar to the teacher-rating scale, and the number of rewards (praise) given by the teachers and recorded by observers in the early part of the term was correlated with parental rating, the correlation being .16. At the end of the term, the correlation between total number of rewards and another parental rating rose to .41, a substantial and significant increase. This result indicates that the children who were rewarded more tended to raise their parental ratings more than those with fewer rewards. *Thus, it appears that the effects of rewarding at school tend to generalize to the home, and the effect of rewards on school-related tasks at home generalize to the school.*

Will the rewarding teachers be rated higher by their own pupils? This question was specifically studied by Clark and Groves (1969) with randomly selected students who were enrolled for a summer session in remedial English and mathematics classes in an inner-city vocational high school. There were two English classes at the same level and two mathematics classes. Teachers trained in the massed-immediate-reward procedure, one English and one mathematics teacher, were assigned at random each to one of the two classes in his field. At the end of the session a teacher attitude scale showed significantly better attitudes toward their teachers for both the high-praise mathematics and English students as compared with the normal-praise group. Attitudes toward school, measured by another instrument similar to the teacher attitude scale, showed higher scores for both experimental classes, though the differences were not statistically significant.

A situational type of rewarding also was tested in this study. The experimental situation was a creative movie-making project participated in by the inner-city school pupils who had signed up for speech-drama classes in this vocational high school. Half of the students were selected at random for the movie project, while half continued with the school's regular English IV speech-drama course. English IV grades and credit were also given in the movie class. The teachers for the movie project had participated in the previous reward training sessions. At the end of the summer session, teacher attitude and school attitude scales were given to the pupils in both groups. The movie-making group scored considerably and significantly higher on both scales.

Conclusions

These studies demonstrate the value of the systematic application of rewards to inner-city schoolchildren, a point made by Havighurst (1970) with regard to the *learning* of children; but they go further in showing that the attitudes of the child toward school, his teacher, himself, and probably the home environment, are also improved by rewards.

There is cause for dismay, however, in the fact that the systematic application of rewards is so seldom applied in the schools beyond isolated studies and projects. In fact, many teachers resist the idea, as those who have worked on teacher rewarding well know. It is particularly hard on the teachers who tend to be punitive, or who are somewhat rigid and perfectionistic, or who have conscious or unconscious prejudice toward minority groups—but these people should not be teaching in the inner city anyway.

What is needed is to incorporate training in the systematic application of rewards in all teacher-training programs, but particularly in colleges that prepare teachers and administrators for the inner-city schools.

References

BROWN, J. W. "The Effects of Varying Amounts of Praise on Aspiration Level and Achievement of Elementary School Children." Thesis, Chicago State University, 1964.

CLARK, C. A., AND DALY, J. D. "Studies of Factors in Scholastic Success." In progress at Chicago State University.

CLARK, C. A., AND GROVES, A. M. "Stimulating a Desire to Learn." Unpublished manuscript on an ESEA Title I Mini-Grant project at Dunbar Vocational High School, Chicago, 1969.

CLARK, C. A., AND WALBERG, H. J. "The Influence of Massive Rewards on

Reading Achievement in Potential Urban School Dropouts." *American Educational Research Journal*, 1968, *5*, 305–330.

CLARK, C. A., AND WALBERG, H. J. "The Use of Secondary Reinforcement in Teaching Inner-City School Children." *Journal of Special Education*, 1969, *3*, 177–185.

HARRIS, L. G. "A Study of Competition in Motivating Achievement of Educable Mentally Handicapped Children." Thesis, Chicago State University, 1958.

HAVIGHURST, R. J. "Minority Subcultures and Law of Effect." *American Psychologist*, 1970, *25*, 313–322.

HURLOCK, E. "An Evaluation of Certain Incentives Used in School Work." *Journal of Educational Psychology*, 1924, *21*, 145–159.

MECH, E. V. "An Experimental Analysis of Patterns of Differential Verbal Reinforcement in Classroom Situations." *Bulletin, School of Education, Indiana University*, Sept. 1953, *29*, 5–24.

THOMPSON, G. G., AND HUNNICUTT, C. W. "The Effects of Repeated Praise or Blame on the Work Achievement of Introverts and Extroverts." *Journal of Educational Psychology*, 1944, *35*, 257–266.

CHAPTER 4

Educational Models for the Disadvantaged

Victor G. Cicirelli

For many years in the United States, most children of the urban poor have been inferior in academic achievement to middle-class children and have suffered the consequences of being rejected by teachers, becoming school dropouts without jobs, and contributing excessively to welfare rolls and incidence of crime, drug addiction, and mental illness. The cost for the individual and society has been staggering.

What was new in the sixties was the greater awareness of and concern for the urban poor—especially the education of their children. Out of the many approaches to the problem have emerged three broad viewpoints about the cause of the achievement gap and the means to eliminate it; for convenience, these may be labeled deficit models, school-disparity models, and deactualization models. The deficit models assert that something is wrong with the children of the poor; they are

31

intellectually retarded or limited in some way and hence cannot attain middle-class levels of achievement without appropriate remedial or preventive intervention programs. The school-disparity models assert that something is wrong with the schools; the children of the poor are different from middle-class children but not inferior, and the schools must change their present ineffective approaches in order to use these children's talents for achievement while simultaneously maintaining their subcultural identities. The deactualization models assert that something is wrong with society; society has a false conception of human nature, and the so-called achievement gap between middle-class and poor children is really a pseudo-problem. Each child is a unique individual whose goals for achievement should be determined by his own needs and interests rather than by the imposition of external goals and standards; the disadvantaged child is restricted in the self-actualization of his potential and needs developmental programs allowing him the freedom to release his potential and develop to the fullest.

This paper will consider each of these models in greater detail as a basis for making recommendations for the seventies.

Deficit Models

Common to all deficit models is the notion that the child is lacking in something essential to his achievement in the mainstream middle-class society; that something must be corrected, improved, or prevented from occurring if the child is to achieve in school and later in life. Hence, diagnosis and prescription become important for remedial intervention programs, and a theory of mental development becomes important to guide selection of appropriate experiences for preventive intervention programs.

Three deficit models can be distinguished: the environmental-deficit model, the nutritional-deficit model, and the genetic-deficit model.

Environmental-deficit model. Of all the theoretical models, the environmental-deficit model is undoubtedly the most pervasive; it underlies the bulk of compensatory intervention programs in existence today. In essence, this model asserts that the achievement gap between poor and middle-class children is caused by intellectual (and accompanying emotional-social) retardation in the children of the poor—retardation resulting from lack of appropriate stimulation in the developing child's environment. This position rests on the idea that intelligence is not fixed but "plastic" and that environmental stimulation plays a major role in intellectual development (Hunt, 1961, 1964).

Also, some hold that critical (Hunt, 1964) or optimal (Bloom, 1964; Deutsch, 1964) periods exist early in life; if the stimulation needed to develop certain intellectual functions is not present at these periods, remediation of the resulting deficits is impossible or quite difficult. Others hold that mental growth is cumulative in nature, building on what has gone before; later development, therefore, will be difficult if earlier development is deficient (Elkind, 1970). Inappropriate early experiences may inhibit new learning through the mechanism of negative transfer (Jensen, 1966) or "harden" the individual in certain intellectual channels, so that new learnng is difficult (Ausubel, 1965). Because of the great difficulty involved in obtaining adequate measures of supposed impoverished environments, evidence in support of this model is largely correlational; causal relationships have not been established to the extent needed to confirm the environmental-deficit model.

Those who espouse the environmental-deficit model assume that the deficits can be remediated or even prevented if intervention begins early enough. With the broad objective of remediating the disadvantaged child's cognitive deficits, a dazzling variety of intervention programs have been mounted, ranging from small experimental efforts to the nationally implemented Head Start program. Such programs or "treatments" have largely been based on common sense, trial and error, traditional nursery school approaches, Piaget, O. K. Moore, Montessori, S-R approaches, and a smattering of theories of learning, motivation, and individual differences. Many of the programs are quite eclectic in approach. For example, Weikart's (1969) cognitive program is a combination of verbal bombardment with an intellectual-development program based on Piagetian theory and Smilansky's sociodramatic play. Meier, Nimnicht, and McAfee's (1968) "New Nursery School" combines the diagnostic approach of Deutsch with the autotelic responsive environment of O. K. Moore and Montessori method. While the majority of the programs begin intervention in early childhood, the less than satisfactory outcomes of the early-childhood programs have led to extensions of the compensatory-education approach both upward into the elementary school (Follow-Through, Title I programs) and downward into infancy (Gordon, 1969; Lambie and Weikart, 1970), where mothers are trained to teach the infants at home or the infants are taught directly.

Most of the intervention programs formulate specific or multiple cognitive objectives, attempt to identify deficits, and devise strategies to overcome these deficits. Just how well the various programs have succeeded is another matter. Many programs have reported improvements in cognitive areas as measured by tests of intelligence, school readiness, and achievement. For example, most of the Head Start centers reported small to moderate pretest to posttest gains, and such experimental programs as Klaus and Gray (1968), Karnes (1969), and Bereiter and Engelmann (Engelmann, 1970) reported IQ gains of up to twenty-five points. These apparent successes have been dimmed by findings of a fadeout effect in the elementary grades, where these children either regress or stay at a plateau while control groups of children who have not had the intervention treatment make a spurt and catch up (Gray and Klaus, 1970; Westinghouse, 1969). Some argue that one cannot expect long-term effects from intervention programs without continuing special environmental stimulation, but such a view implies that more needs to be done than merely remediating certain deficits. In any event, even if long-range effects can be demonstrated, educators must still judge whether the results are worth the costs.

Comparative experimental studies (Karnes, 1969; Spicker, 1971; Weikart, 1969) have provided some valuable information about the merits of the various treatment approaches of compensatory-education programs. Approaches stressing cognitive or academic-skill development produced the largest IQ increases; other programs produced IQ gains when they were highly structured and incorporated language development as an important objective.

Beyond this, we still know little about what constitutes the "appropriate" environmental treatment, the sequencing of curriculum materials within the treatment, the timing of such treatment, or the kinds of treatments needed for individuals with particular kinds of cognitive deficits. Infant, nursery, preschool, and parent-education programs continue to proliferate at a rapid rate, in spite of our present ignorance about proper treatment and doubts about the outcome. Whether such approaches can ever enable the urban poor to "catch up" to more affluent segments of society remains to be demonstrated.

Genetic-deficit model. Another variant of the "something is wrong with the child" hypothesis is the genetic-deficit model, most recently propounded by Jensen (1969) and Shockley (1971). The main (and greatly oversimplified) argument is that existing data (largely from twin studies) show individual differences in IQ to be largely hereditary and that, as a result, differences in IQ between socioeconomic-status groups or between racial groups are also largely hereditary, since the environmental contribution to the variance in IQ is insufficient to explain such group differences. According to Jensen, one can expect little gain in IQ from environmental manipulations such as the many types of compensatory-education programs now in existence. Shockley's main concern is that disproportionate reproduction in lower socioeconomic Negro subgroups is dysgenic for the entire population, and Herrnstein (1971) argues that we are moving not toward a classless society but one of increasing social stratification based on inherited IQ differences.

While a summary of the arguments advanced in opposition to the genetic model is beyond the scope of this paper, these range from arguments that the question is not a proper or valid one for study ("Is Intelligence Racial?" 1971), that data or methods needed to resolve this question are not available (Cavalli-Sforza, 1970), that Jensen's heritability measurements have questionable validity (Crow, 1969), and that interracial IQ differences can be accounted for within a genetic model by assuming a "malicious allocation" of Negroes to the poorest environments (Light and Smith, 1969), to Bereiter's (1970) contention that even within the strictures of Jensen's model substantial differences in IQ can be accounted for by environmental variables. According to Bereiter, a fourteen-point increase in mean IQ (without necessarily changing the population variance) can result from environmental changes; such an outcome would place the attainment of basic academic skills needed for gainful occupation within the capabilities of the great majority of those presently disadvantaged.

While Jensen feels that compensatory-education programs are of little use to disadvantaged pupils, he does not feel that educational efforts should be abandoned. Instead, the educator should consider a broader spectrum of abilities and design curricula suited to these children's stronger abilities. As an example, he cites his own two-level model of abilities; according to this model, low socioeconomic children achieve as well as high socioeconomic children at the first (associative) level of abilities but not at the second (conceptual) level. Low socioeconomic children, then, should be taught in a way that makes use of their associative abilities.

Nutritional-deficit model. The nutritional-deficit model asserts that inadequate protein intake or synthesis during brain development could result in some loss or change of function. Inasmuch as 60 per cent of brain growth is complete by the end of the first year, and 90 per cent by age five, early nutritional adequacy is important. Inadequate nutrition during pregnancy is also implicated in higher incidence of prematurity and complication of pregnancy in low socioeconomic populations (Pasamanick and Knoblock, 1966; Pasamanick, 1969). Just how extensive or severe malnutrition might be among America's urban poor today is not known, but "there exist subclinical states of poor nutrition throughout the world that go unrecognized and may be perpetuating silent destruction upon the learning skills of the world's population" (Kappelman, 1971, p. 160).

Harrell, Woodyard, and Gates (1955), in a classic study, provided nutritional supplements to experimental groups of pregnant women and gave placebos to control groups; later they gave intelligence tests to the offspring. Significantly higher IQ's of experimental-group children resulted in two of the three areas where the studies were carried out; in New York City, this amounted to an IQ difference of eight points at four years of age. Cravioto (1966, 1968) found IQ gains of up to eighteen points in studies of severely malnourished Latin American populations—provided nutrition therapy was instituted by two years of age; he found no change in response to nutrition therapy after four years of age.

If previous research is correct, the time for prevention or remediation comes well before the schools are concerned with the child. School nutrition programs for the children of poverty, while laudable for humanitarian reasons, may thus not be expected to remediate early damage. Effects of improved health and vigor on motivation and school achievement (and long-range effects on the next generation) are of course another matter.

In addition to nutritional problems, children of the poor suffer from a host of health problems, which prevent the children from effective school performance. According to A. F. North, Senior Pediatrician with Project Head Start, "Children living in poverty have more frequent and more severe illnesses and are less likely to receive adequate health care than are more advantaged children, so health assumes an even more important role in the development of socially disadvantaged children" (1968, p. 195). (Children of the poor, particularly in aging sections of large cities, have higher incidence of lead and other heavy-metal poisoning, with its attendant CNS damage.) However, the difficulty of obtaining good data relating to health problems of young children precludes exact documentation of this claim. In a study of 1,467 Head Start enrollees given medical and dental screening in Boston in the summer of 1965 (Mico, 1968), 77 per cent were referred for further diagnosis or treatment for one or more reasons; however, in spite of these difficulties, 80 per cent of the enrollees were given general-health ratings of from good to excellent. Certainly evidence is needed as to whether these health problems can be effectively treated and whether the treatment results in improved intellectual functioning.

School-Disparity Models

These models all have in common two basic ideas. First, the urban poor child is not inferior to the middle-class child, although he may be different in various ways. Second, the schools are responsible for the achievement gap between the poor and the middle-class child, since they fail to reach the different child. The school-disparity models vary in their conceptions of just how the urban child differs from the middle-class child and also in how the school is at fault.

Cultural-difference model. The cultural-difference model, as presented by Baratz and Baratz (1970) and Stewart (1968), refers to language differences between American Negro cultural groups and the middle-class culture, although the model can be extended to other ethnic groups and cognitive functions. Proponents of this model argue that the schools—instead of attempting massive intervention procedures with culturally different children—must eliminate their archaic and inappropriate procedures for dealing with cultural differences. Intervention programs have failed, according to this view, because they are based on nonexistent deficits, black dialect is not a defective linguistic and conceptual system, as charged by many interventionists, but a structurally coherent although different system. In other words, it has all the components of an adequate grammar. Education for these children should not attempt to destroy the experience and cultural forms with which the child is familiar, but use culturally relevant methods and procedures to teach new materials. Thus, in the Baratz program, instruction is begun in the child's dialect and extended to standard English and mainstream culture.

Culture-of-poverty model. The culture-of-poverty model (Banfield, 1971; Gladwin, 1961; Lewis, 1966) refers to a way of life or style of living that is handed down across generations of the poor and transcends social, racial, regional, and national boundaries; thus, urban poor the world over have much the same system of values and style of living.

Presumably, ghetto children have acquired the basic values and attitudes of their subculture early in life, which accounts for their differences in behavior and achievement compared to the middle-class child. These values and attitudes include strong feelings of fatalism and belief in chance, strong present-time orientation and short time perspective, impulsiveness or inability to delay gratification or plan for the future, concrete rather than abstract thinking processes and concrete verbal behavior, feelings of inferiority, acceptance of aggression and illegitimacy, and authoritarianism. Such people have little interest or motivation for schooling and achievement, and are supposedly resistant to change no matter how it is advanced.

Riessman (1962) suggests that a recognition of this different culture can aid the teacher to structure his social-emotional relationships with the child in such a way as to make use of the child's in-group loyalties, informality, humor, and so on, and to structure his teaching so as to take advantage of the child's particular abilities and style of learning.

The idea of a culture of poverty has been sharply criticized (Allen, 1970), in that this position implies a consensus and homogeneity of values and styles of living within the poor that is not borne out by empirical studies. Studies supporting the culture-of-poverty idea have been observational and anecdotal in nature and involved extremely small samples of people; further, values derived from observations of behavior are used circularly to explain that same behavior. Finally, the definition of the poor is not clear-cut; the model may apply only to a small number of extreme poor and not to the majority of ghetto residents.

Bicultural model. The bicultural model, as expounded by Valentine (1971), refers to the ghetto Negro, although it could apply to other ethnic groups as well. According to this view, blacks are simultaneously committed to both black culture and mainstream culture (the two are not mutually exclusive, as often assumed); ethnic socialization comes from the family and other primary groups, and mainstream enculturation comes from such sources as television, mass marketing, and public institutions and amusements. A good deal of the mainstream cultural content remains latent and potential, since there is little opportunity to practice mainstream behavior patterns in everyday life. (For instance, the black may comprehend standard English, even though he uses dialect.) There may nevertheless be psychological allegiance to mainstream cultural values, aspirations, and role models.

If educators, instead of assuming that the black child lacks mainstream culture, would realize that he has acquired a good bit of mainstream culture but may be too inhibited to demonstrate it, they could provide real aid to the biculturation process through attitudes of acceptance and awareness. Those blacks who have genuine difficulties in adjusting to mainstream cultural institutions need special guidance and help in removal of obstacles to biculturation.

Institutional-prejudice model. Proponents of this model (Clark, 1965; Rosenthal and Jacobsen, 1964; Stein, 1971) regard the achievement gap as the consequence of an institutional prejudice against the children of the poor, and not due to any inherent deficiencies on their part. Teachers and administrators prejudge these children as incompetent and difficult to handle; and their low expectancies of poor children's success may act as self-fulfilling prophecies. To discourage the achievement of ghetto children administrators may formulate devious policies, such as tracking, watered-down curricula, nonacademic goals, assignment of ill-qualified teachers to ghetto schools, encouragement of dropping out, excessive suspensions and expulsions, and a policy of accountability to no one for lack of success in teaching. Such an atmosphere discourages both the children and the few teachers who are sincerely trying to teach. Stein terms all of the above "strategies for failure," which may be accompanied by the setting up of many ineffective compensatory programs in the schools. A way out of the situation is seen in the rise of parent groups who seek to control the education of their children.

Deactualization Models

Deactualization models all have a humanistic underpinning: The individual is unique, and his subjective experiences and self-concept are basic determiners of his behavior and development. Human nature is basically good; the individual has the capacity for insight and for sustained motivation to actualize his potentials. The individual is constantly growing and "becoming," and his primary motivation is to actualize his potential and develop into the best version of a person he could become relative to his own values and goals.

The traditional nursery school embodies many of these ideas (Elkind, 1970), such as individualized instruction, discovery learning, and use of intrinsic motivation. This extension of the traditional nursery school overlaps in its viewpoint wth progressive education, Piagetian theory, British Infant School approaches, today's youth movement, certain neo-Freudians, and the humanist-existentialist viewpoint toward human nature and development.

The children of the poor differ in achievement from middle-class children because they have not been motivated to actualize their potentials; instead, they have been frustrated and alienated so that they do not have the basic trust and autonomy necessary to take risks, reach out, grow, and attempt to learn in a meaningful way. A diagnosis-prescription approach is not what is needed to help these children, but rather a self-prescription. What they need is a warm, accepting environment, a prepared environment of many alternatives and opportunities, and freedom to choose accordingly (to play, ask questions, explore, manipulate, and experiment to see what happens). Teachers are to supply the warm interpersonal relations and the environment, and then consult, tutor, advise as the occasion demands. When the children of the poor gain emotional security, they will become free to choose and to release their learning powers and actualize their potential. (At times they may need help, such as specific instruction or drill, but always within the context of ongoing meaningful learning for them.)

Since each child is basically unique, it makes no sense to compare his achievement as he actualizes his potential to that of other children through standardized tests or other normative criteria. Thus, comparison of urban poor children with middle-class children in terms of achievement is really a pseudo-problem.

Examples of programs that can be interpreted as largely concerned with self-actualization are the Bank Street Early Childhood Center (Biber and Franklin, 1967), Cross-Cultural Nursery (Weber, 1970), traditional nursery programs extended to the disadvantaged (Spicker, 1971), British Infant Schools (Rogers, 1971), New School at the University of North Dakota (Silberman, 1970), Summerhill (Neill, 1960), Rochester's World of Inquiry School (Weber, 1970). These schools differ in many ways, including degree of guidance given by the teacher; however, their common essential ingredient is to allow the individual freedom to choose what he wants to learn from many alternatives provided in the environment.

Lack of evaluation and systematic research into educational practices is one of the major criticisms of this approach. There seems to be an overemphasis on arts and crafts, with an isolation from real problems of the outside world. In general, educational goals are vague and ambiguous. Proponents of this approach assume that free selection implies interest and sustained motivation and that teacher selection implies lack of interest and motivation. As yet there is no evidence for this, nor for the goodness of human nature and self-insight. Such programs leave much to chance, for the individual may never get beyond superficial interests or random activities.

New Directions

The problem facing educators in the seventies remains much the same as it was in the sixties: to account for the achievement gap between the urban poor and middle-class children and to find ways to close it. What is new is a growing disillusionment with many approaches tried in the sixties, and with the capabilities of urban school systems to deal with the problem at all. What, then, is the future course of the various approaches discussed here?

Environmental approaches. These models have led to the development of compensatory-education programs whose objectives are to diagnose deficiencies and to remediate or prevent them, if the programs are started early enough. In the early seventies, although Head Start has retrenched somewhat, other programs are proliferating at a rapid rate, with government-sponsored day care soon to become a reality. At this point, we do not know whether these programs will be any more successful than they were in the sixties, although their very proliferation assures their continued existence.

In the sixties these programs were not successful in producing long-range effects or in producing effects at acceptable levels of efficiency (size of effects relative to time and cost). In addition, a successful "delivery system" was lacking, one that could transmit promising experimental programs for wider or mass applications.

Since we still do not know what makes for a successful program, it is imperative that intervention programs be kept experimental, with well-designed evaluation procedures. Many questions can and should be researched in order to determine the limits of modifiability of the human organism and to formulate a prototype program (Sigel, 1971). The most effective time for intervention, the duration of the intervention, and the type of program that is most effective with children of different racial/ethnic backgrounds or with different cognitive deficits are all of great importance. Also, the possible inhibitory or facilitating effects of the same training stimulation at different points in the curriculum sequence or at different ages must be determined (Sigel, 1971; White and Held, 1967). This kind of research will be time-consuming, but there is no alternative unless we are to be satisfied with compensatory programs at their present levels of development.

Various programs are now operating at different age levels; but there is no genuine continuity, since such programs are not articulated with each other. (The abrupt discontinuity of the transition from compensatory preschools into traditional elementary programs—with their different values, expectations, and regimentation—is frequently blamed for fade-out effects.) As everyone knows, intelligence continues to develop at least through the teens without any abrupt shift at puberty. It follows that we need, at least experimentally, articulated programs of sustained duration from infancy through high school graduation. Such planned continuity can best be carried out within the structure of the established urban school system, which could be extended downward to include infant and nursery programs. Such an administrative unit would make it more feasible to carry out longitudinal studies with proper controls and evaluation.

Urban systems must take seriously the employment of an evaluation expert for each school, one who is well versed in research design, measurement, and statistics, and who can involve the faculty in continuing and constructive evaluation of the success of their work.

Nutritional approaches. Although we have been made aware of the importance of adequate nutrition for prenatal and early development, and of the high incidence of nutritional and health problems among the urban poor, it seems unlikely that any great gains will be made without an extensive government commitment to public health and a program that will attract ghetto mothers and children. Educators can help by giving their junior and senior high school students information on the importance of prenatal care and nutrition. Also, well-articulated programs from infancy to high school graduation can provide a vehicle for associated health and nutritional care.

Genetic approach. This model has stimulated no programs in the sixties, but it has stimulated thought to the point where we must take the question of the hereditary background of the learner more seriously. Do different social and ethnic groups have inherently different patterns of abilities and hence require different educational programs? Intergroup profile differences (Jensen, 1970; Lesser, Fifer, and Clark, 1965; Westinghouse, 1969)—although they cannot be attributed solely to differences in heredity—at least suggest that some attention must be focused on these questions.

According to Herrnstein (1971), if compensatory programs succeed in creating equivalent environments for all children throughout their development, then heredity will account for all differences between individuals and we will develop an aristocracy far more permanent than anything in the past. We may then need to take more seriously the notion of genetic engineering (or some sort of sophisticated eugenics program) to attain an egalitarian society. Presently know techniques of population and birth control, coupled with such new advances as artificial implantation into nonbiological mothers (prenatal adoption) of fertilized ova of superior genetic stock and reproduction by cloning (Rorvik, 1971), suggest means of halting dysgenic trends of which Shockley (1971), and others warn. (This may be the ultimate environmentalist position, manipulating an individual's genetic potential as well as his surroundings.) The genetic question is still very much open, and may provide us with new solutions in the future.

If, on the other hand, as Bereiter (1970) suggests, we can—through compensatory education alone—succeed in lifting the IQs of the genetically most poorly endowed to a level that would permit them to undertake a gainful occupation and enjoy a reasonable standard of living, we will have eliminated a major social problem.

School-disparity approaches. Advocates of these models have made us aware that schools in the sixties have not met the challenge of recognizing the cultural differences of the children of the poor and teaching them accordingly; indeed, school practices may actively interfere with and inhibit the children's ability to learn.

If it is correct that something is wrong with the schools and not with the children, then certain recommendations for the seventies emerge. First, a major research effort (given government support of a magnitude at least equal to that given the deprivation hypothesis) should be made to discover the specific subcultural differences of importance to education and the ways of gearing teaching methods and curriculum to these differences to produce relevant educational outcomes. Since most of our major cities contain a number of minority subcultures, this may well imply a much more individualized approach to education than heretofore employed.

Second, if one accepts the school-disparity models, it must be noted that early intervention is not implied. (If there are differences, not deficits, early education has no priority.) Instead, the massive funds now devoted to early intervention programs could be channeled into improvements and research at the primary and secondary levels.

Third, the charge that school administrators and teachers treat ghetto children so prejudicially as to doom them to failure must be investigated and met, where needed, with major reforms. Administrative policies can be changed through administrative reorganizations, with ghetto parents and teachers participating in the decision making. Most would agree that we must improve, rather than eliminate, our public schools.

Actualization approaches. Programs that strive to promote self-actualization are less explicitly advanced and identified than are the various compensatory programs. The very fact that such programs seem to be in tune with both the youth movement and the traditional nursery approach makes it likely that we will see more of them in the future. However, unless we are to accept on faith that such programs will have more desirable outcomes than alternative educational measures, we must have careful evaluations of their worth. Such evaluation, combined with research aimed at discovering the most worthwhile learning options to offer the child at a particular stage of development, is strongly needed in the seventies.

Common trends and recommendations. All of the models—whether they are trying to correct or prevent deficits, to teach to the cultural differences of students, or to release self-actualizing tendencies —seem to be converging on the idea of individualized instruction. If we are indeed moving in the direction of individualized instruction, then it seems important to integrate all three positions as effectively as possible. Thus, students should be given as much freedom as they can handle from infancy through high school; but teachers, armed with knowledge of the students' deficits and differences (where these exist), can use this information to advise, consult, and intervene at the right moment to aid.

Since early-education programs evidently are going to be with us for some time, every effort must be made to develop an articulated total education program, with particular emphasis on improvements in the elementary and secondary programs. Again, all models imply such a need.

Educators must seriously consider the relationship of school achievement to later success on the job and in life. Evidence from a variety of sources indicates that IQ and school achievement are poorly correlated with job success (Jensen, 1970; Kohlberg and Mayer, 1971), although the correlation is greater between these factors and occupational status. It is likely that opportunities for employment and advancement in later life are now too strongly tied to educational qualifications. What is needed is to identify just what is really important and relevant for success in life, and to make sure that proper priorities are established in the schools.

In conclusion, the seventies must be a decade of improvement in the education of the urban poor. The schools themselves can do the job, and they should attempt it. Even if schools have been doing a questionable job in the past, they should not be eliminated in favor of other institutions or reduced in significance, as some would have us believe (Holt, 1965; Illich, 1971). On the contrary, with some measure of relief from the enrollment pressures and scarcity of qualified teachers which characterized the sixties, this is the ideal time to concentrate on quality education for all.

References

ALLEN, V. L. "Theoretical Issues in Poverty Research." *Journal of Social Issues*, 1970, *26*, 149–167.

AUSUBEL, D. P. "The Effects of Cultural Deprivation on Learning Patterns." *Audiovisual Instruction*, 1965, *10*, 10–12.

BANFIELD, E. C. *The Unheavenly City.* New York: Harper & Row, 1971.

BARATZ, S. D., AND BARATZ, J. C. "Early Childhood Intervention: The

Social Science Base of Institutional Racism." *Harvard Educational Review*, 1970, *40*, 29–50.

BEREITER, C. "Genetics and Educability: Educational Implications of the Jensen Debate." In J. Hellmuth (Ed.), *Disadvantaged Child*. Vol. 3. New York: Brunner/Mazel, 1970. Pp. 279–299.

BIBER, B., AND FRANKLIN, M. B. "The Relevance of Developmental and Psychodynamic Concepts to the Education of the Preschool Child." In J. Hellmuth (Ed.), *Disadvantaged Child*. Vol. 1. Seattle, Wash.: Special Child Publications, 1967. Pp. 305–323.

BLOOM, B. *Stability and Change in Human Characteristics*. New York: Wiley, 1964.

CAVALLI-SFORZA, L. L. "Problems and Prospects of Genetic Analysis of Intelligence at the Intra- and Interracial Level." In J. Hellmuth (Ed.), *Disadvantaged Child*, Vol. 3. New York: Brunner/Mazel, 1970. Pp. 111–123.

CLARK, K. B. *Dark Ghetto*. New York: Harper & Row, 1965.

CRAVIOTO, J. "Nutrition, Growth, and Neurointegrative Development: An Experimental and Ecologic Study." *Supplement to Pediatrics*, 1966, *38*.

CRAVIOTO, J. "Nutritional Deficiencies and Mental Performances in Childhood." In D. Glass (Ed.), *Environmental Influences*. New York: Rockefeller University Press, 1968. Pp. 3–51.

CROW, J. "Genetic Theories and Influences: Comments on the Value of Diversity." *Harvard Educational Review*, 1969, *39*, 301–309.

DEUTSCH, C. P. "Auditory Discrimination and Learning: Social Factors." *Merrill-Palmer Quarterly*, 1964, *10*, 277–296.

ELKIND, D. "The Case for the Academic Preschool: Fact or Fiction?" *Young Children*, 1970, *25*, 132–140.

ENGELMANN, S. "The Effectiveness of Direct Instruction on IQ Performance and Achievement in Reading and Arithmetic." In J. Hellmuth (Ed.), *Disadvantaged Child*. Vol. 3. New York: Brunner/Mazel, 1970. Pp. 339–361.

GLADWIN, T. "The Anthropologist's View of Poverty." In *The Social Work Forum*. New York: Columbia University Press, 1961.

GORDON, I. "Early Child Stimulation through Parent Education: A Final Report to the Children's Bureau." Gainesville: University of Florida Press, 1969.

GRAY, S. W., AND KLAUS, R. A. "The Early Training Project: A Seventh-Year Report." *Child Development*, 1970, *41*, 909–924.

HARRELL, R. F., WOODYARD, E., AND GATES, A. I. *The Effects of Mothers' Diets on the Intelligence of Offspring*. Bureau of Publications, Teachers College, New York, 1955.

HERRNSTEIN, R. "IQ." *Atlantic Monthly,* September 1971, pp. 43–64.

HOLT, J. "How to Help Babies Learn—Without Teaching Them." *Redbook,* 1965, *126,* 54–55.

HUNT, J. MC V. *Intelligence and Experience.* New York: Ronald Press, 1961.

HUNT, J. MC V. "The Psychological Basis for Using Preschool Environment as an Antidote for Cultural Deprivation." *Merrill-Palmer Quarterly,* 1964, *10,* 209–248.

ILLICH, I. *Deschool Society.* New York: Harper & Row, 1971.

"Is Intelligence Racial?" *Newsweek,* May 10, 1971, pp. 69–70.

JENSEN, A. R. "Cumulative Deficit in Compensatory Education." *Journal of School Psychology,* 1966, *4,* 37–47.

JENSEN, A. R. "How Much Can We Boost IQ and Scholastic Achievement?" *Harvard Educational Review,* 1969, *39,* 1–123.

JENSEN, A. R. "Another Look at Culture—Fair Testing." In J. Hellmuth (Ed.), *Disadvantaged Child.* Vol. 3. New York: Brunner/Mazel, 1970. Pp. 53–101.

KAPPELMAN, M. H. "Prenatal and Perinatal Factors Which Influence Learning." In J. Hellmuth (Ed.), *Exceptional Infant.* Vol. 2. New York: Brunner/Mazel, 1971, 155–171.

KARNES, M. B. "Research and Development Program on Preschool Disadvantaged Children." Final Report, Vol. 1, University of Illinois, Contract No. OE-6-10-235, U.S. Office of Education, 1969.

KLAUS, R. A., AND GRAY, S. W. "The Early Training Project for Disadvantaged Children: A Report after Five Years." *Monographs of the Society for Research in Child Development,* 1968, *33*(4).

KOHLBERG, L., AND MAYER, R. S. "Report to the Office of Economic Opportunity." Cited in *Report on Preschool Education,* July 14, 1971, p. 6.

LAMBIE, D. Z., AND WEIKART, D. P. "Ypsilanti Carnegie Infant Project." In J. Hellmuth (Ed.), *Disadvantaged Child.* Vol. 3. New York: Brunner/Mazel, 1970. Pp. 362–395.

LESSER, G. S., FIFER, G., AND CLARK, D. H. "Mental Abilities of Children from Different Social-Class and Cultural Groups." *Monographs of the Society for Research in Child Development,* 1965, *30*(4).

LEWIS, O. "The Culture of Poverty." *Scientific American,* 1966, *215,* 19–25.

LIGHT, R. J., AND SMITH, P. V. "Social Allocation Models of Intelligence." *Harvard Educational Review,* 1969, *39,* 484–510.

MEIER, J. H., NIMNICHT, G., AND MC AFEE, O. "An Autotelic Responsive Environment Nursery School for Deprived Children." In J. Hellmuth (Ed.), *Disadvantaged Child.* Vol. 2. New York: Brunner/ Mazel, 1968. Pp. 300–316.

MICO, P. R. "Head Start Health: The Boston Experience of 1965." In J. Hellmuth (Ed.), *Disadvantaged Child.* Vol. 2. New York: Brunner/Mazel, 1968. Pp. 187–215.

NEILL, A. S. *Summerhill: A Radical Approach to Child Rearing.* London: Hart, 1960.

NORTH, A. F. "Pediatric Care in Project Head Start." In J. Hellmuth (Ed.), *Disadvantaged Child.* Vol. 2. New York: Brunner/Mazel, 1968. Pp. 95–124.

PASAMANICK, B. "A Tract for the Times: Some Sociobiologic Aspects of Science, Race, and Racism." *American Journal of Orthopsychiatry,* 1969, *39,* 7–15.

PASAMANICK, B., AND KNOBLOCK, H. "The Contribution of Some Organic Factors to School Retardation in Negro Children." In S. W. Webster (Ed.), *The Disadvantaged Learner: Knowing, Understanding, Educating.* San Francisco: Chandler Publishing Co., 1966. Pp. 286–292.

RIESSMAN, F. *Culturally Deprived Child.* New York: Harper & Row, 1962.

ROGERS, V. R. *Teaching in the British Primary School.* New York: Macmillan, 1971.

RORVIK, D. *Brave New Baby.* New York: Doubleday, 1971.

ROSENTHAL, R., AND JACOBSON, L. F. "Teacher Expectations for the Disadvantaged." *Scientific American,* 1964, *218,* 19–23.

SHOCKLEY, W. "Negro IQ Deficit: Failure of a 'Malicious Coincidence' Model Warrants New Research Proposals." *Review of Educational Research,* 1971, *41,* 227–248.

SIGEL, I. "Developmental Theory: Its Place and Relevance in Early Intervention Programs." Paper presented at biennial meeting of the Society for Research in Child Development, Minneapolis, April 1971.

SILBERMAN, C. E. *Crisis in the Classroom.* New York: Random House, 1970.

SPICKER, H. H. "Intellectual Development through Early Childhood Education." *Exceptional Children,* 1971, *37,* 629–664.

STEIN, A. "Strategies of Failure." *Harvard Educational Review,* 1971, *41,* 158–204.

STEWART, W. "Continuity and Change in American Negro Dialects." *The Florida FL Reporter,* 1968, *6.*

VALENTINE, C. A. "Deficit, Difference, and Bicultural Models of Afro-

American Behavior." *Harvard Educational Review*, 1971, *41*, 137–157.

WEBER, E. *Early Childhood Education*. Worthington, Ohio: C. A. Jones Publishing Co., 1970.

WEIKART, D. P. "Comparative Study of Three Preschool Curricula." Paper presented at biennial meeting of the Society for Research in Child Development, Santa Monica, California, March 1969.

Westinghouse Learning Corporation/Ohio University. *The Impact of Head Start: An Evaluation of the Effects of Head Start on Children's Cognitive and Affective Development*. Vols. I and II. Springfield, Virginia: Clearinghouse for Federal Scientific and Technical Information, Sales Department, U.S. Department of Commerce, 1969.

WHITE, B. L., AND HELD, R. "Plasticity of Sensorimotor Development in the Human Infant." In J. Hellmuth (Ed.), *Exceptional Infant*. Vol. 1. New York: Brunner/Mazel, 1967. Pp. 291–313.

CHAPTER 5

Nonstandard Speech Patterns

Lloyd J. Leaverton

There is vigorous disagreement among and between educators, psychologists, and linguists concerning the acceptability of nonstandard speech patterns as legitimate forms of communication. The "standard English advocates" insist that nonstandard patterns interfere with effective thinking. The "nonstandard advocates" maintain that nonstandard speech patterns permit the user to engage in just as high-level abstract reasoning and overall problem solving as does the standardized dialect.

Bernstein's (1964) research has possibly exerted the strongest influence in support of the first position. After comparing the speech

The psycholinguistic project referred to in this paper has since 1965 been cooperatively supported by the Illinois Plan for Program Development for Gifted Students, State of Illinois and the Board of Education, City of Chicago.

patterns of lower-class and middle-class children, he concluded that lower-class children fail to learn a linguistic code that enables them to deal with the complex and abstract situations they will encounter in formal educaton. The "restricted" code (as Bernstein has labeled it) tends to fixate the child at a limited conceptual level. On the other hand, the "elaborated" code learned by the middle-class child prepares him to function at the abstract conceptual level required for effective problem solving in our complex society. Bereiter and Engelmann (1966) take a similar position. When confronting children from communities where nonstandard speech patterns are used, they conclude, the teacher must "start from zero" and proceed on the assumption that the children have no prior knowledge of English.

A beautiful example refuting the above point of view was recently related to me by Mrs. Olga Davis, a member of our research staff. A practice teacher under her supervision was teaching her first-grade class the concepts *death* and *extinct*. When a faculty member from the university came to observe the practice teacher, she was appalled to find that disadvantaged first-grade children were being expected to distinguish between such abstract terms. Mrs. Davis then approached the class and asked, "Children, you remember we discussed *death* and *extinct* last week? Can you tell me about our discussion?" John raised his hand and said, "Martin Luther King, he extinct." Floyd immediately exclaimed, "That's not right. He just one man. There whole lot of other people still running around. Extinct mean whole lot of things used to be alive and walking around and you don't see them no more—like them dinasars, they extinct." As Fasold (1971) points out, we cannot claim that sentences with double negatives are inherently illogical unless we are prepared to claim that all French speakers think illogically.

Comprehensive discussions of the legitimacy of black nonstandard English are found in the writings of Shuy (1966, 1969), Stewart (1970), and Carroll (1971).

Sledd (1969), an eminent linguistic scholar, questions the wisdom of imposing the standard dialect on children at all. He suggests that the rejection of "black English" may be a form of displaced racial prejudice: "The fact is, of course, that Northern employers and labor leaders dislike black faces but use black English as an excuse" (p. 1311).

A child's self-concept, in Sledd's opinion, can be badly damaged when he is forced to learn standard English by repetitive drill, derived by analogy from structuralist methods of teaching foreign languages: "Professor Troike can argue the success of his methods by showing that after six months of drills a little black girl could repeat 'his hat' after her teacher, instead of translating automatically to 'he hat.' Unfortunately, tapes do not record psychological damage, or compare the effectiveness of other ways of teaching, or show what might better have been learned in the same time instead of learning to repeat 'his hat'" (p. 1312).

Instead, Sledd offers the following recommendations: "Bidialectalism would never have been invented if our society were not divided into the dominant white majority and the exploited minorities. Children should be taught that. They should be taught the relations between group differences and speech differences, and the good and bad uses of speech differences by groups and by individuals. The teaching would require a more serious study of grammar, lexicography, dialectology, and linguistic history than our educational system now provides—require it at least of prospective English teachers" (p. 1315).

Kochmann (1969) has also strongly urged that we should not force standard English speech patterns on black urban children—especially the adolescent living in the black ghetto. Instead, we should focus on intensive language instruction within the framework of the nonstandard forms with which the child can identify.

During the past seven years, I and my colleagues have been testing an approach in language-arts instruction that differs in some basic aspects from the two positions just discussed (Leaverton, 1965, 1967, 1969, 1971a). We feel that the ultimate acceptance of Bernstein's position would force one to conclude that the "elaborated" code used by the columnist William Buckley results in more effective thinking than the "restricted" code frequently used by Samuel Clemens or Will Rogers. We cannot accept this conclusion. On the other hand, the position taken by those who feel that it is undesirable or unnecessary to have children learn the standardized dialect is also unrealistic. Sledd, I feel, is correct in his concern for the psychological damage that can be done by belittling the established speech patterns of the child's home and community. He is wrong, in my opinion, in concluding that standard English cannot be taught in a way that respects the established speech patterns of the child when he enters school. Children—especially primary-grade children—usually want to please their teacher. If standard English is introduced as another way of saying something already familiar to them, the negative results described by Sledd need not occur. In fact, our research has shown that if the children's established speech forms are accepted as legitimate forms of communication while those speech forms used in the school by the teacher and observed in the books are systematically introduced, the children readily accept and enjoy learning the speech forms traditionally fostered by the school.

Our research was initiated to test a model of language-arts instruction based on the following conjectures and assumptions.

The first conjecture is based on substantial research findings concluding that the material to which the learner is introduced should be meaningful to him; that is, in the area of language-arts instruction, the child's established speech patterns must be accepted and used—especially when his speech patterns are different in some basic respects from standard English.

Second, at no time during the learning situation should the child be given the impression that his basic established speech patterns are inferior speech. He is, however, expected to learn to distinguish between his familiar speech patterns and the standard ones, which may be unfamiliar to him. To facilitate this distinction, we introduce in our research model the concepts of *everyday talk* and *school talk.* Everyday talk refers to the nonstandard pattern with respect to verb usage. School talk refers to the statement or story in which the verb form corresponds to the standardized dialect. Since the child feels most comfortable using the everyday talk patterns that are familiar to him, the initial emphasis in the approach we are testing—in beginning reading and oral-language activities—is placed on having the child make a transition from the familiar everyday talk form to the unfamiliar school talk form. Once the child has mastered the school talk form, the teacher may ask him whether a particular statement is everyday talk or school talk. If it is school talk, the child may be asked to change the statement to everyday talk, or vice versa.

In considering programs for children whose speech patterns differ from standard English, we had to ask ourselves what aspect of standard English should be emphasized in the program. Differences occur in grammatical form, pronunciation, and vocabulary. Which pronunciation system can be identified as corresponding to the standard dialect? Also, even if a standard pronunciation system can be identified and justified, will it be educationally feasible with primary children to focus on this aspect of the standard dialect? Even if it were possible and feasible to identify and teach a standard pronunciation system to primary-grade children, there is far more tolerance in our society toward regional variations in pronunciation and vocabulary than toward differences in verb usage. In considering these questions, we concluded that in our research we would focus only on the difference between the standard and nonstandard dialects that existed in the area of verb usage. Pronunciation would be considered only if it determined the form of the verb (for instance, *work, works*).

The decision to focus on verbs *only* as the distinguishing variable between the nonstandard and the standard was also influenced by the fact that transition from the nonstandard to the standard pattern often can be made by *adding* to the nonstandard pattern. For example, the statement "My daddy strong" can be changed to the standard dialect by adding *is*. Similarly, "My daddy work" can be changed to the standard pattern by adding *s*. This aspect of the model is consistent with research studies showing that learning is enhanced if it starts at a point meaningful to the learner and does not force him to unlearn previously learned material. Therefore, in developing our research materials we tried to focus primarily on speech patterns that could be changed into standard forms by *adding* to the nonstandard form.

The reading series (Davis, Gladney, and Leaverton, 1969) consists of eight units. The focus of each unit is on a particular verb form that frequently appears in nonstandard form in the child's informal conversation. The content of the stories focuses on the child, his community, and his ethnic group. The everyday talk story is introduced first, followed by the same story with the verb form changed to correspond to the school talk form (see Table 1).

Each unit is printed as a separate paperback book. As soon as a child has completed a book, it becomes his property to take home and share with his younger brothers and sisters. Space is provided in several of the books for the children to write their own stories. If the child's story uses the nonstandard verb form under consideration, he is asked to change it into the standard form. If the child's story uses "school talk" verb forms, he may be asked to change to "everyday talk" verb forms.

Oral language instructional activities were also developed as a companion program to the reading series (Gladney and Leaverton, 1968). These activities, organized by units, focus on the same verb forms used in the reading materials. Each unit introduces a new verb form systematically to prevent errors of distribution. For example, the verb form *are* is introduced immediately following the completion of the unit dealing with *is* to avoid overcorrections such as *they is*. In introducing each unit, the teacher tells a story or asks a question structured to elicit from the children their speech patterns in the verb area being studied. The children's statements in nonstandard and standard forms are recorded on the chalkboard. For example, some of the responses given by the children in a conversation about their friends during a lesson on the use of *is* in simple sentences were:

Table 1. VERB FORMS IN EXPERIMENTAL READING MATERIALS

Reading Materials		Everyday Talk	School Talk
Unit 1	All about Me	Employs the verb *got*	Introduces the verb *have*
Unit 2	All about Me and My Family	Absence of *is* and *are*	Introduces *is* and *are*
Unit 3	In My House and in My School	Absence of third person singular	Introduces the verb ending -*s*
Unit 4	Yesterday	Absence of -*ed* ending	Introduces the -*ed* ending
Unit 5	Working and Playing	Use of *do*	Introduces *does*
Unit 6	At School	Use of *be* in place of *am, is, are*	Introduces *am, is,* and *are* in place of *be*
Unit 7	I Be (Am) Scared When . . .	Use of *he be, we be, they be*	Introduces standard forms *he is, we are, they are*
Unit 8	Afro-Americans	Serves as a review for the verb patterns introduced in the preceding books. This book has only one set of stories; in the stories the verb slot is left blank and the child is to fill in the blank with the school talk form.	

"Marie my friend." "Timuel is smart." "Robert he bad in school." The teacher then describes each sentence as everyday talk or school talk, pointing out to the children that the sentences omitting *is* are everyday talk and the sentences including *is* are school talk. The teacher explains that school talk and everyday talk are simply different ways of expressing the same ideas, neither one "wrong" or "right" but used in different situations, that is, in school or out of school.

After the activities stemming from the children's own statements are concluded, prewritten sentences and stories in everyday talk and dialogue in school talk which include the verbs being studied are given to the children for practice in changing the nonstandard dialect to the standard dialect in orally spoken sentences. Finally, at the close of each unit, each child is asked to give an informal oral presentation using school talk.

At no time during the lessons is the teacher required to interrupt the child to correct his speech. If a nonstandard form occurs in a child's statement with respect to a verb form studied in a previous unit, the teacher asks the child or the class whether the statement was everyday talk or school talk. If, however, the verb form is one that has not been introduced in the oral language activities, the teacher does not call attention to the nonstandard form.

A comprehensive analysis of the research findings is reported in another paper (Leaverton, 1971b). Hence, it will not be repeated here. The major findings, briefly summarized, are as follows: (1) The group of first-grade children who received both versions of the materials (everyday talk followed by school talk) excelled in nineteen of twenty measures investigated as compared with a matched group of children in the same class who were given only the school talk version of the reading materials (Leaverton, 1971). (2) The children who received the experimental treatment in first grade were retested when they reached third grade. The results were then compared with those of all other third-grade children in the school. Table 2 gives the results of these findings. In all of the subtests the low children in the experimental group were higher than the low children in the control group.

Table 2. Scores of Experimental and Control Groups on Reading Subtests of Metropolitan Elementary Test

	Above 1.5	Above 2.0	Above 2.5	Above 3.0	Above 3.5
			Per Cent		
Reading					
Experimental	100	100	58	36	18
Control	97	89	50	19	04
Word Knowledge					
Experimental	100	71	47	29	17
Control	87	75	48	20	07
Word Discrimination					
Experimental	100	82	47	35	29
Control	96	93	53	28	17
Language					
Experimental	100	94	64	52	17
Control	88	80	64	34	13

N for Experimental Group = 17.
N for Control Group = 76.

Several studies in progress are using the Psycholinguistic Reading materials to replicate and/or investigate our findings in further detail.

Possibly the most significant value of our model is its influence on the attitude and behavior of the teacher toward the children's oral language. The traditional approaches to reading and oral-language programs frequently have not taken into account the effect of the nonstandard dialect on the interaction between teacher and child. Possibly to a large extent, the teacher's attitude has contributed to the difficulty many of the children have had in learning to read and achieve ultimate success in the school situation. In using this model, the teacher is at no time required to criticize the speech of the children while they are beginning to read or during the oral-language activities.

What are the implications of this model for future research? The model places emphasis on the phrase as the initial unit given to the child in the beginning reading situation, as contrasted to the isolated word (emphasized in the "look-see" approach) or the individual sounds contained in the word (emphasized in the phonic approach). When the phrase is used as the primary unit, the variables of pitch and stress also are introduced as possible aids to comprehension. There is essential agreement among scholars of language that in early speech development pitch and stress take precedence over vocabulary as indicators of meaning. Parents, for example, have little difficulty in determining from the early babblings of the child not only what mood the child is communicating but also whether the utterance is a question or a command.

In view of the importance of pitch and stress in early speech development, investigations should be made of the possible effect of the phrase used as the initial emphasis in beginning reading instruction —not only with children whose speech patterns differ from standard English but also with the large group of children who speak standard English.

References

BEREITER, C., AND ENGELMANN, S. *Teaching Disadvantaged Children in the Preschool.* Englewood Cliffs, N.J.: Prentice-Hall, Inc., 1966.

BERNSTEIN, B. "Elaborated and Restricted Codes: Their Social Origins and Some Consequences." In J. Gumphrey and D. Hymes (Eds.), "The Ethnography of Communication," *American Anthropologist Special Publication,* 1964, *66*(6), Part 2, 55–69.

CARROLL, J. B. "Language Development and Reading." International Reading Association Conference, Preconvention Institute VIII, Atlantic City, N.J., April 1971.

DAVIS, O., GLADNEY, M., AND LEAVERTON, L. *The Psycholinguistics Reading Series: (A Bi-Dialectal Approach)*. Chicago: Board of Education, 1969.

FASOLD, R. W. "What Can an English Teacher Do about Nonstandard Dialect?" *English Record*, 1971, *21*(4), 82–91.

GLADNEY, M. R., AND LEAVERTON, L. "A Model for Teaching Standard English to Non-Standard English Speakers." *Elementary English*, Oct. 1968, 758–763.

KOCHMANN, T. "Rapping in the Black Ghetto." *Trans-Action*, 1969, *6*(4), 26–34.

LEAVERTON, L. "An Experimental Language Arts Program for Potentially Gifted Culturally Disadvantaged Primary Children." Proposal to Superintendent of Public Instruction, State of Illinois, March 1965.

LEAVERTON, L. "Identification and Assessment of the Language Potential of Culturally Disadvantaged Negro Children Whose Established Language Patterns Differ from Standard English Usage." Proposal to Superintendent of Public Instruction, State of Illinois, March 1967.

LEAVERTON, L. "In-Service Training Program to Accompany Field Testing and Dissemination of the Psycholinguistic Reading Series." Proposal to Superintendent of Public Instruction, State of Illinois, April 1969.

LEAVERTON, L. "Dialectal Readers—Rationale, Use and Value." International Reading Association Conference, Preconvention Institute VII, Language Development and Reading, Atlantic City, N.J., April 1971a.

LEAVERTON, L. "Follow-Up Three Years Later of 1,400 Children Who Learned to Read Using the Psycholinguistics Reading Series." Proposal to Superintendent of Public Instruction, June 1971b.

SHUY, R. W. "Dialectology and Usage." *Baltimore Bulletin of Education*, 1966, *43*, 40.

SHUY, R. W., AND BARATZ, J. C. (Eds.), *Teaching Black Children to Read*. Washington, D.C.: Center for Applied Linguistics, 1969.

SLEDD, J. "Bi-dialectalism: The Linguistics of White Supremacy." *English Journal*, 1969, *38*, 1307–1315.

STEWART, W. A. "Current Issues in the Use of Negro Dialect in Beginning Reading Texts." *The Florida FL Reporter*, Spring/Fall 1970.

PART II

Evaluation
Perspectives

P_{art} Two raises the following questions: In what ways is evaluation helpful and destructive in the urban schools? How can the evaluator work effectively with community groups? How can alternatives to conventional schools be evaluated?

Block identifies the negative consequences of "judgmental evaluation," a process for identifying individual differences in performance among learners. This kind of evaluation gives little information on learning difficulties, destroys the child's will to learn, and encourages labels such as "slow learners." He recommends the use of evaluation consultants to inform teachers of both the fallibility and the valid uses of measurement, and proposes a model for improving student evaluation. His model provides for feedback, streamlines the instructional correction process, and establishes performance standards.

Stodolsky reviews research on early-childhood problems and distinguishes structured problems, with goals explicit and implicit in materials, and child-centered programs, which exploit the child's interest and exploratory behavior. From available comparative evaluations, it appears that structured programs produce greater gains in cognitive and language growth. Well-defined treatments and closely matched measurements are needed to monitor comparative progress in new programs.

Beck describes the difficulties and pitfalls encountered when university professors try to evaluate and solve the educational problems of urban communities. Because academicians have acted as "colonial administrators" and treated ethnic groups as "target populations," they have often impeded educational progress in the inner city. He gives several examples of the traditional professor's failures in this regard, and describes a new model for university-community collaboration.

Eash and Napolitan evaluate a street academy as an alternative model to the large urban high school. Students are not obliged to attend, although they do sign in and out of learning centers. Nor are there fixed classes and schedules; students have responsibility for pacing their own learning. Learning groups are kept small; and individualized, self-pacing materials and diagnostic tests are used. The authors conclude that placing responsibility for learning on students prevents violence, truancy, and other problems that plague urban high schools.

Rippey specifies the forces that prevent effective evaluation of urban educational programs: the community, the teachers in the schools, and the evaluator's colleagues. From his evaluations of the Woodlawn Experimental Schools and the Teacher Corps Project, he identifies several ways to improve evaluation: using research to improve communication within the bureaucracy of urban school systems; finding the sources of dysfunction within school organizations; and recruiting evaluators truly committed to relevant inquiry. Unless a strong alliance of the academy and the community is created, there is little chance to improve urban schools through evaluation.

CHAPTER 6

Student Evaluation and Promotion of Learning

James H. Block

A critical problem haunting educators throughout the world is how to effectively, efficiently, and economically increase all students' learning. Nowhere is this problem felt more keenly than in the public schools of major cities. In this chapter, several methods are proposed whereby student evaluation techniques might be used to help solve this problem.

Impairment of Learning

Traditionally, student evaluation has been conceived as a process for judging changes relative to a set of educational objectives as the result of some instruction (Tyler, 1950). While in recent years some evaluators (for instance, Bloom, Hastings, and Madaus, 1971; Dressel, 1965) have expanded this conception considerably, many

61

public school personnel continue to view student evaluation as a
judgmental process for identifying and certifying performance differences among learners.

Data documenting the negative effects of this view on student
learning, especially urban student learning, are amazingly sparse.
From the anecdotal (for example, Black, 1963) and empirical data
available, however, it is possible to outline at least three ways in which
this narrow conception can contribute to poor pupil learning.

First, this view leads to the use of student evaluation primarily
for grading purposes. Unfortunately, present grading practices doom
most students to receive average or below-average marks regardless of
how well they might learn. For example, the use of a "normal curve"
ensures that roughly 70 per cent of the students receive a C or lower
grade. Since grades are one of the major types of evidence by which
a student gauges his academic and general personal competence
(Torshen, 1969), many students are bombarded with negative indications of their worth. These students eventually develop negative interest
in, attitudes toward, and anxiety about further learning (Bloom, 1971;
Sarason et al., 1960). Some develop negative academic and even
negative general self-concepts (Purkey, 1970; Torshen, 1969), and a
significant number acquire mental health problems (Stringer and
Glidewell, 1967; Torshen, 1969). These affective traits, in turn, encourage the students to cease striving for learning excellence (see
Stanwyck and Felker, 1971) and even undermine their capacity to
learn the things they are capable of learning (Feather, 1966; Purkey,
1970).

Second, this conception of student evaluation fosters the pre-
dominant use of "summative, norm-referenced" evaluation instruments
in the classroom. The instruments are *summative* in that they are
administered at the end of a long instructional segment (several textbook chapters, a quarter, a term, or a course) to sum up each student's
learning progress (see Bloom, Hastings, and Madaus, 1971). They are
norm-referenced in that each student's progress is determined by
comparing his score with the scores of his classmates or some other
norm group (Glaser and Nitko, 1971).

The use of these instruments can contribute to poor learning for
two reasons. First, they typically are employed for grading purposes
and thus can provide the negative feedback that eventually extinguishes
some pupils' desire to learn and corrodes their learning capacity.
Second, they usually provide too little information too late to help a
student surmount past learning difficulties (Airasian, 1969). Specifically, these instruments ordinarily do not consistently identify *what*
objectives he failed to learn or *where* in the segment he encountered

difficulties. Hence, they usually supply few specific cues to *why* he failed to attain certain objectives. Without answers to the questions of what, where, and why, the teacher cannot reliably design his instruction to best facilitate a student's future learning, nor can the student best organize his subsequent study and review. Even in those rare cases where the instruments do provide the necessary information, they do not encourage the student to complete prior learning before attempting new. As Airasian (1971) points out: "Mastering certain points missed in a summative evaluation may give a student satisfaction, but it does not raise his grade" (p. 79).

Third, the traditional view of student evaluation encourages teachers and other school personnel, such as counselors (Cicourel and Kitsuse, 1963), to use evaluation results for labeling a student's academic potential. Examples of common labels are "smart-dumb," "fast-slow," "overachiever-underachiever," "gifted–educably mentally retarded." All such labels carry an implicit set of performance expectations for the pupils to whom they are overtly or covertly applied. Some studies suggest that, especially in the crucial early grades, these expectations may create and perpetuate a self-fulfilling prophecy in student learning (Baker and Crist, 1972). The teacher subconsciously structures his instruction so that each student is constrained to learn roughly in accordance with the teacher's original expectations. Thus, should the teacher attach a label connoting low performance expectations, as is often the case in urban, especially ghetto, education (Clark, 1965; Gottlieb, 1966; Harlem Youth Opportunities, 1964; Wiles, 1970), then he unwittingly lowers the quality of his instruction and thereby produces the poor student learning expected.

Besides influencing the quality of a student's instruction, labels, like grades, can also affect his willingness to learn and his actual learning ability. Through a myriad of subtle and not so subtle means, including the grading process, the teacher will convince some learners to adopt a particular label as reflecting their true academic potential. Henceforth these students are likely to perform in accordance with the expectations they believe to be implicit in their label (Lecky, 1945). Thus, should they adopt a label connoting their inability to learn, they are likely to exhibit both an unwillingness and an inability to learn, even though they possess the requisite abilities.

Promotion of Learning

Why has student evaluation generally been used in such negative and unproductive ways? One explanation is that most public school teachers, counselors, and administrators have had little formal training in evaluation theory and practice (Brim et al., 1965; Goslin, 1967); hence, they are either unfamiliar with alternative uses (such as diagnosing student learning difficulties, assessing learning readiness, and defining and clarifying instructional objectives) or are unskilled in defining and clarifying instructional objectives) or are unskilled in their application. An obvious key to the more salutary utilization of student evaluation in urban education, therefore, would be to provide more and better evaluation training for *all* pre-service and in-service personnel. Whether it occurs in public school–based clinics and workshops or in university and teacher-training courses, this preparation should stress the following: the variety of possible classroom roles for student evaluation; awareness of the positive and negative effects of each role on students, teachers, the school, and even the community (Bloom, 1969); the fallibility of evaluation results and the sources of fallibility; on-the-job training and practice in the application of various techniques and interpretation and use of results (Ebel, 1967). A second possibility would be for each urban school system, perhaps each school, to hire a cadre of full-time consultants with special competence in both testing and teaching (Ebel, 1967).

But increased training or expert aid, even if exceptionally good, will not be enough. Unless it is possible to convince urban school personnel that the primary goal of student evaluation is *not* the judgment of student learning, then some individuals will continue to use evaluation in the ways described above. To emphasize its many alternative classroom uses, therefore, educators must consider new goals for student evaluation. One such goal is the maximal promotion of each student's learning.

Model for Optimal Quality of Classroom Instruction

Let us begin by sketching a model for classroom instruction of optimal quality. The model derives from research on group and tutorial instruction (Moore, 1971; Rosenshine, 1970; Thelen et al., 1968) and from writings on models of learning (for example, Carroll, 1963; Hilgard, 1965) and instruction (for example, Gage, 1964; Wallen and Travers, 1963). This literature suggests that the quality of instruction for any student can be defined by three sets of highly complex variables: (1) the clarity and appropriateness of the instructional *cues;* that is, "the degree to which the presentation, explanation, and ordering of elements of the learning task approach the optimum for a given learner" (Carroll, 1963, as quoted in Bloom, 1968). (2) the amount of active *participation* in and *practice* of the learning allowed; (3) the amount and types of *reinforcements* or rewards provided.

Under ideal instructional conditions, such as one well-trained tutor per student, each of these variables is manipulated almost automatically to ensure optimal quality of instruction for each learner. Classroom conditions, however, are often far from ideal—usually a single type of instruction, which employs primarily verbal cues; a limited amount of learning time; and a high student-teacher ratio prevail. Under such circumstances, it is unlikely that a teacher's instruction can be of optimal quality for each student no matter how good the teacher may be. Some students may require nonverbal rather than verbal cues; more time to practice; more chance to interact with the teacher; or more than a smile, verbal praise, or the teacher's attention. The problem faced by any model for high-quality classroom instruction, therefore, is how to recreate, under existing conditions, the optimal quality of instruction usually found only under ideal conditions.

Research carried out both here and abroad (for instance, Block, 1971) suggests that the model in Figure 1 will solve this problem. As drawn, the model proposes that feedback and correction techniques are the catalysts required to transform ordinary group-based instruction into instruction of optimal quality for each learner. These techniques supplement the group instruction in such a way that the teacher can make the same kinds of modifications in each of his student's instruction as would a tutor for his tutee. The feedback devices detect gaps in each student's learning at selected intervals in the group instruction. Then, a number of group and/or individual instructional correctives are used systematically to vary the cues and/or the participation-practice and/or the reinforcements until each learner's problems have been surmounted. For example, reteaching is used to overcome learning difficulties shared by a group of students. Small-group study sessions, individual tutoring, and alternative instructional materials (textbooks, workbooks, programmed instruction, audio-visual methods, academic games and puzzles) are employed to handle individual learning errors.

Three major roles for student-evaluation techniques in the promotion of learning follow readily from this model. Each centers on the development of improved classroom feedback/correction techniques.

Feedback. One obvious role is the provision of the necessary feedback information. Here "formative, criterion-referenced" classroom evaluation instruments are required. The instruments should be *formative* in the sense that they are designed to be an integral part of the teaching-learning process and thus to shape the outcomes of the process. They should be short, ungraded, administered as frequently

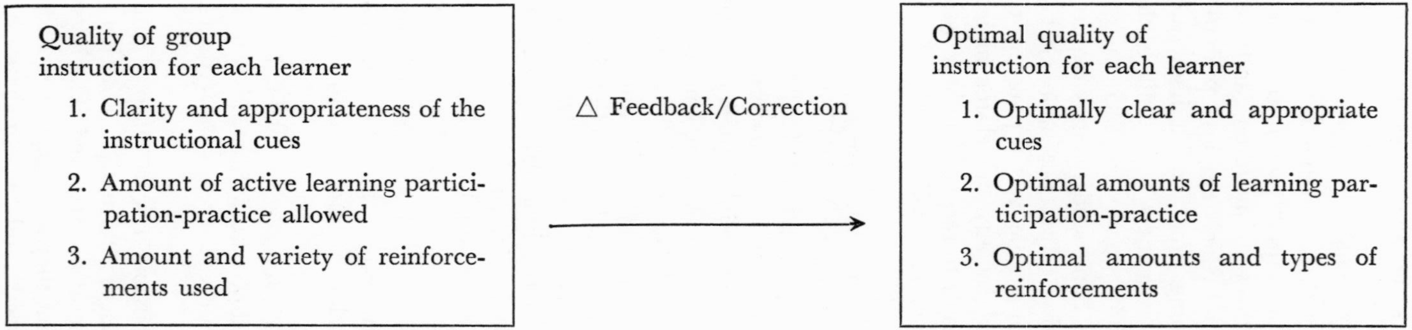

Quality of group
instruction for each learner

1. Clarity and appropriateness of the
instructional cues

2. Amount of active learning participation-practice allowed

3. Amount and variety of reinforcements used

△ Feedback/Correction

Optimal quality of
instruction for each learner

1. Optimally clear and appropriate
cues

2. Optimal amounts of learning participation-practice

3. Optimal amounts and types of
reinforcements

FIGURE 1. A MODEL FOR OPTIMAL INSTRUCTION

as necessary, and diagnostic. Useful formative instruments must provide a continuous flow of information to *both* the teacher and the learner regarding the ongoing effectiveness of the teaching anl learning (Airasian, 1969; Bloom, Hastings, and Madaus, 1971). The instruments should be *criterion-referenced* in two senses. First, they should provide an in-depth picture of what objectives the student did not learn in a given instructional segment and where he encountered learning problems. This information will provide clues to why particular objectives were not attained. Second, they should assess the adequacy-inadequacy of the student's learning with respect to *what* objectives he attained, rather than *how many* he reached relative to his peers (Block, 1971; Bormuth, 1970; Glaser and Nitko, 1971).

Correction process. A second role for student evaluation is the streamlining of the correction process. Here the term *streamlining* does not mean the assemblage of the most efficient and effective, yet parsimonious and inexpensive, corrective battery possible. The construction of such a battery primarily requires the techniques of curricular, not student, evaluation. Rather, it means the development of efficient procedures for translating the learning difficulties evidenced by a student on a feedback instrument into a set of correctives which will most likely overcome these difficulties.

This streamlining will require the creation of what might be called a "corrective contingency management system." One component of such a system must be a battery of evaluation instruments compatible with the classroom instruction in which the student will engage (Cronbach, 1970). These instruments should delimit the cues to be used, the participation-practice to be allowed, and the reinforcements to be provided, and then ascertain each student's status relative to these characteristics. The second component must be a battery of evaluation instruments designed to identify the particular types of cues, the amounts of participation-practice, and the types and amounts of reinforcement each student requires for optimal quality of instruction over the given material.

From information regarding the classroom instruction's major characteristics and each student's status relative to these characteristics, general areas can be identified where the quality of the group instruction will not be sufficient for a particular student. Contingency plans, based upon each student's requirements for optimal instruction, can then be developed. These plans will specify a particular set of correctives likely to remove the incongruence between the quality of instruction provided and the optimal quality of instruction required. Should the student actually encounter learning problems over any segment of the group instruction, the contingency plans would be set in operation.

Consider this example: Suppose the amounts of participation-practice allowed and the amounts and types of reinforcement to be provided by some classroom instruction are satisfactory for a given student. But suppose the cues are to be presented in a mode (perhaps verbally) that the student cannot understand. The instructional cues, then, might be a potential source of learning difficulty for the student. Hence, a set of contingency plans would be drawn up based on information regarding the particular cues this student requires for optimal instruction. Should he actually encounter learning difficulties, the contingency plans would be implemented to present the unlearned material in a cue mode (perhaps nonverbally) he could most easily understand.

Standards. A final role for student evaluation techniques is the setting of performance standards against which the adequacy or inadequacy of each student's learning over a given instructional segment can be judged. Bormuth (1969, 1971) has demonstrated the possibility of empirically setting more objective and realistic standards than those used in the past. Block (1970), in turn, has demonstrated the possibility of empirically setting standards whose maintenance throughout an instructional sequence maximizes selected end-of-sequence learning outcomes. Taken together, therefore, this research suggests the possibility of using performance standards as major instructional variables in the promotion of student learning. If the teacher or administrator can select a particular set of desired learning outcomes, then he should be able to set a standard whose maintenance throughout an instructional sequence will maximize each student's attainments relative to these outcomes. Once set this standard would act as a benchmark for monitoring either the "health" or equivalently what Farquhar (1968) terms the "pathology" of each urban student's learning. At any time the student's learning was substandard, correctives would be applied to return it to par.

To illustrate these ideas, consider the following example. The basic subjects in most elementary school curricula are learned sequentially. Thus, the student's failure to learn adequately one task in a sequence may condemn him to learning failure in all subsequent tasks. The tragedy of this situation is graphically illustrated in a longitudinal study of school achievement conducted by Payne (1963). She found that a student's success or failure in sixth-grade reading or arithmetic could be highly predicted given knowledge of only his first- and perhaps second-grade performance. That is, the student's performance in grades one and two seemed to predetermine his success or failure later in the sequence. As Bloom (1970) points out, had short-term performance standards ("sequential norms") been available in grades one and two, then some students' subsequent long-term learning failure might have been averted. Urban schools should be able to use already existing data to set such standards for all required, sequentially learned subjects. Initially the standards might be set to indicate simply "how much" the student should have learned at each stage in the sequence if his learning is to meet certain end-of-sequence criteria. Later, they might be set in terms of "what" he should have learned.

Implications for Urban Education

Student benefits. Urban students will benefit in at least four ways from the use of student-evaluation techniques to promote learning. First, especially in sequentially learned subjects, most students will learn more effectively. Research (Block, 1971) suggests that classroom use of sound feedback/correction techniques typically can enable 75 per cent of the students to learn selected subjects as well as do only the top 25 per cent at present. Virtually all students learning with the assistance of such techniques can achieve well enough to earn C or higher marks as judged by the same grading criteria used for students learning without such assistance.

Second, most students' learning can be made more efficient. Especially for sequentially learned subjects or topics, there seem to be particular performance standards whose attainment increases the amount of subsequent material students learn in a given time (Block, 1970; Merrill, Barton, and Wood, 1970). The reason is clear. The student who is helped to learn adequately the material in one task in a sequence can concentrate on the new material in the next task. The student who is not helped must spend time learning both the former and the latter material. The further he is allowed to proceed unassisted in the sequence, the more time he must devote to learning old rather than new material.

Third, most students will be partially insulated from the negative affective consequences of present instructional and evaluational practices. On the one hand, they will gain the repeated positive school learning experiences which foster positive interests in and attitudes toward learning, promote the growth of a positive academic and probably general self-concept, and immunize against mental illness (Bloom, 1971; Purkey, 1970; Stringer and Glidewell, 1967; Torshen, 1969). On the other hand, they will obtain new perspectives on the meaning of student evaluation which should reduce its anxiety-provoking qualities and exaggerated importance in student life. In particular, students will discover that evaluation is an integral part of the teaching-learning process rather than the ultimate goal of the process and consequently that grading and evaluation need not be synonymous.

Finally, many students will be freed from the negative scholastic effects of the concept of individual differences. Few ideas have had greater positive impact on urban education than the notion of individual differences as many chapters in this volume attest. But the idea has also provided some urban educators a convenient series of excuses whereby responsibility for poor student learning is shifted from the educational system to the student's genetic and/or environmental background. As these educators have absolved themselves from responsibility for student learning, they have become increasingly lax in providing the conditions under which almost all students can learn.

The use of student-evaluation techniques to develop improved classroom feedback/correction processes should place the concept of individual differences in proper perspective in urban education. Research using relatively crude systems to improve the quality of instruction for suburban, lower-middle class students (Block, 1970) and urban students (Kersh, 1970; Kim et al., 1969) suggests that the commonly observed relationship between individual differences and student achievement may often be a sheer *artifact* of our present instructional practices. These studies show that the degree to which individual differences in such variables as aptitude, socioeconomic status, and IQ are reflected in student achievement is some negative function of the quality of instruction provided each learner. The higher the quality of instruction, the less the effects of these differences. Thus, if these findings are replicated as improved feedback/correction systems evolve, they should caution urban educators against using any student's background as a scapegoat for instructional ineffectiveness.

Let me emphasize that I am not proposing that individual differences may not condition student learning in some cases. Rather, I am suggesting that perhaps the concept of individual differences has been uncritically overused in urban education to explain our inability to teach some students or our ability to teach some better than others.

Teacher benefits. Urban teachers also will receive certain important benefits from the use of student evaluation as proposed. First, they can reap returns of increased learning for most, rather than just a few, students from their instruction. These returns will be greater each time a particular topic, course, or subject is retaught, provided the teachers continue to use the techniques described above to refine and improve their classroom feedback/correction procedures (see, for example, Bloom, 1968).

Second, especially for sequentially learned material, the teachers can make their instruction more efficient. Limited experimental research suggests that the teacher, with the assistance of a good feedback/correction system, may be able to ensure high levels of learning for most students while spending no more, perhaps even less, instructional time than is usually spent helping only some students learn well (Block, 1970; Merrill, Barton, and Wood, 1970).

Third, urban teachers will gain some tools by which to discharge growing public demands for accountability. To date, while teachers have been deluged with demands that they assume greater responsibility for their students' learning, almost without exception they have not been provided with any effective means for reaching this end. The development of improved classroom feedback/correction techniques should provide teachers with the vehicles they have lacked.

Fourth, urban teachers may be able to alleviate some of their classroom disorder problems. In particular, the use of student evaluation in the ways proposed above may help the teacher reduce the hostility and frustration generated by previous instructional and evaluational practices. The teachers can help most students attain consistent academic success and thus both the short- and long-term benefits of such success. High levels of student learning, in turn, should discourage teachers from underestimating their students' capacity for intellectual growth.

School benefits. Urban schools will gain a set of benefits equally as important as those accruing to their students and teachers. First, they will acquire the lever required to increase pupil learning substantially. Hence, like the individual teacher, the schools also can most fully capitalize on their tremendous investment of resources in student instruction. Sound feedback/correction systems have proved to be both an effective and efficient means of individualizing instruction even in classrooms with up to 70 to 1 student-teacher ratios and for samples of thousands and tens of thousands of students (Kim et al., 1969, 1970). So far, development costs have been minimal. For example, teachers working together for an hour or two a day have constructed sound feedback/correction systems for an entire year's work in courses such as mathematics and biology in fewer than ten weeks (Airasian, 1969). Once set up, of course, such systems can be used repeatedly.

Second, the schools may be able to reclaim experienced teachers and to save the inexperienced from the indifference toward teaching and learning excellence prevalent in some urban schools (Clark,

1965; Silberman, 1970). Doubtless such indifference may derive from poor working conditions; for the most part, however, it probably results from many teachers' inability to realize, regardless of their efforts, any tangible, positive student learning results. If the use of student-evaluation techniques to build improved classroom feedback/ correction systems can enable each urban teacher significantly to improve his students' learning, then this indifference can be stemmed.

Third, the schools, within their present organizational and curricular framework, will be able to promote the fullest development of most students. They will be able to provide almost every learner with both those cognitive skills and competencies and those affective traits required for successful entry and residence in the adult world of work and leisure. From this cognitive and affective base, most students will be able to realize any vocational or avocational goals *they choose* instead of only those goals *chosen for them.*

This last argument may be unacceptable to the reader familiar with either Cronbach's (1971) or Ebel's (1970) distinction between training and education. Cronbach, for example, argues that training involves only the shaping of student behaviors in some basic areas while education entails training, the development of analytic and problem-solving skills, and the fostering of creativity and self-expression. On the basis of this distinction, the uses of student evaluation developed here might be misconstrued as fostering the fullest development of the individual with respect only to training and not to educational goals. Remember, however, that the proposed uses are meant for implementation within the framework of present urban educational systems. In this framework, students are typically required to spend ten to twelve years locked for the most part into a training curriculum consisting of long learning sequences for a few required subjects. The teaching of analytic and problem-solving skills and the promotion of creativity and self-expression usually are, in practice, either predicated upon or secondary to mastery of these subjects. Hence, a student's failure to learn these basic subjects and the repeated frustration, humiliation, and despair engendered thereby can make him unwilling or unable or both to participate in "educational'" efforts to develop high-level cognitive skills or to nurture creativity and self-expression. Within such a framework, therefore, both training and educational goals are fostered by any set of procedures that will ensure mastery of the required subjects for most students.   •

Admittedly, the view taken here of student evaluation's latent potential for improving urban education is optimistic. But perhaps the best argument for this optimism is Pascal's argument for the survival of the rational man: "One argument for believing in heaven is that if you are wrong, little is lost, but if you are right, much may be gained."

References

AIRASIAN, P. W. "Formative Evaluation Instruments: A Construction and Validation of Tests to Evaluate Learning over Short-Time Periods." Unpublished doctoral dissertation, University of Chicago, 1969.

AIRASIAN, P. W. "The Role of Evaluation in Mastery Learning." In J. H. Block (Ed.), *Mastery Learning: Theory and Practice.* New York: Holt, Rinehart, and Winston, 1971. Pp. 77–88.

BAKER, J. P., AND CRIST, J. "Teacher Expectancies: A Review of the Literature." In J. D. Elashoff and R. E. Snow (Eds.), *Pygmalion Reconsidered.* Worthington, Ohio: Jones, 1972. Pp. 48–64.

BLACK, H. *They Shall Not Pass.* New York: William Morrow, 1963.

BLOCK, J. H. "The Effects of Various Levels of Performance on Selected Cognitive, Affective and Time Variables." Unpublished doctoral dissertation, University of Chicago, 1970.

BLOCK, J. H. (Ed.). *Mastery Learning: Theory and Practice.* New York: Holt, Rinehart, and Winston, 1971.

BLOOM, B. S. "Learning for Mastery." *UCLA Evaluation Comment,* 1968, *1,* 1–12.

BLOOM, B. S. "Some Theoretical Issues Relating to Educational Evaluation." In *Educational Evaluation: New Roles, New Means.* Sixty-Eighth NSSE Yearbook, Part II. Chicago: University of Chicago Press, 1969. Pp. 26–50.

BLOOM, B. S. "Toward a Theory of Testing Which Includes Measurement-Evaluation-Assessment." In M. C. Wittrock and D. E. Wiley (Eds.), *The Evaluation of Instruction: Issues and Problems.* New York: Holt, Rinehart, and Winston, 1970. Pp. 25–50.

BLOOM, B. S. "Individual Differences in School Achievement: A Vanishing Point?" In *Education at Chicago,* Newsletter of the Department of Education, University of Chicago, Winter 1971, pp. 4–14.

BLOOM, B. S., HASTINGS, J. T., AND MADAUS, G. F. *Handbook on Formative and Summative Evaluation of Student Learning.* New York: McGraw-Hill, 1971.

BORMUTH, J. R. *Development of Readability Analysis.* Final report, USOE, Contract No. OEC-3-7-0700052-0326, Department of Education, University of Chicago, 1969.

BORMUTH, J. R. *On the Theory of Achievement Test Items.* Chicago: University of Chicago Press, 1970.

BORMUTH, J. R. *Development of Standards of Readability: Toward a Rational Criterion of Passage Performance.* Final report, USOE, Project No. 9-0237, Department of Education, University of Chicago, 1971.

BRIM, O. G., JR., et al. *The Use of Standardized Ability Tests in American Secondary Schools and Their Impact on Students, Teachers, and Administrators.* Technical Report No. 3 on the Social Consequences of Testing. New York: Russell Sage Foundation, 1965.

CARROLL, J. B. "A Model of School Learning." *Teachers College Record,* 1963, *64,* 723–733.

CICOUREL, A. V., AND KITSUSE, J. I. *The Educational Decision Makers.* New York: Bobbs-Merrill, 1963.

CLARK, K. *Dark Ghetto: Dilemmas of Social Power.* New York: Harper & Row, 1965.

CRONBACH, L. J. *Essentials of Psychological Testing.* (2nd Ed.), New York: Harper & Row, 1960.

CRONBACH, L. J. "Mental Tests and the Creation of Opportunity." Paper presented at the annual meeting of the American Philosophical Society, April 1970.

CRONBACH, L. J. "Comments on 'Mastery Learning and Its Implications for Curriculum Development.'" In E. W. Eisner (Ed.), *Confronting Curriculum Reform.* Boston: Little, Brown, 1971. Pp. 49–55.

DRESSEL, P. L. "The Role of Evaluation in Teaching and Learning." In *Evaluation in Social Studies.* Thirty-Fifth Yearbook of the National Council for Social Studies. Washington, D.C.: National Education Association, 1965. Pp. 1–20.

EBEL, R. L. "Improving the Competence of Teachers in Educational Measurement." In J. T. Flynn and H. Garber (Eds.), *Assessing Behavior: Readings in Educational and Psychological Measurement.* Reading, Mass.: Addison-Wesley, 1967. Pp. 263–269.

EBEL, R. L. "Behavioral Objectives: A Close Look." *Phi Delta Kappan,* 1970, *52,* 171–173.

FARQUHAR, W. W. "Academic Motivation and Inner-City Schools." In H. C. Rudman and R. L. Featherstone (Eds.), *Urban Schooling.* New York: Harcourt, Brace and World, 1968.

FEATHER, N. T. "Effects of Prior Success and Failure on Expectations of Success and Subsequent Performance." *Journal of Personality and Social Psychology,* 1966, *3,* 187–198.

GAGE, N. L. "Theories of Teaching." In E. R. Hilgard (Ed.), *Theories of*

Learning and Instruction, sixty-third yearbook of the National Society for the Study of Education, Part 1. Chicago: National Society for the Study of Education, 1964. Pp. 268–285.

GLASER, R., AND NITKO, A. "Measurement in Learning and Instruction." In R. L. Thorndike (Ed.), *Educational Measurement.* Washington, D.C.: American Council on Education, 1971. Pp. 625–670.

GOSLIN, D. A. *Teachers and Testing.* New York: Russell Sage Foundation, 1967.

GOTTLIEB, D. "Teaching and Students: The Views of Negro and White Teachers." In S. W. Webster (Ed.), *The Disadvantaged Learner.* San Francisco: Chandler, 1966.

Harlem Youth Opportunities Unlimited. *Youth in the Ghetto.* New York: Harlem Youth Opportunities, 1964.

HILGARD, E. R. *Theories of Learning.* New York: Appleton-Century-Crofts, 1956.

KERSH, M. E. "A Strategy for Mastery Learning in Fifth-Grade Arithmetic." Unpublished doctoral dissertation, University of Chicago, 1970.

KIM, HOGWON, et al. *A Study of the Bloom Strategies for Mastery Learning.* Seoul: Korean Institute for Research in the Behavioral Sciences, 1969. (In Korean.)

KIM, HOGWON, et al. *The Mastery Learning Project in the Middle Schools.* Seoul: Korean Institute for Research in the Behavioral Sciences, 1970. (In Korean.)

LECKY, P. *Self-Consistency.* New York: Island Press, 1945.

MERRILL, M. D., BARTON, K., AND WOOD, L. E. "Specific Review in Learning a Hierarchical Imaginary Science." *Journal of Educational Psychology,* 1970, *61,* 102–109.

MOORE, C. A. "Tutoring, Dyadic Interaction and Interpersonal Processes." Unpublished bibliography, Center for Research and Development in Teaching, Stanford University, 1971.

PAYNE, M. A. "The Use of Data in Curricular Decisions." Unpublished doctoral dissertation, University of Chicago, 1963.

PURKEY, W. W. *Self Concept and School Achievement.* Englewood Cliffs, N.J.: Prentice-Hall, 1970.

ROSENSHINE, B. "Teaching Behaviors and Student Achievement: A Review of Research." Stockholm: International Association for Evaluation of Educational Achievement, 1970.

SARASON, S. B., et al. *Anxiety in Elementary School Children.* New York: Wiley, 1960.

SILBERMAN, C. E. *Crisis in the Classroom.* New York: Random House, 1970.

STANWYCK, D. J., AND FELKER, D. W. "Intellectual Achievement Responsibility and Anxiety as Functions of Self Concept of Third- to Sixth-Grade Boys and Girls." Paper presented at the annual meeting of the American Educational Research Association, New York, 1971.

STRINGER, L. A., AND GLIDEWELL, J. C. *Early Detection of Emotional Illnesses in School Children.* Final report. St. Louis, Missouri: Division of Research and Development, St. Louis County Health Department, 1967.

THELEN, H., et al. *Learning by Teaching.* Chicago: Stone-Brandel Center, 1968.

TORSHEN, K. P. "The Relation of Classroom Evaluation to Students' Self Concepts and Mental Health." Unpublished doctoral dissertation, University of Chicago, 1969.

TYLER, R. W. *Basic Principles of Curriculum and Instruction.* Chicago: University of Chicago Press, 1950.

WALLEN, N. E., AND TRAVERS, R. M. W. "Analysis and Investigation of Teaching Methods." In N. L. Gage (Ed.), *Handbook of Research on Teaching.* Chicago: Rand McNally, 1963. Pp. 448–505.

WILES, D. K. "The Mosaic Composition of Urban School Teachers." *Urban Education,* 1970, *5,* 141–151.

CHAPTER 7

Defining Treatment and Outcome in Early-Childhood Education

Susan S. Stodolsky

Ⅰn the last several years, the field of early-childhood education has greatly expanded. Programs for preschool children, especially children of the poor, have been established across the nation. Since the majority of poor children live in the cities, many of these preschools are located in urban areas. In this country there were a number of significant forerunners to the current wave of school interventions with young children (see Kirk, 1958; Skeels, 1966; Skeels and Dye, 1939; Wellman, 1940). However, massive efforts at compensatory education for the preschool child did not get underway until the mid-1960s, when the federal government and other agencies funded large-scale efforts such as Head Start to intervene in the cycle of poverty by attempting to better prepare poor children for school entrance.

Heavy government funding has led to pressure for solid evidence about the efficacy of preschool interventions. In this chapter I discuss what available evaluation studies have found and explore the scientific adequacy of the current data base for making judgments about program effectiveness.

The discussion will be limited in scope. A number of writers (Cohen, 1970; Scriven, 1967; Stake, 1970; Westbury, 1970) have suggested roles for evaluation which go beyond the traditional attempt to relate student outcomes to some educational experience. Many of their ideas point in important new directions. In early education there are still many problems in the domain of classic evaluation, so I restrict my attention there. In addition, I restrict my attention to problems associated with the evaluation of short-term or immediate end-of-program effects. This limitation arises because at this time there is insufficient data regarding the long-term effects of preschool programs on school achievement and noncognitive characteristics of poor children.

One further special constraint in the field of early education should be signaled. Methodologically, the evaluator in this field faces acute measurement problems. The young child is difficult to test or interview, and group methods are usually inappropriate. Expensive individual assessment is often the only valid and reliable option for measuring attributes of young children. In addition, there are very few measures available in most areas of interest to evaluators. In the noncognitive domain the lack of instruments or other procedures is especially acute. (For reviews of instruments and ideas for new ones see Cazden, 1971; Kamii, 1971; La Crosse, Lee, Litman, Ogilvie, Stodolsky, and White, 1970).

Having noted these limitations, I now turn to data that bear on the effects of preschool programs in the short run. I have selectively reviewed current studies of preschool programs, with particular attention to comparative studies. I cannot claim to have done a comprehensive job, but I believe I have seen a representative array. I want to note two salient generalizations about the existing data and then analyze current approaches to preschool intervention. With a clear view of current programs I return to the evaluation studies. Two initial generalizations about current evaluation studies are presented now.

First, as might be expected, the studies make use of only a few measurement procedures. The most commonly used instruments include the Stanford-Binet Intelligence Test and the associated Hertzig-Birch measures of responsiveness to task demands or the standard rating sheet of test behavior, the Peabody Picture Vocabulary Test, the Illinois Test of Psycholinguistic Abilities, the Preschool Inventory, and, on occasion, the Wechsler Intelligence Scale for Children, the Leiter Performance Scale, the Frostig Test of Visual Perception, the Wide Range Achievement Test, a few Piaget tasks, and some assessments of motor abilities. Occasional attempts, with equivocal or disappointing results, have been made to assess self-concept (Di Lorenzo, Salter, and Brady, 1969; Gray and Klaus, 1970). Similarly, an occasional study includes assessment of other behaviors—persistence, curiosity, and the like. In short, few instruments have been used, and consequently a narrow range of behaviors has been assessed.

Second, in virtually *any* reasonably well-executed program undertaken with disadvantaged children at an early age, the children experience short-term gains on a *general* measure of intelligence. (There are, of course, some programs in which no gains are found; but these are generally poor programs, programs of extremely short duration, and situations in which measurement is confounded by bilingualism.) Such gains, though often sustained by children for some time after the preschool year, are matched by control groups whose first year of schooling is in kindergarten or first grade—thus washing out the supposed advantage of the preschool experience. There are a few seemingly very powerful programs which do not show this pattern of results, but the instances are not frequent enough yet to seriously alter the proposition. The pattern of data which shows the "going to school effect" has been noted and effectively discussed by others (Bereiter and Engelmann, 1966; Datta, 1969; Weikart, 1967; Zigler and Butterfield, 1968). A number of reasons for this data pattern have been offered: that the change in test scores reflects real cognitive change; that the change is attributable to motivational or rapport effects or both; that some combination of cognitive and motivational factors is involved; that the changes are primarily attributable to statistical regression in test scores.

Current Approaches to Preschool Intervention and Comparative Studies

Many approaches to preschool intervention are being tried at present. As White (1970) points out, diversity obtains at both the level of rhetoric and in terms of classroom operations. Programs vary in many ways. There are a number of points of view about what should and should not be taught to young children, what aspects of development to stress in the early years (for example, intellectual, social, sensory-motor, or emotional), and how best to accomplish goals. Maccoby and Zellner (1970), in describing the various models of education contained in Project Follow Through, have shown that some differences center around views about the nature of learning and the role of motivation in the behavior of the child. Differences also emerge in the stress placed on possible outcomes.

While it is difficult to do justice to existing programs by attempting to categorize them, two common distinctions have been made in the descriptive literature and in the comparative evaluation studies to date. One frequently used dimension of comparison is that of *structure*. Di Lorenzo and his associates (1969) operationally define a structured program in the following way: "The teacher emphasizes specific instructional goals. She focuses attention on the objective through defining the time period for the activity, using special materials and prescribing the child's responses" (p. III–4). This definition, although not always made explicit by other writers, seems to conform to the use of the term in the available literature.

Familiar examples of the structured programs would be the Bereiter-Engelmann curriculum; Bushell's behavior analysis program and other highly planned and sequenced programs, such as Karnes's experimental curriculum, the DARCEE Program, and the Perry Preschool Project. Programs at the other end of the structure continuum are usually termed *traditional, child-centered,* or *discovery* programs. These programs may or may not have specific goals (the best of them do), but the teacher attempts to capitalize on the behavior of the child as the child engages in activities which he self-selects to promote goals, as opposed to determining in advance the time and context in which to work with a given child toward some instructional objective. These child-centered programs are not necessarily all self-programmed by the child, but the child's spontaneous behavior and play are considered an important component of such programs. Examples of this approach are the Bank Street program and the open-classroom models, some of which are being developed in cooperation with Education Development Center. Under this definition of structure, a child in a Bereiter-Engelmann classroom as well as a child in a preplanned tutorial would have a structured experience. But a child selecting his own work or play to any significant extent would be in a less structured situation. Thus, many Montessori preschools, although prepared and sequenced in regard to materials, would be moderate to low in structure since the children program their own activities most of the time.

The other contrast usually noted in comparing preschool approaches is whether primary emphasis is on cognitive and language outcomes (intellectual-academic) or on such outcomes as the development of autonomy, social skills, curiosity, and the like (socioemotional). There is no necessity for the degree of structure to converge with differences in educational objectives, but as Di Lorenzo et al. (1969) note, with few exceptions the most structured programs are also those that emphasize cognitive and academic objectives, and the less structured programs typically put more emphasis on noncognitive factors. The cognitive and noncognitive realms are not, of course, the exclusive interest of any program developer.

What are the empirical findings from available comparative evaluation studies? The data (Bissell, 1971; Di Lorenzo et al., 1969; Weikart, 1969) indicate that the more structured (and cognitively oriented) programs tend to produce larger gains on measures of cognitive and language growth than do the child-centered programs. Thus Weikart, reviewing studies through 1969, writes: "The basic conclusion is that the more structured or task-oriented the program, the greater the gains in immediate intellectual competence, and where followup data are available, academic achievement" (1969, p. 3).

Karnes, Teska, and Hodgins (1970) attempted to use the dimension of structure as a basis for comparing four preschool programs. The experimental program they developed was highly structured and emphasized language and cognitive development. It produced marked gains on related measures (Binet, ITPA). A Montessori program, which they thought of as next in structure, did not produce noticeable gains on these measures, whereas a traditional program showed moderate gains in language and cognition. The experimental and traditional classes had a teacher-child ratio of 1:5, a figure lower than that in the other two programs under study.

Weikart (1969) conducted an experiment in which three curricular approaches (a unit-based curriculum emphasizing social-emotional development; the Perry Preschool cognitively oriented curriculum; and the Bereiter-Engelmann curriculum) were implemented with groups of fuctionally retarded disadvantaged children. All three programs stressed language development and used language extensively. The children in all three programs were visited at home regularly by staff members for additional teaching. The staff members chose the curiculum with which they wanted to work, and a very high degree of staff involvement and planning was achieved. Weikart found to his surprise that, under the superb conditions of this experiment, children in all three programs made extremely large intellectual gains;

no differences were detected in the children's performances according to the curricular approach in which they were enrolled. Weikart attributes these findings primarily to the staff model and the mode of operation, which was invariant across the three programs. Also, the measurements were fairly closely articulated to the objectives of the three programs. In any case, the study does seem consistent with the notion that a high degree of teacher control, here at least at the planning level, is effective.

One last comparative study bears mention because it is an example of the direction I believe such studies should take. Miller and Dyer (1970) experimentally assigned children to one of four programs: DARCEE, Bereiter-Engelmann, Montessori, and Traditional. They then predicted a variety of outcomes, *different* for each program, based on their understanding of the objectives of each of the approaches. They also attempted to monitor each curriculum while it was in progress. These aspects of their work are most appreciated. Their findings did not always confirm their hypotheses. Relevant here is the fact that they also found that the more structured programs (DARCEE and Bereiter-Engelmann) were most effective in producing cognitive change in the children. There are, however, many other interesting aspects to their study since they attempted to study curiosity, independence, persistence, and other attributes which have rarely been examined in preschool evaluations.

These illustrative findings from comparative studies adequately convey the thrust of the literature. It is now appropriate to recast these findings in a sophisticated methodological frame. Two new generalizations and associated corollaries emerge from these data. These propositions have not been adequately explored previously; and I believe they substantially account for the findings from studies of short-term effects of preschool interventions. These propositions assume that a given educational experience produces the same effect in all children (compare Cronbach and Snow, 1971).

Defining Outcomes and Treatments

In comparative evaluation studies and many single-model studies of preschool programs, *the programs that appear more successful on the basis of the data are those whose objectives or curricular emphases come closest to the measured outcomes.* For example, in the Di Lorenzo et al. (1969) study, the programs with most emphasis on language and cognitive outcomes did produce most gains on measures in these areas. Or in the Karnes et al. (1970) study, the lack of growth, particularly in the language area, in the Montessori classrooms studied is probably due to the lack of verbal experiences in these Montessori classrooms, a curricular quality noted by the authors.

In comparative evaluation studies and many single-model studies of preschool programs, *the programs that appear to be more successful on the basis of the data are those whose treatment is most under control—that is, most homogeneous with respect to the children's experiences.*

I discuss these two points in detail subsequently. Three obvious corollaries from them should be noted at this juncture: (1) The more homogeneous the treatment, the more likely that effects will be found, assuming some relevant outcome measures. (2) The more heterogeneous the treatment, the more likely that effects will not emerge *for the group as a whole,* even if effects exist for some subpopulation who have experienced a relatively homogeneous treatment. (3) The more control one gains over treatment, through either experimental manipulation *or* empirical description, the more likely that the outcomes can be related to specified treatments. Let me turn now to each of these main points in depth.

The first central point addresses the issue of articulating outcome measures with the program. If it were possible at this time to specify on a priori grounds what effects should be produced by any successful preschool program, the measurement articulation problem would become irrelevant. Some in the field believe that such a determination can be made now. I do not find it possible to subscribe to any one set of objectives as obviously superior to another in the early-childhood field. Too little is known about the interface between early experiences and later functioning in the child. In view of this problem, it seems essential to approach evaluation work with as differentiated a set of probes as possible. At a minimum, a satisfactory evaluation of a preschool project should make every effort to assess as sensitively as possible the intended outcomes of the program.

An important methodological advance in this direction can be made by spending enough time in classrooms, in addition to talking to teachers and looking at materials, so that the evaluator can tentatively convince himself that the activities in the classroom do seem to have the potential for developing the attributes in children which he proposes to measure in the evaluation study. A somewhat similar plea was made by Swift (1964) in reviewing nursery school research before the new wave of research dealing with disadvantaged children had

begun. It deserves restatement. Taking this additional step in attempting to define the likely outcomes of a program can be very salutary.
An example from my own work is relevant here.

A few years ago, I assumed responsibility for a small-scale
evaluation of a contemporary Montessori program which, with OEO
funding, had integrated a small number of black Head Start children
into the middle-class, racially integrated classrooms of the preschool.
The first research studies in the school used the Stanford-Binet as the
primary instrument for measuring intellectual change, along with some
Piaget measures, measures of social interaction, and teacher ratings
of various qualities of the children's behavior (Jensen and Kohlberg,
1966; Kohlberg, 1967).

Not unexpectedly, as research in the school began to accumulate (Stodolsky and Jensen, 1969), it became clear that the Stanford-
Binet results at the Montessori site were highly similar to those being
obtained elsewhere. First-year children tended to show significant gains
on the Stanford-Binet; children in subsequent years in the school did
not. Importantly, the early work did show that the Piaget tasks were
not affected by the Montessori experience, a finding which was replicated over a number of years and has theoretical import (Kohlberg,
1968).

Simultaneous with the evaluation project, my students and I
were doing observational studies in the school, looking at the way in
which children used the free-work structure. We wanted to know how
they selected activities and what they selected (Stodolsky, 1969, 1971).
Having spent a fair amount of time in the classrooms, we began to ask
ourselves in subsequent planning for the continuing evaluation study
just why the Stanford-Binet results looked as they did and what, if
anything, was remaining unexamined in terms of the effects of the
Montessori preschool. With a small initial sample, Kohlberg (1967)
had found a strong relationship between IQ gains and increases in
attention in the children. For reasons which are not entirely clear,
subsequent groups of children entering the program were rated as
less distractible at the beginning of school: so the relationship Kohlberg unearthed was not replicated.

When we examined the Montessori materials and curricular
arrangements in detail, it seemed very clear that the major emphases
of this particular curriculum were not on general cognitive growth,
certainly not on verbal concept development (an important part of the
Stanford-Binet); rather, the curriculum seemed oriented toward the
development of fine-motor coordination; sorting, matching, and clas-
sificatory skills; and number concepts. On a global level, many experi-

ences seemed to be classifiable in the realm of performance rather than verbal intelligence. We posited, on the basis of this analysis, that the Stanford-Binet increases found in the first-year children were probably due more to rapport, motivational, or work-set skills than to cognitive changes. (We would place Kohlberg's findings on attention in this cluster.) We felt that this hypothesis should be tested in our subsequent evaluation study by giving both the Stanford-Binet and performance measures (we chose the WPPSI for children over four and the performance scales of the Merrill-Palmer for younger children) to children in their first, second, and third years in the preschool. If our analysis was correct, the first-year children would experience gains on both sets of measures, but the children beyond their first year in the program would show continued growth only in the performance area and no changes on the Stanford-Binet.

The report of this research is available in detail elsewhere (Stodolsky and Karlson, 1972). It is sufficient here to indicate that our hypotheses were strongly supported. We found differential outcomes of the Montessori curriculum. In terms of Stanford-Binet performance, this particular program seems no better or worse than most well-implemented programs for children in their first year of schooling. Gains are made, but we are really not able to say what, in particular, is responsible for them. However, we are able to point to probable reasons for continued growth on the performance measures. Many specific activities in classrooms are oriented in this direction, and the findings for the group indicate that the grading of activities is adequate to challenge both middle-class and disadvantaged children through at least two years of a Montessori experience. As we noted in our report of this work, the development of performance strengths in the disadvantaged children may or may not facilitate their future academic performance in the typical verbal elementary school. But at least the data are in hand to make choices about how to proceed in the further schooling of the children or to go back and rework the preschool experience in different directions if this course seems desirable.

Although this illustration is limited to the cognitive domain and to gross measurements, I believe it points in the direction that assessment of short-term effects should take. It is also heuristic in terms of the position I took regarding measurement articulation in the existing literature. If measurement is well articulated with a program, the program is likely to look effective. Thus, if we had judged the Montessori program in 1968, we would have concluded that it is possibly effective in promoting intellectual growth in children in their first year of school, but it certainly is not effective in sustaining or continuing growth in children beyond their first year. In 1970 we reached a very different conclusion, couched in different terms.

To reiterate, I would argue that outcome measures should be closely tailored to the curriculum under review. The decision rests on whether one has a priori criteria to impose in terms of student outcomes or is trying to find out how and in what ways a particular approach is producing change in students. For the most part, the latter is what I think we should be doing at this time in the field of early-childhood education.

I believe the second proposition I put forward has profound implications in terms of future evaluations and the decision making that must come from such studies. I asserted that available data suggest that the more effective programs are commonly termed structured programs. I have noted that the operational definition of structured in most of the studies is teacher-directed. But I believe an appropriate way to think about this is to recognize that the structured programs are those which are most under control and therefore most homogeneous with respect to the behavior of the children. With this reinterpretation, the findings show that the more homogeneous programs are the more successful ones. Thus, the Bereiter-Engelmann program (Di Lorenzo et al., 1969; Karnes et al., 1970; Miller and Dyer, 1970), the Karnes experimental program (Karnes et al., 1970), the Perry Program (Weikart, 1967), the DARCEE program (Miller and Dyer, 1970), and in general the "preacademic" programs (Bissell, 1971) would appear to achieve the most growth in the cognitive and language areas in which they place emphasis.

I would argue that this is the case, at least in part, because these programs have met one essential ingredient of any good research design. These programs have a well-defined treatment. We are measuring the effects of something that is specifiable and largely the same for the participating children. In less structured programs—for example, the discovery models or the traditional child-centered nursery—the behavior of the children is much more diverse. Although materials and general orientation are provided, the children are free to self-select their activities in these programs. Proponents of these open methods consider self-selection a vital part of the curriculum, and it may well be. The question becomes: What is known about the behavior of children under a free-choice regimen, and what does this knowledge imply for evaluation studies?

During the 1930s a series of studies were done on the behavior of children during free play in nursery schools. At that time most nursery schools served middle-class children and were child-centered (hence the term *traditional*). It is very clear from this early work (Bott, 1928; Bridges, 1929; Gutteridge, 1935; Van Alstyne, 1932) that children make use of free-choice opportunities in unique ways. When given a selection of activities from which to choose, some children concentrate their efforts in one direction, others in another. Some children become very specialized and repetitive, others scatter their efforts. Although the early researchers were interested primarily in finding out what materials were most appealing to young children, the data very clearly show individual patterns of activity. There are, too, age and sex differences in activities chosen, a point also investigated by Shure (1963).

These early studies, though highly suggestive, were fraught with a number of difficulties and were generally restricted to short periods of time during the school year. Most important here is that there was no way to connect the patterns of activity observed with possible changes on psychometric or other indices of growth. In an attempt to make up some of these deficiencies a student of mine, Alfred Karlson (1972), launched a dissertation project which had two major objectives. The first was to provide an empirical year-long description of the activities of a group of middle-class and disadvantaged children in a preschool. The second was to attempt to relate the specific patterns of activity of the children to their cognitive growth as measured by psychometric instruments. The study was conducted in the Montessori preschool described earlier. In this school almost the whole session is free play or work, during which the children select their own activities. It is a special case because the environment is prepared and the materials are largely self-correcting and sequenced. However, the sequenced nature of the curriculum should mitigate against individual patterns of activity.

Karlson categorized activities according to similarity of content of the materials in use and by incorporating some of Montessori's categories of activity. Fourteen categories were identified—among them, practical life, art, sorting and matching, insets, construction toys, unit blocks and table blocks, sociodramatic play in the doll corner, math, reading. Forty-three children ranging in age from three to six, half Head Start and half middle class, were studied. Each child was observed on a nearly daily basis over the whole school year for a period of five minutes during free-work time. A running narrative of behavior was obtained. Since we had earlier established that children in free-play situations are engaged in both activity and in-between behaviors (Stodolsky, 1969, 1971) the records were coded for segments of activity time as opposed to transition time. The activity time was then placed in the relevant category. In addition, ratings of attention to the activity and of the child's mastery of the task were also made.

This time sampling procedure is based on about 2 per cent of the time a child was in school, but we hoped that the data would be representative of the patterns of activity in which the children were engaged. The analysis of the data clearly showed that children were participating differentially in the activities available in the classroom. The most consistent group differences emerged in regard to sex and age. For example, younger children spent more of their time doing practical life exercises and using construction toys than did older children. Boys spent more time using blocks and construction toys and engaged in special projects, while girls did practical exercises and sorting and matching tasks. There were no sex differences in art or the frequency of sociodramatic play, findings inconsistent with earlier work. There were few differences attributable to social class alone. Middle-class children engaged in the more academic activities (mathematics and reading) more often than did the Head Start children; but when initial intelligence level is controlled, the social-class effect washes out, suggesting that the brighter children, regardless of social class, engaged in these activities.

Although group differences in patterns of activity were evident in the Karlson (1972) data, there was considerable individual variation in patterns of activity in the preschool. These data make apparent that each child is defining his own curriculum. The patterns of activity are not a random sample of the available activities. Each child must be considered as having his own treatment.

This finding is extremely important. We were able to show some general effects of the Montessori curriculum by narrowing our focus to the performance areas of intellectual growth because it was in that area that the activity choices converged. Nevertheless, the lesson of the descriptive study would seem to be that empirical descriptors of the experiences of individual children in free-choice programs are essential for making connections between the school experience and outcomes.

In Karlson's (1972) research, the key question was: Is there a connection between the activity patterns of individual children and the extent of change experienced by the children on the tests administered? The simple argument that there should be a direct connection between what children did with their time in the preschool and the changes they experienced on relevant psychometric instruments was being made. The answer was sought statistically by using the children's time allocations to the fourteen categories of activity (expressed in percentages and properly transformed) as predictors of IQ change scores in a multivariate regression analysis. No test regression effects were present in these data. That is, there was no association between the child's initial level on the intelligence test and the extent of change the child exhibited.

With the data for the WPPSI Performance IQ as an example, for the most adequate sample was available in this case, the regression analysis strongly supported the presumption of a relationship between time allocations to certain activities and the gain or loss scores of the children. Covarying on age, sex, social class, and initial IQ does not change this pattern. Using all allowable categories of activity as predictors of WPPSI change scores, Karlson obtained a significant F ratio ($P < .02$) with a multiple R of .92. In other words, all the categories account for 85 per cent of the variance in change scores. Using a strict criterion under which each category is significant singly, he found that five predictors account for about 76 per cent of the variance.

To emphasize this point, Karlson attempted to predict Stanford-Binet change scores on the basis of the activity patterns. Here we would expect little or no connection because we could not theoretically make one between the classroom activities and what the Stanford-Binet measures. The multivariate regression for the whole sample with all the activity categories is not significant. Only one category of activity has a significant single-order correlation with Stanford-Binet change.

The Karlson (1972) study is an example of the use of empirical treatment descriptors in an evaluation plan. It is only a first step in a line of work which I believe could radically alter our understanding of preschool experiences. This study would have been enhanced if other expected outcomes had also been measured. For example, some children may have developed in the areas of persistence, orderliness, or self-confidence, noncognitive outcomes to which the curriculum is also addressed. Certain activity patterns might be predictive of such developments.

One critical implication of this work is that any curricular approach which allows self-selection of activities cannot be evaluated as a program for a group of children. There are a series of programs in operation, depending on the activity patterns and other varying factors in each child's experience. No wonder group results are unclear. If one believes in the efficacy of self-selection, provided that a good environment of materials and people is available to the child, then a diversity of outcomes emerges from such programs. In order to understand and judge such programs, empirical treatment descriptors and additional measurements of children are essential. Only by launching such evaluation efforts can valid assessments of the open methods be made.

Some might be tempted to take the activity categories Karlson found to be most predictive of growth in the Montessori preschool and to say "these are the ones that work." Certainly one could experimentally expose a group of children to just those activities and see whether they proved equally effective under such imposed conditions. At the present, I feel it is more important that these activities were self-selected. The children who engaged in the activities which relate to cognitive growth spent some of their time in activities which, on a statistical basis, appear less effective for promoting the performance gains observed. But perhaps those activities, the balance the child was able to strike, provided confidence, pride, and the needed resources to go on to challenging tasks.

These issues are complex. Some are empirically resolvable. At this juncture I believe that the evidence regarding the structured versus the traditional preschool methods is not adequate. The more structured programs are clearly more efficient; they do not leave much to chance in the allocation of time and experiences for children. A position which favors such economy of effort is certainly tenable. However, if one opts for a diversity of viable objectives for young children, the more open methods deserve more study.

I have tried to show that the interpreter of current evaluation data is faced with an array of findings which in a certain sense are all loaded toward making the structured and cognitively oriented programs look effective. This is the case primarily because the measurements used are most closely articulated with the objectives of these programs and because the structured programs meet the important methodological criterion of being a treatment to be evaluated. Before accepting existing data as veridical, we must study the less structured programs in terms which are adequate for them. This means utilizing more assessments of the children, looking carefully at the nature of the experiences provided in the classrooms, and empirically identifying the treatments which individual children or groups of children experience. Then one can begin to adequately judge the less structured programs in terms of their effectiveness for a range of children.

The evaluation strategy I have outlined is awesome. However, anything less makes the interpretation of evaluation data regarding open methods an impossible task. The data available are, in my opinion, close to meaningless for directly addressing what is being accomplished in free-choice programs. Proponents of open methods for preschool and elementary school children must come to terms with the diversity they are creating and address their evaluations to it. This effort will involve considerable thought about what the options children have mean with respect to a variety of outcomes. The studies proposed here will probably be exhausting and expensive at first. Nevertheless, if such efforts are not launched, the more "efficient" curricula will certainly carry the day. I believe that such an educational policy decision would be seriously premature. But if the "softies" don't get tough methodologically, the climate of the times will sweep past them. We will, I fear, forego an important opportunity to learn about the growth and education of young children. And, in the long run, the children may be the losers. Let us not spare the needed effort now. Intelligently planned diversity in educational practice, consistent with the diversity of children, is surely what is most needed.

References

BEREITER, C., AND ENGLEMANN, S. *Teaching Disadvantaged Children in the Preschool.* Englewood Cliffs, New Jersey: Prentice-Hall, Inc., 1966.

BISSELL, J. S. *Implementation of Planned Variation in Head Start. I. Review and Summary of the Stanford Research Institute Interim Report: First Year of Evaluation.* Washington, D.C.: Office of Child Development, U.S. Department of Health, Education, and Welfare, April 1971.

BOTT, H. MC M. "Observation of Play Activities in a Nursery School." *Genetic Psychology Monographs,* 1928, *4,* 44–88.

BRIDGES, K. M. B. "The Occupational Interests and Attention of Four-Year-Old Children." *The Pedagogical Seminary,* 1929, *36,* 551–570.

CAZDEN, C. B. "Evaluation of Learning in Preschool Education: Early Language Development." In B. S. Bloom, J. T. Hastings, and G. F. Madaus (Eds.), *Handbook on Formative and Summative Evaluation of Student Learning.* New York: McGraw-Hill, 1971. Pp. 345–398.

COHEN, D. K. "Politics and Research: Evaluation of Social Action Programs in Education." *Review of Educational Research,* 1970, *40,* 213–238.

CRONBACH, L. J., AND SNOW, R. *A Perspective on the Problem of Aptitude and Instruction.* Stanford University, 1971, draft manuscript.

DATTA, L. "A Report on Evaluation Studies of Project Head Start." Paper presented at American Psychological Association Convention, Washington, D.C., 1969.

DI LORENZO, L. T., SALTER, R., AND BRADY, J. T. *Prekindergarten Programs for Educationally Disadvantaged Children.* Final Report, Project No. 3040, Contract No. OE-6-10-040, New York State Education Department, December 1969.

GRAY, S. W., AND KLAUS, R. A. "The Early Training Project: A Seventh-Year Report." *Child Development,* 1970, *41,* 909–924.

GUTTERIDGE, M. V. *Study of the Duration of Attention in Young Children.* Australian Council for Educational Research Series, No. 41, 1935.

JENSEN, J., AND KOHLBERG, L. "Report of a Research and Demonstration Project for Culturally Disadvantaged Children in the Ancona Montessori School." Submitted to Office of Economic Opportunity, August 1966.

KAMII, C. K. "Evaluation of Learning in Preschool Education: Socio-emotional, Perceptual-motor, Cognitive Development." In B. S. Bloom, J. T. Hastings, and G. R. Madaus (Eds.), *Handbook on Formative and Summative Evaluation of Student Learning.* New York: McGraw-Hill, 1971. Pp. 281–344.

KARLSON, A. L. "A Naturalistic Method for Identifying Behavioral Aspects of Cognitive Acquisition in Young Children Participating in Preschool Programs." Unpublished doctoral dissertation, University of Chicago, 1972.

KARNES, M. B., TESKA, J. A., AND HODGINS, A. S. "The Effects of Four Programs of Classroom Intervention on the Intellectual and Language Development of Four-Year-Old Disadvantaged Children." *American Journal of Orthopsychiatry,* 1970, *40,* 58–76.

KIRK, S. A. *Early Education of the Mentally Retarded.* Urbana, Ill.: University of Illinois Press, 1958.

KOHLBERG, L. "Assessment of a Montessori Program." Paper presented at American Educational Research Association Convention, New York, February 1967.

KOHLBERG, L. "Montessori with the Culturally Disadvantaged: A Cognitive-Developmental Interpretation and Some Research Findings." In R. Hess and R. Bear (Eds.), *Early Education: Theory, Research and Action.* Chicago: Aldine Press, 1968. Pp. 105–118.

LA CROSSE, E. R., LEE, P. C., LITMAN, F., OGILVIE, D. M., STODOLSKY, S. S., AND WHITE, B. L. "The First Six Years of Life: A Report on

Current Research and Educational Practice." *Genetic Psychology Monographs,* 1970, *82,* 161–266.

MACCOBY, E. E., AND ZELLNER, M. *Experiments in Primary Education: Aspects of Project Follow Through.* New York: Harcourt Brace Jovanovich, 1970.

MILLER, L. B., AND DYER, J. L. "Experimental Variation of Head Start Curricula: A Comparison of Current Approaches." Annual Progress Report submitted to Office of Economic Opportunity, 1970.

SCRIVEN, M. "The Methodology of Evaluation." *AERA Monograph Series on Curriculum Evaluation,* No. 1. Chicago: Rand McNally, 1967.

SHURE, M. B. "The Psychological Ecology of a Nursery School." *Child Development,* 1963, *34,* 979–992.

SKEELS, H. M. "Adult Status of Children with Contrasting Early Life Experiences." *Society of Research in Child Development Monographs,* 1966, *31*(3), whole.

SKEELS, H. M., AND DYE, H. B. "A Study of the Effects of Differential Stimulation on Mentally Retarded Children." *Proceedings of the American Association of Mental Deficiency,* 1939, *44,* 114–136.

STAKE, R. E. "Objectives, Priorities, and Other Judgmental Data." *Review of Educational Research,* 1970, *40,* 181–212.

STODOLSKY, S. S. "Transition Behavior of Children during Free Play in Nursery Schools." Paper presented at the Society for Research in Child Development convention, Santa Monica, 1969.

STODOLSKY, S. S. "How Children Find Something to Do in Preschools." Department of Education, University of Chicago, 1971. Mimeo.

STODOLSKY, S. S., AND JENSEN, J. "Final Report: Ancona Montessori Research Project for Culturally Disadvantaged Children." Submitted to Office of Economic Opportunity, October 1969.

STODOLSKY, S. S., AND KARLSON, A. L. "Differential Outcomes of a Montessori Curriculum." *Elementary School Journal,* 1972, *72*(8), 419–433.

SWIFT, J. "Effects of Early Group Experience: The Nursery School and Day Nursery." In M. L. Hoffman and L. Hoffman (Eds.), *Review of Child Development Research.* Vol. 1. New York: Russell Sage, 1964. Pp. 249–288.

VAN ALSTYNE, D. *Play Behavior and Choice of Play Materials of Preschool Children.* Chicago: University of Chicago Press, 1932.

WEIKART, D. P. "Preschool Programs: Preliminary Findings." *Journal of Special Education,* 1967, *1,* 163–181.

WEIKART, D. P. "Comparative Study of Three Preschool Curricula." Paper presented at Society for Research in Child Development convention, Santa Monica, 1969.

WELLMAN, B. "Iowa Studies on the Effects of Schooling." *Yearbook of the National Society for the Study of Education,* 1940, *39,* 377–399.

WESTBURY, I. "Curriculum Evaluation." *Review of Educational Research,* 1970, *40,* 239–260.

WHITE, B. L. "Informal Education during the First Months of Life." In R. Hess and R. Bear (Eds.), *Early Education: Theory, Research and Action.* Chicago: Aldine Press, 1968. Pp. 143–171.

WHITE, S. H. "The National Impact Study of Head Start." In J. Hellmuth (Ed.), *The Disadvantaged Child.* Vol. 3. New York: Brunner/Mazel, 1970. Pp. 163–184.

ZIGLER, E., AND BUTTERFIELD, E. C. "Motivational Aspects of Change in IQ Test Performance in Culturally Deprived Nursery School Children." *Child Development,* 1968, *39,* 1–14.

CHAPTER 8

Professorial Involvement in Cities

Armin Beck

$$◈◈ ◈◈ ◈◈ ◈◈ ◈◈ ◈◈ ◈◈ ◈◈$$

When Pogo said, "We have met the enemy and they is us!" he may have had reference to the disparity between what professors in urban institutions feel they should do to help communities and what the communities feel they need from the urban university. During recent years, large numbers of professors have gone into the different city communities, on their own terms and with their preconceptions of community needs—preconceptions, for the most part, not based on community definition. They made so many frightful blunders that in some instances universities have been forbidden by community groups and organizations to come into poor communities to "do good."

The community/university issue was joined at a meeting of the Tri-University Conference on Education (1968). The education dean of an eastern urban state university described the ways in which he was encouraging his 500-plus professors to involve themselves in

95

community affairs. After hearing him out, community representatives from around the country agreed that, instead of becoming social activists, the professors should stay in their office rooms. Rather than spring themselves into the community, they should stay in their hallowed halls, for they could do the least amount of harm there. The values that they would bring to the community were generally not those of the community itself. The community people did not want to support an army of education professors flooding the communities with good will and good intentions so that they could become "involved in social action," or so that they could become relevant for their students, or so that they could formulate "successful" programs to perpetuate themselves in government or university programs. The potential harm was too great.

The main reason for community rejection of university involvement is that the university's perception of need seldom seems to coincide with the community's perception of its own need. Professors want to study the people to find out more about them, so that governmental and university programs can be devised, proposed, and funded to take care of the needs uncovered by those studies. Community people want the money themselves, so that they can devise programs to define their own needs and desires and to set wheels in motion to correct the problems uncovered by their need definition. That difference tends to make professors "natural enemies" of the people, especially in their role as institutional agents.

This chapter discusses responses to these questions concerning urban education: Who are "the people" of the communities, and whence derives professorial knowledge about them? Who are the professors in universities that serve urban populations? What are some conditions that should be met before professors should be formally "allowed" into the communities?

The People and the Professors

My purpose here is not a redefinition or analysis of "the people," but an examination of some ways in which information is gleaned about them. From whom do we accept our information? Scholars such as Robert J. Havighurst years ago pioneered in and provided us with the research necessary to carry on action programs in urban education. Many of the new researchers, however, have been detrimental to successful action programs in urban communities and even to the community people themselves.

Daniel P. Moynihan (1967) studied the Negro family and

supplied proof of its social and familial inferiority; national policy was made. James S. Coleman (1966) focused on comparative black and white educational achievement and supplied proof of educational inferiority of black students; national policy was made. Arthur Jensen (1969) studied native intelligence and supplied proof of the genetic intellectual inferiority of blacks. Continuing national policy is being made. Thomas F. Pettigrew (1969) was paid a goodly sum from an Office of Education contract to discuss racial separateness or together-ness at a recent convention of the Society for the Psychological Study of Social Issues. He concluded that one society is better than two (regardless of the murderous consequences of the white man's insti-tutional and personal behavior toward the black man).

The policy that was developed resulted inevitably in programs for the "poor" or for the "defined population" or for the "targets"— programs designed by nonpoor, nontarget, nonoppressed middle-class professors. It is not suggested here that the numerals used by the profes-sors went awry or that the formulas they used to feed their computers to test their hypotheses were wrong and they therefore came up with wrong answers. No, the numbers are correct. It is the hypotheses and conclusions that are not credible. Because the hypotheses were almost always formulated in a race-oriented context, the professors usually arrived at conclusions that support white university hypotheses and denigrate the people who are hypothesized about, or who are studied.

The question of who defines whom is not substantially different from the discussion carried on by Carter G. Woodson (1963):

> There can be no reasonable objection to the Negro's doing what the white man tells him to do [in the context of schooling and education] if the white man tells him to do what is right; but right is purely relative. The present system under the control of the whites trains the Negro to be white and at the same time convinces him of the impropriety or the impossibility of his be-coming white. . . . History does not furnish a case of the eleva-tion of a people by ignoring the thought and aspiration of the people thus served. . . . The educational system as it has devel-oped both in Europe and America is an antiquated process which does not hit the mark even in the case of the needs of the white man himself. If the white man wants to hold onto it, let him do so; but the Negro, so far as he is able, should develop and carry out a program of his own [pp. 23–24].

It is difficult for a Moynihan (1967), for example, to study data and draw conclusions about the Negro family and come up with anything but a negative response, no matter how benevolent he is or appears to be. He brings his whole background of Irishness, professorness, middle classness to bear on a Negro question. Not surprisingly, his findings denigrate the studied population. Moynihan can, however, as reported by Fuchs (1968), talk successfully about the Irish of New York from their initial immigration to the present time. The Irish looting, burning, draft-dodging, rioting, and hard drinking notwithstanding, when a reader finishes "The Irish of New York" his response is different from his response to *The Negro Family*. The former is laden with ethnic pride; the latter, with sympathy. The reader is invited to view with suspicion every scientific or social scientific study that ends with negative conclusions about oppressed, "target" populations, whether or not the research is reported in refereed journals.

So we have "traditional" university scholars studying oppressed minorities as a prelude to involvement in urban social action. The studies, however, often result in even greater oppression for the minorities. That is, because of the additional knowledge gleaned by the scholars, correct or not, the minorities have even less opportunity to define their own condition and prescribe programs to alleviate that condition.

On the other hand, when Richard A. Goldsby (1971) examines the field of genetics from what many consider a neutral viewpoint, and when his determination on race is that it is a "breeding population," with different but neither superior nor inferior characteristics, and when this thesis stands in opposition to the thesis held by some white biologists, no national policy, or even discussion, results. When black educational achievement is related to the black experience in the urban ghettos of America as discussed by psychiatrists Grier and Cobbs (1971), and when, based on their conclusions, they make certain prescriptions for education, no national policy results. When Carmichael and Hamilton (1967, 1969) study successful political organization of black people and therefrom make certain recommendations, no national policy results. When Harold Cruse (1967) reports on his studies of the effects on black people of interethnic power, no national policy results. When Deluvina Hernandez (1970) raises serious academic questions concerning not only the appropriateness but the cultural accuracy of Anglo-university research on Chicanos, not only does no policy result but no serious academic discussion ensues. When Vine Deloria, Jr. (1970), excoriates the concept of the neocolonialist anthropologists as advisers to the government in Indian affairs, national policy remains as it was.

Who are the traditional white university scholars? What makes them "the enemy" of the communities? What serves to put them continually into positions of power and influence, when usually in their own context they deny that they even want such things? Some students and professors have referred to it as white-skin privilege. But it goes deeper than skin. Many readers of this paper gained influence, power, and privilege by being born into the kinds of families into which they were born and by growing up in the life style and with the alternatives that are thereby open to them. Frequent informal tests reveal that people who control policy for urban education and thereby control definitions of the educational needs of urban communities are over thirty years old, members of the middle class, nonfundamentalist Protestants, Caucasian, and male. These five characteristics, taken together, provide the recipients with power and influence in educational matters in the United States, and they have nothing to do with anything that has been earned. People are born with them, grow up with them, and use them as tools of their trade. Although some professors have achieved high position without one or more of these characteristics, they have had more to overcome than people who have all five.

Empirical questions that can, informally at least, test the thesis of the previous paragraph, as the reader observes a local college or university, are these: Proportionately, how many women are employed in faculty positions and what is their status? How many black, Chicano, Puerto Rican, Native American, or other colored minority professors are there? How many Catholics or Jews are in positions of influence in the college's administration? How many lower-class or upper-class people are employed in professorial capacities? How many "youngsters" are on the faculty?

If a professor wants to become a social activist in an urban setting, he must take this power into consideration. When psychologists, who generally fit the five power categories, study nonwhite or poor youngsters and conclude, for example, that the children lack the capacity for delaying reward gratification, and when local or national curriculum policy is based on these findings, the residual power of the testers should be considered. When psychologists say that poor young people cannot delay this gratification and that therefore the poor young people behave as they do, it is assumed that psychologists' children *can* live with such delay. The major difference is that psychologists *know* that their children generally can get Ph.D.s and/or go on to an affluent life if they want to, and the poor people know just as clearly that they and their children cannot. In effect, then, the psychologists' children's rewards are not delayed either.

One method whereby "others" can get these residual rewards

is to emulate the old, white, middle-class, male Protestant professors and administrators. The more that "others" act this way, the more they tend to be included. Minority groups know this, and until the past few years they have been willing to play by those rules. They still must play the game to get in; but once in, they have more and more behaved like minority group people, much to the consternation of the people who employ them. This behavior, by the way, is not always safe for personal survival within the institution, but it is the role often taken in recent years.

An interesting case in point is a recent experience at a large midwestern urban state university. The number of colored ethnic faculty in one of the colleges decreased from sixteen to four between one school year and the next. The colored ethnic faculty members had allied themselves with their racial counterparts in the various communities. The issue was college program definition for these communities and whether the communities would have a voice in the programs that affected them. When an impasse was reached between the college and the communities, most of the colored ethnic faculty members resigned or were fired, or their contracts were not renewed.

In sum, as long as academicians act toward communities like "colonial administrators," which they can do by virtue of their influence, they would be well advised to stay out of the urban communities and not become social activists. Unless they take steps to divest themselves of "who they are" before they become involved with community activism, they should remain in their academic cells and not try to program themselves and others by use of government or private money.

The dilemma is that we may not be able to survive as a nation —our educational systems may not be able to survive within that nation—without direct and vigorous involvement in the city's communities on the part of the academic profession. However, if professors continue as they have in the past, either they will drive community activists even further away from the universities and the schools or an academic wall—impenetrable by anyone on either side of it, regardless of good will or intentions—will be built up.

What then is necessary? How can academicians be of positive worth to the communities they purport to help without adding to the colonization of the people within those communities?

Conditions for Involvement

There are difficulties in store for an academic man if he wishes to become a positive social activist in urban communities, primarily because of the strictures placed on him by both academic society and the outside society which produced him. These strictures provide the very core of his existence. Without them, the professor loses status, both academic and in his home community; he loses money because he probably will not receive private or government funding for his projects; he loses caste; and he becomes like "one of them," the people without society's normal supports. To gain, or to regain, all these things, he must work in cooperation with government, education, business, industry, and labor, and not in cooperation with the indigenous community.

Some of the strictures that have been observed in various activities and projects are listed and discussed below.

rational behavior	irrational behavior
legal or civil	illegal or human
social research	social action
responsible	irresponsible rabble-rousing
legitimate organization	illegitimate organization
discussive	disruptive

In each case the first term (as defined by those who have power) represents an acceptable behavioral characteristic. The opposite term represents unacceptable behavior. Thus, it is considered rational behavior for some universities to require high school graduates to have two years of a foreign language prior to college entrance. It is considered irrational behavior when students whose high schools offer no foreign language try to lie to overcome that requirement or when their parents, as members of community organizations, try to "storm the barricades" of the university to pressure it either to modify the requirement or to help influence the school to include two years to satisfy the requirement. Individuals and community groups in the inner city consider the former requirements irrational and their own attempts at change rational; but their definition, not having societal or academic support, comes to naught. When law and order is restored, it is at their expense, not at the university's. The net effect is that the university, using the idea of "rational" behavior, drastically reduces entrance of inner-city youth to its halls and remains overwhelmingly a white institution. Whether it is intentional or not is immaterial. One thing, then, that academicians must be willing to do is to behave in a "rational" manner as defined by the community ("irrational" as defined by the university) in order to become relevant to the community's definition of its educational needs and desires.

It is considered legal behavior for school districts to try every form of interposition known to our judicial system to keep black students from attending school with white students. It is also considered legal behavior for black parents or organizations to go to court in city after city to try to have the courts force the school districts to follow the patterns of school desegregation laid down by courts all over the country. This legal behavior is acceptable to the white community, and by the time the case is successfully concluded, new ways have generally been found in the legal profession to circumvent the court's rulings. It is considered illegal behavior for black individuals or groups, recognizing the limitations of the laws, to mount some form of protest in an effort to force compliance with the law. Perpetrators of such behavior are jailed or fined. Which behavior, however, is legal? According to many black victims, if they are allowed to define, the latter behavior is legal behavior. Professors who wish to become involved in a positive way in black communities should be willing to adopt the definition of the communities themselves.

Another example may help to clarify the distinction between legal and illegal behavior. Every civil rights struggle that has taken place with white support or white leadership has been structured to limit the white man's behavior toward the black man, determining in each case "how much of a man we are going to let him be this year." Then the new civil rights law is passed—and who immediately breaks it? Is it the black man trying to find a home in a neighborhood heretofore not open to him? Or is it the white real estate dealer who still maintains his own traditional version of the law? A Human Relations Commission, or a Fair Housing Commission, is then set up to deal with complaints that come from the blacks. The blacks are expected to go through the legal complications necessary to resolve the issue. Very few blacks are willing to do that, and the city's conclusion, therefore, is that progress in open housing has been made since passage of the law. Now why should black people go through this demeaning "legal" process when the law itself says it is a crime to discriminate? In other words, society now expects the oppressed person to act in a gentle, legal manner when *he* is the one who is suffering from *il*legal actions.

It is considered proper behavior in universities to engage in social research as a prelude to social action. The latter, taken without the former, is generally less effective, even though the plight of the victims is well known. Poor people often need food. Just as often, however, they cannot get it until a consulting firm employed by the city or state welfare has studied them and the results are tabulated. The consultant's conclusions usually are to the effect that the people are hungry. Then food may become available. Or, as is clear from simple observation, children in a given inner-city school are not reading at grade level, and there is no library or learning center. Before emergency supplies are moved in, or at least concurrent with their being moved in, it is deemed necessary to study the pupils: their home and neighborhood backgrounds, their physical condition, their intelligence scores. Then the school has some data to compare after all the money has been spent. The point here is that often action is needed prior to the study—action to alleviate conditions. Such action, in the view of the community, takes precedence over studies of their children. Study as a prelude to action is academically acceptable; action, regardless of study, is acceptable to the community. Definitions of research and action, however, are in the hands of the academicians, not community residents.

It is considered responsible behavior for teachers in an inner-city school to work "within the system" to redress conditions that result in a physically dangerous setting: broken windows, walls peeling their leaded paint. It is considered rabble-rousing, or irresponsible behavior, for them to join parents and children in closing the school down and picketing it. Teachers in a medium-sized midwestern city recently faced this dilemma. They said, in effect, "We know that the parents' grievances are real, from the falling ceilings in several of the classrooms to the irrelevant curriculum; but where is our place? Do we march with the parents, or do we work within the system to get these things changed and go back to our classes on Monday morning?" After considerable discussion, the teachers chose not to go with the parents. The teachers thereby did not accept the definition of "responsible" behavior as used by the parents, who really needed their help. The community needed "irrational" behavior from the teachers; instead, it received sympathy and a lecture in semantics, neither of which was able to repair the falling ceilings.

It is considered acceptable behavior for a university to accept programmatic advice from a legitimately constituted community organization. If the organization is illegitimately constituted, the university will not accept such advice. Here again, however, the question arises: Who may define "legitimate" for the community? Common practice is that university administrators choose the representatives of the community, or they choose the organizations which in turn appoint representatives or spokesmen. Organizations or ideas not legitimized by the university are not accepted by it, whether or not they have credence in the community. Universities have used this technique frequently and successfully to maintain their own programs as they define them, although they sometimes employ residents of the community to carry out their definitions and wishes. Other organizations are then branded as illegitimate. Professors, to become social activists in urban communities, should cast their lot with the illegitimate organizations. They are the ones that generally need and cannot have the support of the established institutions.

In academic halls discussive behavior is correct behavior; disruptive behavior is wrong behavior. Therefore, it is a recurring fashion for biologists, psychologists, or educators to test nonwhite people and to draw conclusions such as those described in the first part of this paper. That sort of behavior on their part is not considered disruptive, even though the conclusions describe a vast portion of the world's population. When black scholars respond in ways that cut off debate, their behavior is viewed not only as anti-intellectual but as disruptive. According to the view of some black scholars, however, it is neither anti-intellectual nor disruptive, nor indeed is it improper behavior at all to discuss social research before it takes place with the view in mind of altering the nature of the research before it damages the studied population. It is not enough to suggest that anyone is free to do any research as long as he is willing to submit it to the marketplace of ideas for acceptance or rejection. Until such time as minority scholars and the communities for which they purport to speak can have at least equal influence in universities, professors should submit to prior approval of certain types of research. This approval, too, should be a condition for involvement in the communities of the city, even though some attempts by minority scholars to gain equal influence sometimes results in what universities consider to be disruptive behavior.

As important as it is for individual faculty members to become active on the terms described above, it is just as important for institutions themselves to develop, with the community, a set of community-defined goals for which the university can supply support. Universities and communities, working in cooperation, may develop the following types of guidelines for professorial and institutional behavior: The university will (1) provide laboratories in various neighborhoods of the city and environs wherein faculty and students can examine community responses to many aspects of the total educational endeavor and where they can examine education's response to many aspects of community life and needs; (2) examine with faculty and students their personal accountability so that it can at least be shared between the institutions which support them and the people they purport to serve; (3) help provide support and resources for individuals, groups, and organizations who need, but otherwise would have no access to, institutional, established resources; (4) aid local communities in the definition of their problems and in the search for their own solutions; (5) help established institutions bring about a redefinition of their responsibilities with respect to loyalty and accountability to people and communities that they are obliged to serve but in fact do not.

The university, with such a policy, can supply the milieu in which professors can become social activists on terms acceptable to the community. Such activism will seldom, if ever, lead to harm to the residents because of the immediate opportunities they have for corrective definitions. It is not the job of the professors to try to turn the community people into rational, legal, responsible, legitimate, discussive individuals, except by the community's definition of those terms. Communities have been rationalized too long. They need people who, as Lerone Bennett (1964) has suggested, will say such things as this (paraphrased): "Discrimination is evil. Kill it. Do not set up a human relations committee, do not set up an investigatory research board, do not organize brotherhood week, do not schedule a faculty meeting to discuss it, do not change the law only, but kill it" (p. 158).

Who shall preside over the leadership in a movement to be of real service to communities? Shall it be the traditional professor, who periodically concludes from his rationally based studies, for example, that if black children go to school with white children, their achievement level improves? Or shall it be people of a black community, who say: "I do not care what your research says about my children and their schooling. You have not even raised the right questions. Why did we have to wait until white youngsters came to our black school for the walls to be painted, for the textbooks to be updated, for the teachers to have human relations workshops, to have regular teachers instead of substitutes?"

The traditional professor—for all his logical, rational, and "responsible" research—is not qualified to provide leadership in urban education. Therefore, the black person or the Chicano or the Native American, or the poor person, or the community person must do so. Professors of today usually do not know the correct questions to raise because they do not understand the community *Weltanschauung*. They must be willing to sacrifice some of their powers of leadership to the people of the communities, even though colleagues would suggest that such behavior is "irrational." Nothing less can be done as a prelude to a serious reevaluation of the role of the academician in urban education.

References

BENNETT, L., JR. *The Negro Mood.* New York: Ballantine Books, 1964.

CARMICHAEL, S., AND HAMILTON, C. V. *Black Power.* New York: Random House, 1967.

COLEMAN, J. S., et al. *Equality of Educational Opportunity.* U.S. Department of Health, Education, and Welfare. Washington, D.C.: Government Printing Office, 1966.

CRUSE, H. *Crisis of the Negro Intellectual.* New York: William Morrow, 1967.

DELORIA, V., JR. *Custer Died for Your Sins.* New York: Avon Books, 1970.

GOLDSBY, R. A. *Race and Races.* New York: Macmillan, 1971.

GRIER, W. H., AND COBBS, P. N. *The Jesus Bag.* New York: McGraw-Hill, 1971.

HAMILTON, C. V. "Conflict, Race, and System-Transformation in the United States." *Journal of International Affairs,* 1969, *1,* 106–118.

HERNANDEZ, D. *Mexican-American Challenge to a Sacred Cow.* Los Angeles: University of California at Los Angeles Mexican-American Cultural Center Monograph Series No. 1, 1970.

JENSEN, A. R. "How Much Can We Boost I.Q. and Scholastic Achievement?" *Harvard Educational Review,* 1969, *39,* 1–123.

MOYNIHAN, D. P. *The Negro Family: The Case for National Action.* Cambridge: MIT Press, 1967.

MOYNIHAN, D. P. "The Irish of New York." In L. H. Fuchs (Ed.), *American Ethnic Politics.* New York: Harper and Row, 1968.

PETTIGREW, T. F. "Racially Separate or Together." *Journal of the Social Sciences,* 1969, *25,* 43–69.

U.S. Office of Education Tri-University Project in Elementary Education. *A Pride of Lions,* report of the fourth national conference. Washington, D.C., 1968.

WOODSON, C. G. *The Mis-Education of the Negro.* Washington, D.C.: Associated Publishers, 1963.

CHAPTER 9

Insights and Alternatives from a Black Street Academy

Maurice J. Eash and James T. Napolitan

Springing up in many large cities today are a number of alternative schools that have refashioned curriculum. These scattered innovations suggest that the problems of the inner-city secondary school may be more curricular than administrative and that the way out may lie in a major curricular reconstruction. But the experiences of these schools are largely inaccessible to public school educators because of a lack of evaluation and study of their practices. Moreover, although many of these schools are started, they quickly die and leave relatively few records of their existence. One of these alternative schools, however, has been in existence since

1967, and a comprehensive curriculum evaluation of its program has been undertaken.

This school, the Christian Action Ministry Academy (CAM Academy), located on the west side of Chicago in a black ghetto, was founded in 1967 as a self-described second-chance school for high school dropouts (Eash, 1970). The evaluation research undertaken for this school, by the Office of Evaluation Research of the University of Illinois in Chicago, points to viable curriculum alternatives to present practice in inner-city high schools. The evaluation gathered data through a study of the school records on curriculum and admissions, minutes of meetings, interviews with teachers, questionnaires from graduates now attending college, and an analysis of pre- and postscores on achievement tests. From these data an analysis of the functioning of the school was made to determine the reasons for its success with a population that had rejected more formal school settings. Full details of the evaluation methodology can be found in a prior report. This chapter presents the main substantive findings of the evaluation.

Curriculum Design

Most alternative schools' students attend voluntarily. At CAM no records are kept of students' attendance, and no report is made of their coming and going. Students account for their presence in school by signing into learning centers and listing the program of learning they are pursuing for that day. For the students, voluntary attendance makes for an atmosphere that is not oppressive; students feel "free" at CAM Academy. In the judgment of the students this atmosphere has helped to lower the aggression and hostility that are often pronounced among students who are not very successful in school. Notably missing are problems of student aggression, drugs, alcohol, gangs, and vandalism. One of the most striking aspects of the large-city high schools is conflict between students and between students and faculty (Havighurst et al., 1970). That kind of conflict is conspicuously absent at the CAM Academy.

The attendance rate at CAM Academy compares favorably with the average attendance in other inner-city high schools, which have the assistance of attendance officers (Stein, 1970). In both instances, attendance is roughly between 60 and 70 per cent of the total student body.

Leaving the matter of attendance exclusively up to the students seems to contribute to motivation; it also puts the student in the position of assuming responsibility for his learning. At CAM Academy, the guidepost on whether a student is making progress or not is his ability to pass certain intermediate steps enroute to taking the General Education Development Test (GED), which serves as the equivalent of a high school diploma. Where students were infrequent in attendance and not making progress, they also soon saw that they had diminished sharply their opportunities for passing the GED. Many of these students had had extensive experience in being unemployed and were fully aware of the significance of a high school diploma.

A second major component in the curriculum design is the establishment of learning centers—instead of a fixed classroom schedule and a structured curriculum for a group of students. CAM Academy has four learning centers: language arts, arithmetic, social studies, and science. These learning centers are supplied with a wide variety of material, and students are encouraged to select and study materials on their own. Once a student starts work on materials, a record is kept on file of his efforts; and from his work samples an individual program is developed. The students also encourage each other to try new materials, which they might otherwise have avoided.

A third component of the curriculum design is the matter of keeping learning centers small (ten to twenty students). There is very little teacher lecturing and formal teaching. Flexible arrangements permit students to shift freely from one learning center to another. The teacher works individually and talks informally with students. Possibly as a result of the small learning centers, as well as the size of the school, there seems to be a feeling of community among students. Of fundamental significance is the students' assumption of responsibility for maintaining an orderly learning environment. They have prevented nonstudents from coming in to sell drugs and gamble.

Instructional Design

A number of practices in instructional design seem to speak directly to the problems of the inner-city schools. Individualization of instruction has been a primary goal. Access to a large variety of materials permits students to be self-pacing in their approach to instruction. The teachers—prevented by irregular attendance and shifts in student population from conducting group instruction—are forced to use individualized approaches that allow students to be self-pacing. The variety and range of instruction used and the way the learning centers are physically organized make the self-pacing approach possible. Moreover, students, through self-selection of subject matter, engage material at their interest level and at their level of instructional competency, thus circumventing a problem very common in total-class instruction, where the middle of the class is the focus and both ends of the continuum are largely ignored.

Students' choices of learning materials and resulting self-pacing are important constructs in the instructional design for establishing the objectives for learning. The wide range of materials and their appeal to several learning styles permit innumerable points of entry for student interest. Materials programmed into small steps as well as completely open-ended instructional materials permit students to evaluate both the type and range of response required. In general the staff has found that programmed materials are favored by students who are less secure and have more limited skills while less structured response materials are more attractive to students who have the fundamental skills.

Instructional methods are more flexible and numerous than those customarily observed in high school classrooms. Individualization is practiced but other approaches enter in: teaming, small-group work, lectures, and films. As mentioned, small classes permit teachers to be flexible in the learning centers. Ten to twenty students are generally in attendance in the learning centers unless a lecture or outside consultants are scheduled. The students engage in a variety of activities in the learning center while the teacher moves around assisting students or handling small groups. Of considerable importance is the student-to-student interaction, whereby students introduce and encourage fellow students to try new materials and books. It seems particularly important as a motivating force for reluctant learners, stimulating them to interact with materials without the usual artificial motivational devices applied by teachers in regular classrooms. The range of methodology does not let the students wallow in failure. In small classes the teachers know when difficulty is encountered. The students in the learning center gain a sense of accomplishment, since instructional methods are designed for them to make progress, and failure is limited. Through this process self-confidence to complete future tasks is established.

Evaluation procedures support the main objectives of the academy. First, there are no group tests given or intergroup comparisons made among students. The student evaluation process is essentially a positive assessment of performance on specific tasks, with the results used to direct students toward mastering needed skills. Monitoring is carried through student records containing work samples. These work samples, particularly in the area of fundamental skills, represent direct tasks related to the external criterion measures of the GED. The work samples are evaluated, and the results are used as feedback and guide to the students. The specter of failure often associated with evaluation is removed; in fact, the students learn to value feedback data from the teachers as assistance in planning their future instructional program. Of equal significance is the relationship that prevails between student and teacher under these conditions, for now they are joined in a mutual task of improving student performance to gain an external goal. The judgments rendered by the teacher in this evaluation process are to help the student in progress toward these goals, rather than to undermine his confidence—as comparisons and emphasis on ranking and scores in evaluation frequently do, especially for the low achiever. This approach stands in sharp contrast to evaluation approaches generally followed in high school classrooms, where comparisons are made among students to produce abstract scores that assume more importance than what is learned.

At first the staff tried to use an instructional design predicated almost exclusively on programmed instruction. They soon found that students had great need of small-group activity in order to develop motivation for pursuing academic goals. Discussion in small groups in a secure environment permits both learning of problem solving and exploration and testing of one's identity. Problem-solving approaches from subject-matter disciplines are also used. Moreover, practices within small groups permit encounters ordinarily too painful to be faced in life to be confronted in a manageable context. Language is clarified, thinking is tested, and priorities are ordered through these small-group experiences. This feature of the instructional design also results in gains in standardized test scores, particularly in language abilities.

This academy is showing outstanding results on measures of academic achievement. Test scores were available on twenty-two of the original sample of thirty-two students interviewed. Only test scores of students who had been in attendance five months were analyzed. Significant gains in mathematics and language arts and limited gains in reading, as measured by the standardized tests, have been recorded. A comparison of pretest and posttest scores on the Test of Adult Basic Education was made to determine the achievement gains for twenty-two students. An eleventh-grade norm was used, since most students had dropped out in eleventh grade at sixteen years of age. The gains in mathematics and language were over two years, and the gain in reading was four months. These scores all represent a reversal of the usual pattern of minimal achievement gains after junior high school.

Conclusions

What alternatives are presented to the public secondary school through this model? It seems that the academy's curriculum meets the personality needs of a segment of students who are disaffected by the structure of the curriculum prevalent in the public secondary schools.

The academy evidently builds upon basic personality needs, which are being denied in large part by the American culture (Slater, 1970). Specifically the academy fosters a humane, participatory group in which the students share their problems with one another and help one another to solve them.

The academy's founders, in devising a curriculum for inner-city youth, have capitalized upon the factor of size. Because of the small size of the learning centers, and the limited size of the student body, intimate relationships between students and faculty are possible. Furthermore, although the curriculum does make demands on students, it avoids much of the humiliation that individuals experience within the setting of a large, impersonal, time-oriented structure. Students and faculty members are on the same side of the line in the academic race and are working against external criteria; thus, the faculty member does not function as gatekeeper on the students' desires, and the grade grind is circumvented. The academy thus avoids becoming moralistic about student behavior and places the responsibility upon students for selecting their goals and directing their own behavior.

What is suggested, then, from this alternative school is a need for reorientation of public high schools—at least for a large segment of our youth in the inner city. We should reconsider many of our traditional procedures: fixed schedules, integrated schools, comprehensiveness, even much of the elaborated curriculum that we have put together through an additive process over the many years. If the data of this alternative school document anything, it is that we must question many of the fundamental assumptions that have guided practice in secondary education, especially in the inner city.

References

EASH, M. J. "A Comprehensive Curriculum Evaluation of the Christian Action Ministry Academy." Office of Evaluation Research, University of Illinois, 1970.

HAVIGHURST, R. J., SMITH, F., AND WILDER, D. "Profile of the Large City High School." National Association of Secondary School Principals, 1970.

SLATER, P. The Pursuit of Loneliness. Boston: Beacon Press, 1970.

STEIN, M. "Truancy Overwhelms the Truant Officers Here." New York Times, February 2, 1970.

CHAPTER **10**

Is the Urban Evaluator Accountable?

Robert Rippey

❧❧❧❧❧❧❧❧

When the roll is called up yonder, will evaluators be there? Not if I read the latest reports correctly. The sins of evaluators have been listed in public with increasing frequency. In the literature one finds evaluation referred to in terms such as "going through . . . an identity crisis" (Dyer, 1969) or suffering from "low prestige, a sense of alienation, and feelings of impotence" (Rossi, 1969). Others (McDill, McDill, and Sprehe, 1969) conclude that evaluation studies are grossly inadequate and question whether these evaluations, as currently conceived, are of any value at all.

If the role of the evaluator is so questionable, why not give evaluation a speedy coup de grace? Perhaps because it still has a unique and powerful role to play—though not necessarily the role that the evaluator has traditionally accepted for himself. The alternative productive role proposed here is neither that of a stool pigeon nor that

113

of a judge. The evaluator, in our view, is a person who is concerned primarily with recording and reporting on the pulse and general condition of the social system into which educational improvements are inserted.

Urban Paradox

The urban setting in which the evaluation researcher finds himself is a challenging paradox. Although urban school systems, because of their size, offer the greatest possibility for advancing knowledge about education, thereby solving many of their own problems, they are also beset by the most severe inhibitions—some fiscal, some political, and some organizational.

For the production of new knowledge about evaluation, the big cities have many advantages: they have large numbers of pupils; they have many schools that offer the possibility for experimental designs in the testing of solutions to educational problems; they have personnel resources to develop the knowledge we need in order to educate thoughtfully, effectively, and humanely. Yet not much new knowledge gets produced: "We lack information . . . we don't know much for sure, and on some questions (such as effective compensatory education), we don't know enough to plan ourselves out of a lunch bag" (Gorham, 1967).

Sound knowledge is badly needed—knowledge of the complexity of the teaching process and of the sensitive relationship between student and teacher—if we are to improve conditions in our big-city schools. Silberman (1970) finds our schools "grim and joyless places." As far back as 1961, Havighurst and Stiles (1968) reported high percentages of alienated youth. Eash (1971) suggests that in some areas of big cities the figure approaches 85 per cent. Perhaps the time will come when all youth are alienated—alienated because of the directionless games they are asked to play, and frustrated by the inconsistent and erratic system of rewards they experience in school. White (1968), studying schoolchildren in New York City, reports that "the view from the pupil's desk is very different from that of romantic intellectualism. . . . Why he is made to learn this and not that . . . is [a] mystery to him; nor does he know what the alternative choices might be . . . he rarely asks why he has been asked to learn them . . . the daily chores, the demands, the inspections become the reality, not the voyage, nor the destination." And anyone who thinks that retention, corporal punishment, defensive teacher behavior, and mindless busy work are but memories of a less enlightened age has not been in many classrooms, urban or otherwise. These conditions are the predictable consequences of a teaching profession that is high in hopes and surrounded by expectations, demands, and challenges, yet devoid of two extremely useful components—the knowledge to make sound decisions and an organizational structure for implementing them.

Are there alternatives to punishing students for nonperformance? What activities on the part of the teacher are rewarding and motivating to students? How can materials of instruction be adapted to individual needs? What policies within the school force teachers into defensive postures, rather than helping them become responsive and adaptable to the many messages that students are sending them—messages that often go unreceived? Are there ways of teaching teachers to be patient, to stay with a child until he accomplishes his work and not keep piling it on as he becomes more and more discouraged? These are questions that groups of teachers in schools need to be encouraged to attack—perhaps along lines suggested by the University of Chicago's Ford Training and Placement program.

Causes of Inadequate Evaluations

The lack of knowledge produced by innovative programs in urban settings can be attributed to at least three causes: the state of the art of evaluation, the state of grace needed to pursue the evaluation of action programs without losing one's composure (Fox, 1968) or scalp (Erickson, 1970), and the state of mind of the evaluator.

State of the art. The state of the art is, of course, deplorable. Now, when I say "the state of the art," I do not mean "the state of the science." The problem is not a lack of statistics (parametric or non) or measures (obtrusive or un); it is faulty application of the techniques. The application of principles of inquiry to current action programs in urban settings has been neither consistent across projects nor integral within. Lengthy criticisms of methodology are available and not too helpful. In fact, the view is growing that some persons in the field of research make their reputations on the basis of the amount of venom they can inject into the body of someone else's research. As Proger (1971) suggests, "Some . . . criticisms advance the state of thinking in the area in question. On the other hand, certain examples of this serialized criticism possess qualities akin to the daily soap opera."

State of grace. The state of grace refers to the kind of divine protection that the evaluator needs in order to survive the pressures from three sources: the community, teachers, and colleagues. Illustrations of these pressures will at times be taken from the Woodlawn Project and the Teacher Corps Project. Other illustrations will be taken from projects in Boston, Cincinnati, and New York.

The Woodlawn Experimental Schools Project is a federally funded intensive effort to improve education in a small area of Chicago. The initial aim of the project was to bring students, parents, and teachers from Wadsworth Elementary School, Wadsworth Upper Grade Center, and Hyde Park High School into a working relationship. This new relationship would then determine new goals and new programs.

The Cooperative Teacher Corps Program was organized for the purpose of developing a model for training teachers from a community to serve in that community. Planning began in 1967, and the program went into operation in the summer of 1970, with thirty-two interns and six team leaders. The program was arranged by means of a collaborative agreement between the University of Illinois at Chicago Circle, District 19 of the Chicago Public School, and a Community Advisory Council. I have worked on the evaluation of both of them.

The community, in its attitude toward both projects, was never really destructive. Although at times feared and castigated by the schools, communities—even angry ones—are concerned about evidence of success of programs. Nevertheless, ever since the time of White's Street Corner Society, most researchers have realized that they must not endanger the authority or prestige of indigenous leaders. On the other hand, it is easy for the researcher to have his prestige and authority cut down by indigenous leaders. And this is something White did not prepare us for. Yet it is something we are going to have to learn to live with. Furthermore, attacks on the researcher are not all of a kind, and one must learn to categorize attacks with discrimination. Some may be harmful, some may be benign, and others may be helpful to the attainment of the goals of a program, or to the accuracy of the research.

A significant incident, in which resistance promoted good ends, occurred at one of the Woodlawn Community Board meetings. Following the reading of a four-page attack on the project by a group of the high school students, the topic of the budget came up. An extremely influential woman from the community began the discussion by saying, "What is this $26,000 for research for? That would buy three more teachers, and all kinds of new equipment." She went on to list other possible uses of the money amidst occasional expressions of "Right on." Recovering from my faint just in time to hear the chairman say "Would you explain that to us, Mr. Rippey?" I gave a straight description of our plan and our intent to provide feedback to the project, to be a part of the change process, and to help with the training of blacks interested in research and evaluation. Although the question from the floor seemed threatening at first, it developed that the community component of the project was interested in having an additional participant-observer attached to its operation. A committee was then appointed to proceed with modification of the budget. Thus, what started out to be an attack resulted in greater community interest and understanding of our research aim, a more comprehensive picture of the project for our research reports, and an additional $7,000 for our budget.

In a similar manner, as part of the Teacher Corps evaluation, the Pilsen community is providing $1,500 for the training of indigenous persons to do interviewing in the community survey, which is part of the evaluation of the Teacher Corps project. This was money granted to the community to do with as it saw fit.

One of the primary sources of resistance to evaluation research in a community comes from nonproductive experiences with research, which communities have suffered in the past. Some of the people in Woodlawn have coined a phrase for the peripheral involvement of the past. They talk about "hit-and-run research." They are wary of the student who spends a few months in the community writing a critical paper, which they may never see. They wonder if this paper will ever bear a dividend for the community. On my first day in Woodlawn, two Rangers asked me what I was doing. I said, "Research." Their reply was, "Oh, a tourist. Would you like us to show you around?" The first question I was asked after I introduced my research and evaluation staff to the parents and teachers of Wadsworth School was "Which one of you is going to write the book?"

Community resistance, then, is real; but it can be dealt with. If the researcher states his case openly and tries to be helpful, he will encounter few problems.

Teachers, as another source of resistance, can be formidable. In the case of the New York City More Effective Schools evaluation, the teachers' union conducted an extensive counterevaluation when the original report showed that reduced class size had pleased parents and teachers but had not resulted in substantial gains for the students.

The evaluator is a prime threat to the teacher's autonomy and privacy. After all, people snooping around classrooms and asking questions of students can be most threatening. Teachers can and do eject researchers from their classrooms occasionally. Teachers also play games with the inquiry process by falsifying answers on questionnaires and by introducing ad-lib modifications into the new programs. This means that all tests must have validity items, and all programs need to have classroom observations made. A new program may look just like the old one in spite of its new title and catalog description.

These threats to teacher autonomy can be minimized or eliminated, and this is a responsibility that the evaluator must take on. First of all, he can try being helpful to teachers. For example, in the Woodlawn Project one of my research assistants, who had lived in Africa for several years, spent some time teaching Swahili to some of the classes. Another assistant, who had experience in the theater, talked to the classes about the production of plays. I spent some time talking with students about computers. The research assistants canvassed the community with community organizers and took lunchroom and playground duty when asked. They got to know the students and the teachers from the inside rather than as spectators. Furthermore, they found themselves co-opted into a role which none of us had expected.

The isolation of teachers from each other, and the weakness of communications channels in schools, has been well documented. The research assistants, however, had a mobility greater than that of anyone else in the system. They found themselves being asked to transmit information to everyone from the project director to the school dentist. Although these requests were a valuable source of information to us, our response to the requests required serious thought. We decided that we could not deliberately obstruct the transmission of vital information, although we needed to be very careful not to damage our neutral role by becoming informants. At times we were able to arrange a meeting between parties in need of communication.

Another way in which evaluators can obtain more cooperation from teachers is by using their expertise to help probe dysfunction in the social system of the school, by means of transactional evaluation (Rippey, 1971). This type of evaluation explores both the anticipated victories of the protagonist and the apprehensions of the antagonist to the project. Such evaluation is perhaps an essential ingredient for the success of any effective change in schools. Yet it is an aspect of evaluation that is almost totally neglected.

The third threat to evaluation research, and perhaps the greatest, comes from one's own colleagues. I am not referring here to the general disdain expressed in faculty meetings about the nonsense of working in schools. I am talking about the kind of unethical and dishonest undercutting which Erickson (1970) decries in his report on the evaluation of the Navajo Indian Project. I am talking about faculty members at one university, who, under the guise of community action, fed false information into the community and the school system. I refer to the attempts of faculty to control or limit the research of their colleagues on the basis of race.

As a final concern about interference with evaluation research, I would suggest that one should scrutinize his research assistants carefully. G. K. was one of my research assistants; at least, he was so employed until he left town in a volley of gunfire. He seemed to be an unusually productive worker, considering his pay. However, not all his effort was devoted to the research, according to this passage from the *Chicago Tribune:*

> *Washington, D.C. August 6, 1969. The influence of the Communist party on the militant Students for a Democratic Society is "quite high," a Chicago youth who spent four years as an undercover agent for the Federal Bureau of Investigation told a House committee today.*
>
> *G.K., 20, who was graduated from the University of Chicago last spring, said, however, that the S.D.S., of which he also was a member while an informant, is moving toward becoming part of the Communist party.*
>
> *G.K., who testified publicly before the Subversive Activities Control Board last month, told the House Internal Security Committee that the S.D.S. hopes to polarize Americans into varying groups that will only promote more unrest.*

Such infiltration can be terribly destructive. Not only can it amount to an unethical invasion of privacy; it can also prove to the community that research is essentially a form of meddling. Perhaps no other research experience of mine has been more traumatic than that one. Luckily, during G. K.'s short tenure, I had collected all information of a confidential nature on a daily basis and kept it at home under my bed.

This raises a terribly important question: to what extent must the research community make a stand against the encroachments of powerful independent agencies?

State of mind. In an age when change, rather than transmission of a fixed heritage, is the demand, conflict and frustration are the order of the day. And this conflict and frustration take their toll on the composure of the evaluator. Furthermore, injection of an evaluator into the scene of the action may cause more trouble than change itself. Thus the anxieties of the evaluator and his identity crisis (Dyer, 1969) may deter him from making the demands necessary for a sound evaluation to take place. Appropriate evaluations may be scrapped or never proposed. The evaluator must be able to discern which threats to sound evaluation are from within and which are external.

The evaluation researcher must place his work in the context of the entire change situation. Evaluation research simply cannot be pasted onto a program for change. It must be an integral part of it. This involves three conditions. Without these three conditions, the evaluator probably will continue to be ineffective.

First, he must be able to work in a truly experimental situation. Projects worth evaluating must have sufficient control over personnel and budget that real change can take place and that both process and outcomes can be observed clearly. This means that innovations aimed at really serious educational problems might best be undertaken in an experimental district operating within an urban system. This district would have its own superintendent, a lay advisory board, and a technical advisory board. The lay board would make certain that community interests were represented in policy making; and the technical board, made up of respected scholars, would provide stimulus and guidance to the project staff. The district would have its own budget and a set of personnel policies which would reflect its experimental orientation. It would not consist of a fixed set of schools. Schools in the district would be selected on the basis of two considerations: (1) an invitation from a population to have its school be a part of the experimental district and (2) technical considerations such as type of student population, incidence of particular learning problems, and long-term experimental plans. Movement of schools in and out of the district and movement of faculty from regular schools to experimental schools would be kept flexible and functional.

Models of this district are hard to find. Perhaps the closest example to this ideal would be the Community Council for Educational Development, an independent district operating within the city of Boston and financed by the State of Massachusetts and the Ford Foundation.

The purpose of an experimental school district is to allow for the flexibility necessary for thoughtful innovation. Perhaps crucial to this flexibility is the ability to recruit personnel committed to and helpful to the new program, persons who agree in advance to the thoughtful scrutiny required to develop and modify a new program. Furthermore, an experimental district should encourage the development of alternate solutions to the problems of education. Confining an experimental district to a single project is debilitating.

Second, a much wider range of persons needs to be involved in evaluation. Parents, students, and teachers should have opportunities to express their perceptions of the new program. Not only the expected but the unexpected should be tested. Not only achievement but a wide range of variables should be sampled.

Third, evaluation should be employed in its transactional form, to help alleviate resistance to change. This requires an understanding on the part of the evaluation researcher not only of his own specific technology but also of the social and political issues which are a part of his milieu.

This view of evaluation may appear closer to administration than to science. But the new tasks I am suggesting are currently not being done, or are being done badly, by either the administration or the evaluator. Administrators are prone to assume the good health of even the sickest organizations, and evaluators eschew sampling any but the overt, objectified manifest goals of programs they associate themselves with. Conflict is avoided by the administrator because it is too dangerous to his reputation and ignored or averaged out by the evaluator because it is too subject to random variation.

Furthermore, failure to deal with the organizational, social, and emotional health of a school in times of change and turmoil results in an intensified resistance to change. New programs are subverted. Teachers defend their anxieties until a new program is different from the old in name only.

This defense against change of course has implications both for us old evaluators and for training the wave of the future. It suggests that there may be a new breed who—in addition to having at least a utilitarian grasp of validity, multivariance, unobtrusive measurements, and interviewing skills—will also know a substantial amount about political forces and social systems.

Getting back to the original question, when the roll is called up yonder, will the evaluator be there? My answer is: "That's anybody's guess." If evaluators mend their ways, if persons in charge of change realize the potential for evaluation, and if dissension within academia does not stamp out this half-breed quasi-disicipline, then the evaluator may be there, toting up his points along with the swindlers, grave robbers, prostitutes, and any nice guys who also happen to be around. On the other hand, if the conflict between objectivity and involvement remains unsolved, if evaluators do not develop more internal fortitude and receive more external encouragement from both the academy and the community, then they will not be there. They will follow the trail of the buffalo, the dodo, and the greater yellow-tailed boonswoggler. They will be an extinct curiosity.

References

DYER, H. "Evaluating Educational Programs." *Urban Review,* 1969, *3*(4), 10–12.

EASH, M. J. "A Curriculum Evaluation of an Academy for Black Dropouts." Paper delivered to AREA, New York, February 1971.

ERICKSON, D. "Custer Did Die for Our Sins." *School Review,* 1970, *79,* 76–93.

FOX, D. "A Reply to the Critics." *Urban Review,* 1968, *2*(6), 27–34.

GORHAM, W. "Testing and Public Policy." *Proceedings of the 1967 Invitational Conference of Testing Problems.* Princeton, N.J.: Educational Testing Service, 1967. Pp. 76–84.

HAVIGHURST, R., AND STILES, L. "National Policy for Alienated Youth." In M. Smiley and H. Miller (Eds.), *Policy Issues in Urban Education.* New York: Free Press, 1968. Pp. 134–147.

MC DILL, E., MC DILL, M., AND SPREHE, J. *Strategies for Success in Compensatory Education.* Baltimore: Johns Hopkins Press, 1969.

PROGER, B. "The Fine Art of Educational Research Muckraking." *American Educational Research Journal,* 1971, *8,* 163–166.

RIPPEY, R. "The Use of Reinforcement in Inner City Classrooms." *Integrated Education,* 1970, *8,* 28–33.

RIPPEY, R. "Can Evaluation and Innovation be Integral?" *Curriculum Theory Network,* in press.

ROSSI, P. "Evaluating Educational Programs." *Urban Review,* 1969, *3*(4), 13–15.

SHUTZ, R. E. "Methodological Issues of Curriculum Research." *Review of Educational Research,* 1969, *39,* 359–366.

SILBERMAN, C. *Crisis in the Classroom.* New York: Random House, 1970.

SKINNER, B. F. "Superstition." *Journal of Experimental Psychology,* 1948, *38,* 168–172.

Urban Review, 1969, *3*(6), 6–7.

WHITE, M. A. "The View from the Pupil's Desk." *Urban Review,* 1968, *2*(5), 5–7.

PART III

Sociological
Perspectives

⟨⟩⟨⟩ ⟨⟩⟨⟩ ⟨⟩⟨⟩ ⟨⟩⟨⟩ ⟨⟩⟨⟩ ⟨⟩⟨⟩ ⟨⟩⟨⟩ ⟨⟩⟨⟩

Part Three asks a number of vital contemporary questions: Under what conditions can racial integration be brought about effectively? What is the effect of schools on learning relative to other social institutions and programs? How does religion affect urban education?

Coleman, from the perspective of his large-scale research on educational equality, sees racial integration as the primary means of improving the schools. Integration demonstrably helps the disadvantaged through stimulating contacts with middle-class children; in addition, the school can serve as a melting pot for young blacks and whites. According to Coleman, integration works well when school authorities retain strong control, when the school climate is strongly middle class, and when the treatment of all students is fair and equitable. His examination of the differences in integration in the United States and Israel, where cultural integration of Eastern and Western Jews is higher than that of blacks and whites in this country, gives us fresh insights into social policies in this country.

St. John, following Coleman's more speculative insights, describes analytically and in detail the research findings on dimensions of desegregation. The review leads to nine propositions regarding effective desegregation. She goes on to describe the effects of desegregation on white students.

Cohen analyzes the failure of compensatory education and questions whether special schooling is more important for urban blacks than income maintenance, work training, and job creation. Like Bettelheim, he emphasizes the importance of socialization, as contrasted with book learning, for school and job success. He points out that school differences in size, budgets, and teacher qualifications have very little effect on students' test performance; rather, test performance is highly related to social inheritance and family background. After reviewing exemplary programs, however, he concludes that highly structured programs with very specific cognitive goals do produce considerable gains in test performance.

Greeley notes the appalling lack of contemporary research on religious education. If religion is fundamental and underpins other meaning systems, such as science and common sense, those concerned with education ought to be much more aware of religious factors. He cites ministers and important leaders in the black movement, the Middle American's concern with his church, and the suburban child's search for meaning. More study is required of religion as one of the several institutions encountered by the urban child.

CHAPTER 11

Social and Cultural Integration and Educational Policy

James S. Coleman

In part as an attempt to overcome inequalities of opportunity and in part because of the desire to integrate more fully a society which has a deep racial cleavage, much effort in the United States has been directed in recent years toward racial integration of schools. The aims, if I correctly summarize the guiding forces which propel the efforts at school integration, are two: First, in accordance with some evidence that disadvantaged children achieve at a higher level in socially and economically integrated schools, integration is seen as a major means of increasing achievement levels of the disadvantaged. Second, with very little control over other aspects of social and economic life in which the racial chasm is quite wide, the aim is to use the schools to create a social bridge between the races—to create sufficient social interaction at a sufficiently early age that the discrimination and cleavage of their parents' generation will not be replicated in their own.

The force of these two arguments has seemed very conclusive to a great many people in recent years; and despite enormous obstacles, both political and operational, racial integration of schools has gone forward. Obstacles include those who are not convinced by the arguments: conservative whites, who see the "good schools" of middle-class whites invaded by lower-class blacks; and militant blacks, who fight to gain control of all-black schools as a cultural and institutional base to strengthen black identity. Even with this antiintegration coalition, policies have moved toward greater school integration. At this point there is paradoxically much greater racial integration in the South than in the North; and in the large cities there are special problems of logistics, but the widespread conviction of the necessity of this change has continued to push the effort forward despite the obstacles.

To describe briefly the ways in which racial integration or racial balancing of schools has been attempted or carried out, these are the principal means: In some places, school boundaries have been redrawn so that previously all-black and all-white schools have become racially mixed. In places where this is less possible, schools can sometimes be combined, with the resulting schools having larger catchment areas. This has in some places been done by reducing the grade span of each school to cover only three or four years instead of six or eight. Where neither of these patterns of reorganization is possible, children have been bused to schools outside their local neighborhoods, to create racially mixed schools despite racially separate neighborhoods. This change has produced, as might be anticipated, the greatest opposition from parents. In addition to these changes, some attention has been given to ensuring that classrooms are racially mixed and not separated into white and black classes within the school.

Under some conditions, racial integration of the schools, bringing together low-achieving lower-class blacks and high-achieving middle-class whites, has produced social turmoil in the schools. It is useful to consider just what these conditions are and what are the conditions under which school integration has gone well.

First of all, it is important to distinguish what is meant here by school integration "going badly" and "going well." The distinction is *not* in terms of scholastic achievement but in terms of social order. Integration "succeeds" when whites do not flee the schools but the schools remain racially mixed; when there are not fights in the halls or on school grounds; when black students and white students get along together reasonably well. It "fails" when there is disorder, conflict, and a rapid movement of whites out of the school.

When school integration succeeds in the sense described above, then in general the scholastic-achievement results have been successful as well. The performance of white children does not go down, as their middle-class parents feared; and the achievement of disadvantaged black children goes up, though not as spectacularly as their parents had hoped. Thus, there are modest but definite achievement gains, without counterbalancing losses; and the social aim of integration is gained, along with some academic results as well.

The social conditions under which this pattern of success occurs can best be described by some observations: (1) Success is most likely to occur in the elementary schools. Social turmoil in integrated schools occurs perhaps most in the junior high schools, beginning about age thirteen; and it occurs in the high schools as well. (2) School integration is most successful where the percentage of middle-class students remains above 60. When the percentage of middle-class whites is between about 20 and 60, there is a continual struggle for "control of the school" between whites and blacks. In addition, when the percentage of middle-class children is less than about 60, the achievement gains described earlier do not occur, and the disadvantaged students are in a school that is little different from a school with all disadvantaged students. (3) Success occurs where people cannot easily move, so that there cannot easily be a rapid exodus of whites or a sudden influx of blacks. (4) Success is most likely when the school is small and when it is not overpopulated. Success is increasingly unlikely as the size of the school exceeds one thousand children. (5) Success is most likely in less densely populated areas: in suburbs, small towns, and rural areas. (6) Success is higher in the South than in the North. This is especially striking because southern whites are more racially prejudiced than northerners, and southern blacks are worse scholastically than northern blacks. (7) Integration succeeds better in private schools than in public ones.

A few general principles emerge from these results. The most important is that social success of school integration depends very much on strong control of the school by the school authorities. Control is greater in the South than the North, greater in private schools than in public, greater in elementary schools than in secondary, greater in small towns than large cities, greater in small schools than large ones, greater where the stduent population is stable than where it is uncontrolled and rapidly changing. A second principle is that social success is more likely when the norms that control the school are not in question and when it is the middle-class norms, set by the middle-class students, that dominate the climate of the school.

There are a number of other principles that emerge when these situations are examined more closely: for example, a strong school principal is important; very explicit and careful fairness to all students on the part of teachers, and attention to making this fairness evident to all students, is important. Sensitivity to unfair treatment, particularly by disadvantaged students and their parents, increases greatly in an integrated school.

In the context of the intensity of efforts toward school integration in the United States, it may be useful to examine different approaches to problems of the disadvantaged elsewhere. I want to focus on the approach that has been characteristic of Israel. Israel confronts, with Eastern Jews, a different problem of absorption of culturally disadvantaged immigrants than does the United States, but nevertheless a problem that has many of the aspects of the absorption of rural blacks into urban industrial America. Consequently, it is surprising to find that with some exceptions, the organization of education in Israel could be described as characterized by: (1) ethnically homogeneous neighborhood schools; (2) little attempt to create school-district boundaries which maximize economic and ethnic integration or to create economically integrated neighborhoods; (3) almost exclusive concentration on solving the educational problems of the culturally disadvantaged within essentially unchanged homogeneous school and social environments.

The first reaction of an American, upon seeing the strikingly different patterns and the strikingly different assumptions on which these patterns are based, is one of puzzlement: Is Israel truly attempting to solve the educational problems created by cultural disadvantage? Are Western Israelis simply fooling themselves that they can integrate Easterners fully into the society while keeping them at a distance? Are the efforts therefore doomed to fail?

But the matter is more complicated than this, for despite the low level of effort to create integrated education, the integration of Eastern immigrants into Israeli society is proceeding far more effectively than the integration of rural black immigrants into urban America. The parallel seems rather more to America's earlier absorption of European immigrants, which was remarkably successful.

It is probably not fruitful to speculate too broadly on why this is true—why the effective integration of Eastern Jews into Israeli society seems to be proceeding successfully, despite the relative indifference to social integration in the schools. Certain points, of course, are obvious: the extreme social cohesion generated by continuing threats to national security, a cohesion that brings Israelis together in spirit, regardless of background; the effectiveness of the army as an educational and socializing institution. But such points merely reiterate matters that are already evident.

I would like to consider instead a distinction that is evident in the contrast between the United States and Israel. The distinction is between *social* integration and *cultural* integration. By *social* integration I mean full-scale participation and social intermixing by each group in all the institutions of a society at all levels—in occupations and professions, in politics and government, in the same religious institutions. No society has complete social integration of its ethnic groups; in fact, complete social integration is probably neither possible nor desirable. But, equally, without a certain level of social integration of all groups, an industrial society cannot cohere over a long period of time. By *cultural* integration I mean an identity of values, beliefs, and attitudes toward the major institutions of society—a feeling of being one nation, with everyone full members of that nation and proud to be so: the same heroes, the same folk culture, the same literature and music. Cultural integration, like social integration, is necessary for the long-term coherence of a society. But it is a distinct and separate kind of integration than social integration as I described it earlier.

When we examine the United States and Israel in the presence of this distinction between social and cultural integration, some of the differences in educational problems and educational strategies become clearer. By any measure, Western and Eastern Jews in Israel are far more culturally integrated than are blacks and whites in the United States. The comparison of social integration in the two countries is not so clear. In some few respects, social integration may be higher in Israel; in most, I suspect it is higher in the United States.

Viewed in this context, the educational strategy in the United States becomes clearer: Given the low level of cultural integration between blacks and whites, the strategy is to use the schools to create social integration, through closeness of association between blacks and whites and through the social mobility of blacks, made possible by a better education. The implicit assumption is that this will then lead to a sufficiently high level of cultural integration to enable the society to cohere.

The relative lack of attention to school integration in Israel also becomes clearer in this perspective. In the presence of a high level of cultural integration among all ethnic groups of Jews in Israel, less need is seen for specially fostering social integration through the schools. Middle-class whites in America are plagued by the vision of a nation split into two hostile camps, and the use of the schools is a desperate attempt to prevent this vision from attaining reality. There is no such vision among Israelis; and given the high level of cultural integration, such a vision would be totally unwarranted. Thus, one of the two principal goals of school integration in the United States is largely stripped away in Israel, leaving only the other—the goal of providing equal educational opportunity. As long as there seem to be possibilities of achieving this equal opportunity in ethnically homogeneous schools, then these less disruptive avenues are likely to be preferred.

Some reflection, however, suggests that both these strategies— that of the United States and that of Israel—may be less than optimum. It may not be possible, when cultural integration is at as low a level as in the United States, for social integration through the schools to be successful. It is cultural integration—the sense of a common identity and a common purpose, the shared values, the shared attitudes toward social institutions—that provides the motive force, for both the advantaged group and the disadvantaged group, that helps to make school integration successful.

Perhaps this can be better seen by considering other points on the continuum of cultural integration. If the cultural integration among ethnically different Jews in Israel is high and that among blacks and whites in America is lower, that among French and English in Canada is much lower still. Some of the problems of the United States strategy of social integration through the schools can be seen in sharp perspective by imagining the conflict in Canada if such a strategy of French-English integration through use of the schools were attempted there. Such an approach for Canada is hardly imaginable. If the weak cultural integration in the United States often fails to provide sufficient motive power on the part of blacks and whites to make school integration successful, the cultural separation in Canada creates motive power in the reverse direction, which would make any attempts at school integration sure to fail.

Still another point on the continuum of cultural integration is provided by the example of Arab Israelis. Their cultural integration into Israeli society is quite low. At present, they have in many ways the status of nonpersons in the society. A similar situation prevailed with regard to blacks in American society thirty years ago. I believe the cultural integration of Arab Israelis with other Israelis lies somewhere between that of the position of the United States in black-white integration and that of the French and English Canadians. The cultural separation is not inherently so difficult as that of Canada. It is, however, a problem that cannot be easily solved at present because the very external threats that strengthen the cultural integration among Eastern and Western Jews in Israel weaken it among Israeli Jews and Arabs.

The defects of the American strategy, with school integration as the first step in a process leading finally to cultural integration, do not mean that the Israeli strategy with regard to Eastern Jews, which assumes that social integration will automatically come through an existing high level of cultural integration, is a correct one. When external threats to national security diminish, social cleavages give rise to cultural cleavages. At such a time it is much more difficult to bridge the chasm between social groups if the chasm has not already been bridged by a high level of social integration. Thus, one could well say that a time of national unity, when the need for such integration is less apparent, is precisely the time when deliberate attempts at social integration through the schools will be most successful—precisely the time when both the advantaged and the disadvantaged will have the motivation and will to make it succeed.

A number of caveats are necessary. One of the most important is that school is in many ways a poor institution for the disadvantaged to overcome their handicaps. Educators often mistakenly see it as the principal such institution and sometimes even as the *only* means by which the disadvantaged can gain upward mobility in the society. But it is the one institution in which the disadvantaged are most at a disadvantage. In the army, people from different walks are on a much more equal footing. In the labor force, men are on a more equal footing as well, for jobs require a much broader range of skills than schools do: the ability to act decisively, inventiveness when confronted by obstacles, skills in interpersonal relations, and many others. For these reasons, an exclusive focus on the schools as the avenue for social integration is probably quite harmful. It is important to ensure that there are many paths to mobility despite failure in school. In the early part of the twentieth century, many European immigrants to the United States became successfully integrated in spite of the schools —largely because of the alternative paths to success, provided mainly by the openness of the occupational structure.

In every society today, social integration entails explicit attention to these alternative channels. It is necessary to maintain an open occupational structure, one that depends more on job performance than on school credentials. It is necessary to develop on-the-job training programs and part-time evening educational activities. Recent research in the United States has shown, for example, that although whites benefit from full-time schooling more than blacks do, blacks benefit more than whites from part-time education after entering the labor force; that is, the part-time education has more effect on later income for blacks than for whites. Schools, then, are only one agency for bringing the disadvantaged into full participation in the society. In any rational social policy, other agencies will be used as well.

The principal point of this chapter, however, is to make explicit the implicit assumptions behind policies of school integration in America. These implicit assumptions are brought into bolder perspective when viewed against the very different policies being pursued in Israel. These contrasting policies show the clear distinction between social integration, through which the United States policies of school integration attempt to increase societal cohesion, and cultural integration, which in Israel provides that cohesion *without* a high level of social integration. The contrasting policies raise questions for both Israel and the United States: for Israel, the question of whether the cohesion will persist without greater social integration; and, for the United States, the question of how cultural integration might be increased, both to augment the success of school integration and to make its success less critical for the long-term cohesion of the society.

References

BEKER, J. "A Study of Integration in Racially Imbalanced Urban Public Schools." Report to the U.S. Office of Education, May 1967.

CHESLER, M., et al. *Planning Educational Change.* Vol. 3. *Integrating the Desegregated School.* Washington: U.S. Office of Education, 1970.

DOWNS, A. "Achieving Effective Desegregation." Washington, D.C.: Systemetrics Corp., 1971. (Mimeographed.)

U.S. Commission on Civil Rights, *Racial Isolation in the Public Schools.* Washington, D.C.: U.S. Government Printing Office, 1967.

WEINBERG, M. *Desegregation Research: An Appraisal.* (2nd Ed.) Bloomington, Indiana: Phi Delta Kappa, 1970.

CHAPTER 12

Social-Psychological Aspects of School Desegregation

Nancy H. St. John

𝕊𝕍ℂ 𝕊𝕍ℂ 𝕊𝕍ℂ 𝕊𝕍ℂ 𝕊𝕍ℂ 𝕊𝕍ℂ 𝕊𝕍ℂ 𝕊𝕍ℂ

For more than two decades school desegregation has been a major political and educational issue in this country, and yet understanding of its influence on children has progressed very little. Three recent reviews of empirical research in this area—on the effects of desegregation on academic achievement (St. John, 1970), on racial cleavage (Carithers, 1970), and on self-concept (Zirkel, 1971)—each conclude that the evidence is neither clear nor consistent.

A likely reason for conflicting findings is that desegregation is a many-sided phenomenon, whose effects may be simultaneously beneficial and harmful to children. Whether the potential benefits out-

133

weigh the potential harm probably depends on the individual pupils involved and, above all, on how desegregation is implemented. And yet courts, legislatures, and schoolmen continue to be obsessed with questions of quantity rather than quality—with mathematical ratios, quotas, balance, rather than with the educational process; in short, with *desegregation* rather than with *integration,* as Pettigrew (1969b) and others use the term.

This chapter represents a search for explanations of the conflicting evidence and for clues to conditions under which desegregation would be more clearly beneficial to children. A brief examination of the findings and criticisms of those who have reviewed research in this area will be followed by an attempt at a theoretical analysis of desegregation as a concept.

Reviews of Research

Educational decision makers can learn little from research to date on the effects of desegregation on academic performance. It is true that longitudinal studies (comparing achievement before and after desegregation) report that white children are generally unaffected and that black children perform no worse and in most instances somewhat better in the new setting; similarly, cross-sectional studies (comparing segregated and integrated children at one point in time) usually report somewhat higher scores for both races in schools over 50 per cent white. However, confidence in these findings is, with few exceptions, weakened by inadequate control on all relevant variables, especially the original equivalence of segregated and desegregated children. Neither the very large Coleman study (1966) nor the well-designed Wilson study (1967) found that school percentage white had an effect on achievement when the social background of children and their classmates was controlled. On the other hand, the U.S. Commission on Civil Rights (1967) found a positive correlation between achievement and classroom percentage of whites, but that is probably because test scores govern classroom placement rather than because classroom racial mix affects test scores. (But see McPartland, 1968, and Pettigrew, 1969a, on this subject.)

Carithers (1970) reports that studies of racial preference, cleavage, and association in desegregated schools have produced conflicting results. "Some have found that, with contact, there is more interracial acceptance, less prejudice, and a raising of Negro self-esteem. Other studies have not supported these findings, noting instead that there is less interracial acceptance" (p. 36). Regarding the effects of ethnic-group mixture on self-concept, some studies have found higher self-concept for segregated Negro students, and others have found higher self-concept for integrated Negroes; but the most usual finding is "no significant difference" (Zirkel, 1971).

Other psychological outcomes of desegregation have been studied, in particular aspiration and anxiety. A review of this literature (St. John, 1971a) reveals that, in ten studies of the relation of school desegregation and aspiration, six found a negative relation and four found a positive relation. Little evidence of serious emotional stress for transferred black children has appeared, in spite of the grave concern of many psychologists contemplating the onset of desegregation. Although anxiety may be partially responsible for the failure of many desegregated black children to show achievement gains, this proposition is difficult to test because of recursive feedback between attitudes and performance, and to date is not proved. (See Weinberg, 1970, for a review of further studies comparing the attitudes of segregated and desegregated pupils.)

The contradictions in the literature on the effects of desegregation cannot be resolved by noting the dates or geographical locations of the studies, nor the age level of subjects, nor the methods of achieving desegregation. Zirkel (1971) attributes the inconclusiveness of findings on self-concept to lack of precision in definition of concepts, ineffective instrumentation, and the diversity of research designs employed. Carithers (1970) criticizes studies of racial cleavage for their correlational design and for not focusing on the social groupings and social processes accompanying desegregation. And Pettigrew (1969a) has called attention to the political impediments that beset any type of desegregation research and to the difficulty of securing samples that are completely unbiased.

There is undoubtedly much truth in each of these analyses. Rather than pursuing this methodological line of inquiry, however, I would like to turn to a more theoretical analysis of desegregation as a concept.

Dimensions of Desegregation for Black Children

I intend to examine, one at a time, several dimensions (meanings, aspects) of school desegregation for black pupils and to suggest that each can be enlightened by reference to a body of social-psychological theory. (See Table 1.) For each a different criterion variable appears to be the most appropriate measure of outcome. I will look both at the possible meanings of a desegregated school in contrast to

Table 1. DIMENSIONS OF SCHOOL RACIAL COMPOSITION

Dimension	Key References	Attitudinal Outcome	Conditional Factor
Symbolic message	Rotter, 1966 Gurin, 1969	Sense of control	Black self-determination
Stigma, aura	Fauman, 1957 Goffman, 1963	Self-esteem	Access to quality schooling and programs
Relative deprivation	Stouffer, 1949 Pettigrew, 1967	Morale	Nondiscriminatory treatment
Expectations of significant others	Brookover, 1965 Clark, 1965	Aspiration	Nonracist staff
Normative reference group	Merton, 1957 Kemper, 1968	School-related norms	SES integration No tracking
Interracial contact	Allport, 1954	Cross-racial attitudes	Equality of school status and noncompetitive atmosphere
Minority-group position	Katz, 1964 Carmichael and Hamilton, 1967	Anxiety	Staff protection against social threat
Marginality	Stonequist, 1937 Fishman, 1961	Group identity	School commitment to pluralism
Academic standards	Katz, 1964 Pettigrew, 1967	Motivation	Individualization of instruction

a segregated school and also at the essential conditions that must therefore obtain in the desegregated setting if pupils are to benefit in that regard.

Symbolic message and sense of control. One aspect of school segregation is symbolic, and it was this that the Supreme Court stressed in its 1954 decision. Until recently at any rate, the segregated school stood as a symbol of the powerlessness of the black community. Whether segregated by law, by administrative gerrymandering, or by discriminatory housing, schools have not been one-race because of the wishes of most black parents. Repeated polls have testified to their preference for integration (Brink and Harris, 1964; Campbell and Schuman, 1968; Marx, 1967). The segregated school therefore acted as a signal to the ghetto child that he could not expect to get equal treatment in life or to control his own destiny. The message to him was, as Pettigrew (1964) puts it, "Know your place."

In contrast, minority pupils in majority white schools might be expected to develop a stronger sense of environmental control (Gurin, Gurin, Lao, and Beattie, 1969). However, many militants now argue that parents who put their children into integrated schools are supporting black powerlessness. They are acting, say Carmichael and Hamilton (1967), "on the assumption that there is nothing of value in the black community" and "that in order to have a decent house or education, black people must move into a white neighborhood or send their children to a white school" (pp. 52–54). Moreover, being in a minority, such parents have perhaps even less influence on the policies of the white school than they have in the ghetto. (See Handlin, 1965, and Piven and Cloward, 1967, on the political suicide of desegregation.)

A segregated school is not necessarily a symbol of powerlessness, nor a desegregated school a symbol of powerlessness denied. The essential condition appears to be self-determination, both on an individual and a community level. The black child who attends a racially mixed school will benefit on this dimension only if desegregation is voluntary, or achieved through community effort, as in the case of Boston's "Operation Exodus" (Teele, Jackson, and Mayo, 1967), or if it leads to political gains in the control of the mixed school. On the other hand, if a black community achieves control of its local school and manages it successfully, and if parents consciously choose that school over an equally available desegregated one, their children might experience more sense of power than former classmates who have fled the ghetto.

Stigma, aura, and self-esteem. Students share in the reputation of their schools, with presumed consequences to their self-esteem. Segregated schools have, historically, been inferior schools. They probably still are, in spite of compensatory education and the impulse toward equal-though-separate status. (See Coleman et al., 1966; National Advisory Commission on Civil Disorders, 1968; and Mc-Cauley and Ball, 1959.) Moreover, the racial composition of a predominantly black school also tends to give it a reputation for low standards, poor equipment, and inexperienced staff, which reputation outruns the facts and acts as a self-fulfilling prophecy (Fauman, 1957; Pinderhughes, 1964). The stigma (Goffman, 1963) of attending such schools might depress pupil self-esteem, and the aura of a mostly white school might raise it. However, children's sense of their own worth will not be enhanced by a low-status racially mixed school or a high school in which they are accorded low status or tracked into a low-status program.

Relative deprivation and morale. Closely related to the sense of powerlessness or stigma is the perception of one's own deprivation relative to that of another. For example, the morale of American soldiers in World War II depended on a comparison between their own situation and that of some other group with which they chose to compare themselves (Stouffer, Suchman, De Vinney, Star, Williams, 1949). If ghetto residents perceive that, in comparison with residents of other sections of the city, they are not getting their fair share of the school pie, one might expect them to develop debilitating frustration and lowered motivation.

Attendance at an integrated school, however, will not always reduce perception of discrimination on the part of black pupils, any more than it will mitigate their powerlessness or stigma. In fact, their sense of deprivation in relation to the white pupils with whom they are in daily contact might be even more acute than that of ghetto children in relation to unknown white pupils in distant schools. Several factors might govern whether or not consciousness of discrimination develops: their reception and continued treatment by staff and classmates, whether they and not others have a long bus ride to school, whether they have equal opportunity in choice of courses and extracurricular activities, and whether they receive no more disciplinary action and as many academic and social honors.

In view of the long history of racial discrimination in our society, perception of injustice on the part of minority people can probably be assuaged *only* by conditions that are for some years clearly better than equal. In predominantly black schools, this means facilities, staff, and curricula that are visibly and dramatically superior;

in racially balanced schools, treatment of minority-group pupils must perhaps be actually preferential to be equal in their eyes. (See Pettigrew, 1967, for further applications of relative-deprivation theory to race relations today.)

Expectations of significant others and aspiration. The expectations of both participants and observers tend to be low for the pupils of a ghetto school. Often neither principals nor teachers nor community residents (in general) nor parents (in particular) believe that such a school will maintain high standards or prepare children to compete on an equal footing for college entrance or jobs (Clark, 1965). Since there is evidence of a correlation between (1) the parents' or teacher's estimate of the ability of a child, (2) the child's perception of such estimates, (3) the child's rating of his own ability, and (4) the child's actual performance (Brookover, LePere, Hamachek, Thomas, and Erickson, 1965; Davidson and Lang, 1960; Schwarz and Tangri, 1965), children in the typical ghetto school probably are affected by low expectations for themselves as a group and as individuals.

In an integrated school, however, a black child does not necessarily escape the depressing effect of low expectations of others. The expectations of staff and pupils may here be low—not for all, as in the ghetto school, but merely for the "culturally deprived," the bussed, or the black pupil. The effect could be all the more devastating for a child —particularly since, in such a school, his parents' expectations for him are usually high (Katz, 1967). To allay his anxiety the black child in a desegregated school needs expectations from his teacher that match those of his parents.

Public demonstration of the competence of black students in interracial teams increases white partners' expectations for them and their own assertive behavior (Katz, 1964; Cohen, Lohmann, Hall, Lucero, and Roper, 1970). Even in a predominantly black school, however, sustained high expectations on the part of staff can probably have a facilitating effect on pupil motivation—as evidenced by the extraordinary gains of pupils in the New York Demonstration Guidance program (Wrightstone, 1960) and the initial gains for pupils in the Banneker schools in St. Louis (U.S. Commission, 1967).

Peers as reference group and school-related norms. Another dimension of school racial composition is exposure to classmates with certain ways of thinking and acting. The pupils of a ghetto school are usually reported to be deficient in school-related skills, motivation, and self-discipline (Becker, 1952; Herriott and St. John, 1966). *If* white children are less deficient in these respects, and *if* we accept the proposition that the majority group in a classroom will become the normative reference group for all members, *then* we would predict improved attitudes for black children who move to a school in which white pupils are in the majority. The viability of this assumption rests on at least three (somewhat questionable) assumptions: (1) That the norms of the white children involved are indeed more achievement-oriented than those of the desegregating black children. This will be a function of social class rather than racial differences between them. Association with lower-class white pupils will contribute little to the education of black pupils. (See Havighurst, 1963, on the importance of social-class integration.) (2) The degree to which white and black children are integrated into a single social group. If SES or racial groups are separated, either formally through academic tracking or informally through social distance or hostility, then association and the "homogenization" of attitudes will be within, rather than between, groups (Wilson, 1968). The probable importance of interracial friendship for high achievement in integrated settings is stressed by Pettigrew (1967) and Katz (1964) and is supported by the findings of the U.S. Commission (1967). (3) Whether blacks maintain a black rather than a white reference group (Shibutani, 1967), however friendly their cross-racial relations become.

Interracial contact and acceptance. Attendance at a biracial school exposes a child not only to the attitudes *of* the other group but also to a change in his own attitude *toward* the other group. The hypothesis that interracial contact leads to reduced prejudice has received confirmation from research with adults and in other institutional areas. The important conditions, according to Allport (1954), are that contact be prolonged and that the individuals have equal status and are in pursuit of common goals. We would therefore expect black and white children to develop favorable attitudes toward each other after some months or years together—provided that academic competition is not stressed and that the children are fairly similar in social class and academic status. However, Carithers (1970), who reviews this literature, reports that "there is no general agreement about the effects of interracial contacts on attitudinal change. Some studies have found heightened tolerance; some heightened resistance; some no change" (p. 41).

It is likely that the important precondition, equality of status, has in most cases not been met. However, this condition runs counter to one of the conditions stipulated under the previous dimension: Adopting the norms of peers will be functional for school achievement only if peers are of *higher* SES background and display more achievement-oriented behavior. What is perhaps necessary to satisfy both conditions is that lower-class newcomers adopt the culture of the majority group through "anticipatory socialization" (Merton, 1957). Friendship and reduction in prejudice can then follow.

The presumption for each of the six dimensions so far considered is in favor of the desegregated school. For three other dimensions, the presumption is in favor of the segregated school.

Minority-group position and anxiety. The black child who is desegregated is usually in a minority-group position for the first time as well as being a newcomer and a stranger in an unfamiliar setting (Simmel, 1950). The Group for the Advancement of Psychiatry (1957) has warned that such a situation is bound to be stressful— often producing "emigration neurosis," the near-paranoid interpretation of majority-group behavior by the newcomer who expects rejection. The child's fear of social threat, be it mere rejection or physical harm (Katz, 1964), will be mild or severe depending on the community, the circumstances surrounding desegregation (Coles, 1967), his own ego strength (Milner, 1953), and his prior interracial experience. Whether or not anxiety continues beyond the first weeks of school will depend on staff support and the interracial climate of the school, as well as his own interpersonal skill.

Marginality and group identity. The black child in a white classroom is not only in a minority-group position; he is also a marginal man, bridging two social worlds (Park, 1950; Stonequist, 1937). His loyalty to and identity with his own racial group may be threatened. Moreover, to the extent that there are real differences in values and mores between these worlds, the child may be torn between feeling he both should and should not, in Hamilton's words (1968), "attempt to be a carbon copy of the culture and ethos of another racial and ethnic group." Pettigrew (1969b) suggests that the values of black and white families are more similar than they realize. Desegregated children have the opportunity of making this discovery, and their values will converge still further as a result. Nevertheless, faced with a choice between separatism and acculturation (Fishman, 1961), the child risks both estrangement from his own racial group and rejection by the other group, as well as confusion about his identity and resultant normlessness. Crain (1971) found that black adults whose childhood experience with integration was inconsistent (in that neighborhood, elementary school, and high school were one of them integrated and the others segregated) had low self-esteem and sense of control, presumably because they had not been able to develop a stable identity.

Many black children, however, also experience marginality in all-black schools. The culture of the school is typically that of white, middle-class America and does not encourage healthy racial identity. The cure for marginality in schools of whatever racial mix is a move toward the recognition of cultural pluralism through encouragement of black identity, curricular emphasis on the Afro-American experience, and staff integration.

Academic standards and self-evaluation. Peers serve as comparative as well as normative reference groups (Kemper, 1968). When a child moves from a segregated to an integrated school, he may leave a relatively protected colony and face what Pettigrew calls "universalistic standards" of excellence and the opportunity for cross-racial evaluation (Pettigrew, 1967). Katz (1967) believes that such cross-racial comparisons can have both a high incentive value and a high informational value. The black child wants to succeed in the interracial classroom and there learns that not all whites are better students than he. Moreover, the level and pace of instruction may be more stimulating than in his previous school.

But the advantages of realistic competition can be offset by fear of failure. Katz goes on to postulate that in view of generally inadequate early training, either at home or in segregated schools, a desegregated child will often have a low probability of success. In addition, he may suffer from unrealistic feelings of inferiority. He is therefore not able to live up to expectations of his parents and his own motivation to do well. Anxiety and lowered self-concept follow.

The younger the age at which children are desegregated, the less they should be handicapped by inadequate early training and feelings of inferiority. And, in fact, achievement is generally found to be highest for those who were desegregated from first grade on (Coleman et al., 1966; Mahan, 1968; Purl, 1971; St. John, 1971b).

Several factors will probably determine whether the desegregated classroom is, on balance, threatening or facilitating. Among these are the initial difference in achievement level of black and white children, the supportiveness of school staff, the availability of school academic policies that favor overcoming handicaps, and above all individualization of instruction. But, as we have noted above, many of these same factors could potentially transform a ghetto school into a setting in which a strong, yet realistic academic self-concept is fostered.

The foregoing consideration of various meanings of school racial composition leads to the proposition that black children will benefit from desegregation for the following reasons and under the following conditions:

Desegregation, as a symbol of equality affirmed and powerlessness denied, will raise black sense of control—*provided* desegregation is achieved through individual or community self-determination.

Desegregation to a school of higher status will enhance self-esteem—*provided* black pupils are not accorded low status in the new school.

Desegregation, by reducing sense of deprivation relative to pupils in other schools, will raise the morale of black pupils—*provided* they do not feel deprived in relation to white pupils in the same school.

Desegregation may raise the expectations of significant others and so the aspirations of black pupils—*provided* such expectations are for white and black pupils alike.

Desegregation brings association with peers from whom favorable norms may be acquired—*provided* the majority is middle class and there is no within-school segregation.

Desegregation brings interracial contact, which may reduce prejudice—*provided* the individuals involved have equal status and are not placed in direct competition.

On the other hand:

Desegregation places black pupils in a minority-group situation, which may induce anxiety—*unless* the peer group is friendly and the staff is supporting.

Desegregation exposes black pupils to cultural marginality and confusion about their own identity—*unless* pluralism is stressed by the school.

Desegregation allows self-evaluation against academic standards that may in some cases discourage motivation—*unless* instruction is individualized.

Many of these conditions would also temper the potentially negative impact of majority black schools. Moreover, on several dimensions segregated black children appear to be in the stronger position. On other dimensions, only "true integration" in racially balanced schools will probably realize the desired outcomes.

Dimensions of Desegregation for White Children

The pupils in a segregated white school are less aware than those in a segregated black school of their participation in the symbolic denial of American democratic ideals of equality for all citizens. In the North, until recently, distance from the ghetto and a "conspiracy of silence" have quarantined most white children from realization of the existence and nature of ghetto schools. This is no longer true except for very young children. Press and television have brought the desegregation controversy home to suburban children and exposed them to a false sense of superiority because of their privileged position. Rescued from ignorance, they are now exposed to the more dangerous rationalizations of their elders and a sense of de facto implication in an institution which denies the democratic ideals they are being taught to revere. So this symbolic dimension of segregation can harm white children by encouraging hypocrisy and prejudice.

The meaning of desegregation to white pupils would depend very much on black-to-white ratios and on expectations as to future change in ratios. As long as the proportion of black pupils is small (under 20 per cent) and expected to remain so, there would be no reason for white pupils to experience stigma, relative deprivation, social threat, marginality, or a change in norms, standards, or the expectations of their significant others. Prejudice might be reduced if black pupils are not too different in social background.

On the other hand, a school that is 20 to 50 per cent black could have negative influence on white children on some dimensions—especially if further racial change is expected. Whites in schools 20 to 50 per cent black might sense stigma, deprivation, and lowered expectations relative to pupils in all-white schools. If they were bussed to such schools against their will, they might feel conscripted and resentful. And they might experience social threat if blacks were aggressive or united. If black students were accepted as leaders or their norms proved attractive, the values and norms of white students might be affected (white parents might say "for the worse").

Schools over half black would probably not benefit white pupils for the same reasons that they would not benefit black pupils, and whites would thereby lose the advantage of numerical and cultural dominance. White children will be adversely affected, just as black children are, by attending a school with low status in the eyes of the community or one in which parents and teachers have low expectations for academic accomplishment. On this dimension, then, they will ordinarily suffer from attending a majority black school. White pupils who attend majority black schools with mediocre or low academic standards will be handicapped by those standards as much as the black children in attendance. If their prior training has been strong, however, they might enjoy being "big frogs in a little pond" (Davis, 1966). But though their grades and self-esteem might thus be enhanced, objective test scores will often suffer.

According to the theory of differential association, the larger the percentage of black children in a school, the more likely that white children will adopt their attitudes and behaviors. But one should not leap to the unwarranted conclusion that the more blacks in a school, the less desirous will be the attitudes and behavior of white children. In the first place, there is probably little difference between the norms of the two groups of children, once social class is controlled; and any differences that exist are not necessarily to the exclusive advantage of one racial group. For instance, studies repeatedly find that Negroes report higher aspirations but show less realism or knowledge about the world of work. If white youth learned aspiration for further education at the same time as black youth learned realism about how to achieve it, both could benefit from mutual association. Though there is the possibility that desegregation will hurt white children by exposing them to the victims of social disorganization and discrimination, there is also the likelihood that they will either resist or benefit from homogenization of norms.

The point should be made, however, that isolated white children in majority black schools are as liable to social threat and constricting-fear as are black pioneers in predominantly white schools. The chief difference is that the former are usually low-SES children in low-SES schools and the latter are upwardly mobile children in middle-class schools. The realistic risk of physical molestation might therefore be greater for the white child in the ghetto; the risk of well-bred ostracism, greater for the black child in suburbia. Either social situation is stressful; whether or not it results in increased hostility or lowered self-confidence would depend on many factors, especially basic personality structure and family support.

The conditions under which school desegregation could be expected to bring maximum benefit and minimum harm to white students are similar to those mentioned above for black students: some choice between schools, access to quality schooling and program, nondiscriminatory treatment, nonracist staff, SES integration—no tracking, noncompetitive atmosphere, staff protection against social threat, school commitment to pluralism, individualization of instruction; and, in addition, maintenance of quotas to prevent majority white schools from becoming majority black.

This discussion of the theoretical meanings of school desegregation and the conditions under which it will be most beneficial to children is admittedly speculative and in need of testing. However, the fact that empirical findings on the relation between desegregation and achievement, prejudice, or personality are inconclusive and conflicting should probably be accepted at face value and not explained away as the result of the difficulties of research in this area. Still better research will probably continue to produce the same ambiguous results as long as the independent variable is defined as mere change in racial proportions. Until schools take more seriously the implementation process and learn to translate desegregation into integration, losses will probably continue to be as frequent as gains.

In 1935 DuBois wrote that a hostile mixed school and a poor segregated schools are both bad, that other things being equal a mixed school is better for all youth, but that "other things seldom are equal and in that case sympathy, knowledge, and truth outweigh all that the mixed school can offer" (p. 288). Is it not time to shift the spotlight of social research to an analysis of the process of mixed schooling and of the situations in which black newcomers do or do not find "sympathy, knowledge, and truth"?

References

ALLPORT, G. *The Nature of Prejudice*. Cambridge: Addison-Wesley, 1954.

BECKER, H. "Social Class Variations in the Teacher-Pupil Relationship." *Journal of Educational Sociology*, 1952, *25*, 451–465.

BRINK, W., AND HARRIS, L. *The Negro Revolution in America*. New York: Simon & Schuster, 1964.

BROOKOVER, W. B., LE PERE, J. M., HAMACHEK, D. E., THOMAS, S., AND ERICKSON, E. L. *Self-Concept of Ability and School Achievement*. Final Report, Project No. 1636, ER 31. Michigan State University, College of Education, 1965.

CAMPBELL, A., AND SCHUMAN, H. S. *Racial Attitudes in Fifteen American Cities. Supplemental Studies for the National Advisory Commission on Civil Disorders*. New York: Praeger, 1968.

CARITHERS, M. W. "School Desegregation and Racial Cleavage, 1954–1970: A Review of the Literature." *Journal of Social Issues*, 1970, *26*, 25–47.

CARMICHAEL, S., AND HAMILTON, C. V. *Black Power*. New York: Vintage Books, 1967.

CLARK, K. B. *Dark Ghetto: Dilemmas of Social Power*. New York: Harper & Row, 1965.

COHEN, E., LOHMANN, M., HALL, K., LUCERO, D., AND ROPER, S. "Expectation Training I: Altering the Effects of a Racial Status Characteristic." Technical Report No. 2. Stanford University, School of Education, 1970.

COLEMAN, J. S., et al. *Equality of Educational Opportunity*. Washington, D.C.: U.S. Department of Health, Education, and Welfare, 1966.

COLES, R. *Children of Crisis: A Study of Courage and Fear.* Boston: Little, Brown, 1967.

CRAIN, R. "School Integration and the Academic Achievement of Negroes." *Sociology of Education,* 1971, *44,* 1–26.

DAVIDSON, H. H., AND LANG, G. "Children's Perceptions of Their Teachers' Feelings toward Them Related to Self-Perception, School Achievement and Behavior." *Journal of Experimental Education,* 1960, *29,* 107–118.

DAVIS, J. A. "The Campus as a Frog Pond: An Application of the Theory of Relative Deprivation to Career Decisions of College Men." *American Journal of Sociology,* 1966, *72,* 17–31.

DU BOIS, W. E. B. "Does the Negro Need Separate Schools?" *Journal of Negro Education,* 1935, *4,* 328–335.

FAUMAN, S. J. "Housing Discrimination, Changing Neighborhoods and Public Schools." *Journal of Social Issues,* 1957, *13,* 21–30.

FISHMAN, J. A. "Childhood Indoctrination for Minority Group Membership." *Daedalus,* 1961, *90,* 329–349.

GLASER, D. "The Differential-Association Theory of Crime." In A. Rose (Ed.), *Human Behavior and Social Processes.* Boston: Houghton Mifflin, 1962. Pp. 425–442.

GOFFMAN, E. *Stigma: Notes on the Management of Spoiled Identity.* Englewood Cliffs, N.J.: Prentice-Hall, 1963.

Group for the Advancement of Psychiatry. "Psychiatric Aspects of School Desegregation." Report No. 37, New York, 1957.

GURIN, P., GURIN, G., LAO, R., AND BEATTIE, M. "Internal-External Control in the Motivational Dynamics of Negro Youth." *Journal of Social Issues,* 1969, *25,* 29–54.

HAMILTON, C. V. "Race and Education: A Search for Legitimacy." *Harvard Educational Review,* 1968, *38,* 669–684.

HANDLIN, O. "The Goals of Integration." *Daedalus,* 1965, *95,* 268–286.

HAVIGHURST, R. J. "Urban Development and the Educational System." In A. H. Passow (Ed.), *Education in Depressed Areas.* New York: Columbia University, Teachers College, 1963. Pp. 24–45.

HERRIOTT, R. E., AND ST. JOHN, N. H. *Social Class and the Urban School.* New York: Wiley, 1966.

KATZ, I. "Review of Evidence Relating to Effects of Desegregation on the Intellectual Performance of Negroes." *American Psychologist,* 1964, *19,* 381–399.

KATZ, I. "The Socialization of Academic Motivation in Minority Group Children." In D. Levine (Ed.), *Nebraska Symposium on Motivation, 1967.* Vol. 15. Lincoln: University of Nebraska Press, 1967. Pp. 133–191.

148   Nancy H. St. John

KEMPER, T. D. "Reference Groups, Socialization and Achievement."
American Sociological Review, 1968, *33,* 31–45.
MAHAN, T. W. "Project Concern—1966–68: A Report on the Effectiveness of Suburban School Placement for Inner-City Youth." Hartford, Conn.: Board of Education, August 1968.
MARX, G. T. *Protest and Prejudice: A Study of Belief in the Black Community.* New York: Harper & Row, 1967.
MC CAULEY, P., AND BALL, E. D. *Southern Schools: Progress and Problems.* Nashville: Southern Educational Reporting Service, 1959.
MC PARTLAND, J. "The Segregated Student in Desegregated Schools: Sources of Influence on Negro Secondary Students." Report No. 21. Johns Hopkins University, Center for the Study of Social Organization of the Schools, 1968.
MERTON, R. K. *Social Theory and Social Structure.* New York: Free Press, 1957.
MILNER, E. "Some Hypotheses Concerning the Influence of Segregation on Negro Personality Development." *Psychiatry,* 1953, *16,* 291–297.
National Advisory Commission on Civil Disorders. *Report to the Commission.* New York: Bantam Books, 1968.
PARK, R. E. *Race and Culture.* New York: Free Press, 1950.
PETTIGREW, T. F. *A Profile of the Negro American.* Princeton, N.J.: Van Nostrand, 1964.
PETTIGREW, T. F. "Social Evaluation Theory: Convergences and Applications." In D. Levine (Ed.), *Nebraska Symposium on Motivation, 1967.* Vol. 15. Lincoln: University of Nebraska Press, 1967. Pp. 241–311.
PETTIGREW, T. F. "The Negro and Education: Problems and Proposals." In Katz and Gurin (Eds.), *Race and the Social Sciences.* New York: Basic Books, 1969. Pp. 49–112. (a)
PETTIGREW, T. F. "Racially Separate or Together?" *Journal of Social Issues,* 1969, *25,* 43–70. (b)
PINDERHUGHES, C. A. "Effects of Ethnic Group Concentration upon Education Process, Personality Formation, and Mental Health." *Journal of National Medical Association,* 1964, *56,* 407.
PIVEN, F. F., AND CLOWARD, R. A. "The Case against Urban Desegregation." *Social Work,* 1967, *12,* 12–20.
PURL, M. C. "The Achievement of Pupils in Desegregated Schools." Riverside (Calif.) Unified School District, March 1971.
ROTTER, J. B. "Generalized Expectancies for Internal versus External Control of Reinforcement." *Psychological Monographs,* 1966, *30,* 1–28.
SCHWARZ, M., AND TANGRI, S. S. "A Note on Self-Concept as an Insula-

tion against Discrimination." *American Sociological Review,* 1965, *30,* 922–926.

SHIBUTANI, T. "Reference Groups and Social Control." In A. Rose (Ed.), *Human Behavior and Social Processes.* Boston: Houghton Mifflin, 1967. Pp. 128–147.

SIMMEL, G. *The Sociology of Georg Simmel.* K. Wolff (Ed.) New York: Free Press, 1950.

ST. JOHN, N. H. "Desegregation and Minority Group Performance." *Review of Educational Research,* 1970, *40,* 111–134.

ST. JOHN, N. H. "The Effects of School Desegregation on Children." Mimeographed Paper. The Radcliffe Institute, Harvard University, 1971. (a)

ST. JOHN, N. H. "School Integration, Classroom Climate and Achievement." U.S.O.E., Final Report, Project No. OA-026, 1971. (b)

STONEQUIST, E. *The Marginal Man.* New York: Scribner's, 1937.

STOUFFER, S. A., SUCHMAN, E. A., DE VINNEY, L. C., STAR, S. A., AND WILLIAMS, R. M., JR., *The American Soldier.* Vol. 1. Princeton: Princeton University Press, 1949.

TEELE, J. E., JACKSON, E., AND MAYO, C. "Family Experiences in Operation Exodus." *Community Mental Health Journal,* 1967, Monograph Series, No. 3.

U.S. Commission on Civil Rights. *Racial Isolation in the Public Schools.* Washington, D.C.: U.S. Government Printing Office, 1967. 2 vols.

WEINBERG, M. *Desegregation Research: An Appraisal.* (2nd ed.) Bloomington, Indiana: Phi Delta Kappa, 1970.

WILSON, A. B. "Educational Consequences of Segregation in a California Community." In U.S. Commission on Civil Rights, *Racial Isolation in the Public Schools.* Vol. 2. Washington, D.C.: U.S. Government Printing Office, 1967. Pp. 77–84.

WILSON, A. B. "Social Class and Equal Educational Opportunity." *Harvard Educational Review,* 1968, *38,* 77–84.

WRIGHTSTONE, J. W. "Demonstration Guidance Project in New York City." *Harvard Educational Review,* 1960, *30,* 237–251.

ZIRKEL, P. A. "Self Concept and the Disadvantage of Ethnic Group Membership and Mixture." *Review of Educational Research,* 1971, *41,* 211–226.

CHAPTER 13

Compensatory Education

David K. Cohen

◈◈◈◈◈◈◈◈◈◈◈◈◈◈

For the past two or three years public education has been mired in disaster, conflict, and failure. The passage of the 1964 Civil Rights Act lent renewed force to the drive for school desegregation, but within a few years many black leaders were questioning integration. The inception of Project Head Start and Title I of the 1965 ESEA stimulated efforts to improve education for poor children, but by 1969 both programs were officially pronounced failures. The "failure" of such efforts at improving education for poor children is by now not only comfortably ensconced in the public mind, it is firmly bound up with other current notions, including the "necessity" for decentralization and the "impotence" of social programs. This is a situation which contrary facts—if indeed they exist—would be unlikely to alter. Nonetheless, the facts would be useful. At least they could help us to see clearly just what the schools have done or

This paper was written for the U.S. Department of Health, Education, and Welfare (purchase order no. OEC-0-70-5107).

150

might do, and to decide whether the many inferences from their "failure" are warranted.

Program Aims

The place to begin is where the programs do, with some idea of their objectives. This is less easy than it seems. Improving school performance, after all, has not been the sole aim of such endeavors as Title I and—if we think of congressional intent—perhaps not even their main purpose. In addition, the programs have often been carried out with astonishing clumsiness: often the amount of money spent on individual children is trivial, and sometimes the funds have been misspent entirely (Cohen, 1970). Despite all this, better education *was* an important aim of these efforts, and not *all* the funds were badly used.

What do these programs seek in the way of improved school performance? For the most part, local Title I projects announce improved reading or mathematics achievement as their principal goal, but this is far from the only program aim. Many of the reading and mathematics programs also seek to improve the student's self-concept, and a small proportion focus entirely on this problem. Others claim to be concerned mostly with truancy or school retention, and still others aim at improved school-community relations or greater parent involvement. In fact, one really remarkable aspect of local Title I programs is the diversity of aims most projects choose to announce.

But this diversity is only skin deep. Whether it is test scores or truancy, the real (and avowed) aim of Title I programs is to eliminate inequalities in educational opportunity. Almost uniformly this is taken to imply eliminating race or class disparities in the outcomes of schooling. What is more, the program materials envision the elimination of both school and class disparities as a means to another more important end—the elimination of poverty. Thus, the programs differ only in their conception of the mechanisms that will lead to better school performance. They are as one in the view that improved performance is important solely because it will lead to more education, better jobs, more income, and less poverty.

Title I programs, then, make several important assumptions about schooling and its situation in the social order. One is that school performance has a direct causal impact on adult social and economic status. Another is that the chief obstacle to eliminating poverty is the inadequate training or bad manners of the poor. The first point rests on well-established ideas about education; ever since the turn of the century, when Americans began to see their society as one built on technology, schooling has been regarded as the crucial determinant of adult success. And while there is less agreement on the second point, the main drift of opinion has been that stupidity and bad manners are the consequences of poverty rather than the results of selection of the fittest. It follows from both assumptions that, if deprivation and discrimination are eliminated, those with ability can rise as far as their talents will permit. The assumption was that there has been plenty of room at the top and that schooling was the appropriate escalator.

The programs also assume, of course, that the school can improve students' performance. Some programs assume that the main problem is students' discouragement over their poor chances in life; most hold that the problem arises from cognitive deficits due to environmental deprivation, but still others assume that the problem lies in children's poor self-evaluations. Whatever the view, the educators who design and implement Title I programs assume that these difficulties can be repaired by the schools. It will surprise no one to find that these ideas were not probed before Title I was launched. Had they been, the results would have been surprising; for all the available evidence either is ambiguous or runs contrary to the assumptions.

The availability of room at the top is doubtless the most important issue; it is also the most difficult. There is, for example, plenty of evidence that occupations at the top of the social structure have been expanding steadily since the turn of the century. But this proves only that there are more good jobs; the question is—Who gets them? If the patterns of social inheritance are such that they are virtually closed to all but the children of professional and technical workers, the abundance of jobs means absolutely nothing. Though there is little research on this point, the one extant study (Blau and Duncan, 1967) concludes that there is much greater recruitment to white-collar jobs from the ranks of white-collar than blue-collar workers. But this proves only that those at the bottom of the occupational ladder tend to stay there. It does not show that they stay there *despite* superior education. Does schooling tend to equalize life chances among broad social-class groupings?

Unfortunately, there is no evidence directly on this point. Blau and Duncan (1967), studying the impact of schooling on mobility among the nearly one hundred occupations that sociologists survey in such studies, found that educational attainment (years of school completed) has a stronger impact on occupational achievement than several measures of social inheritance (fathers' occupation and education). The problem is that most mobility is short-range and may have little relation to movement across major class and occupational barriers. The evidence on the role of intelligence in occupational mobility suggests that early IQ is moderately related to educational attainment (years spent in school) (Duncan, 1968a) but has no direct impact whatever on occupational attainment once variations in years of school completed are accounted for. Does this mean that improving IQ will improve occupational status? The answer is by no means self-evident.

Furthermore, the studies cited had the entire American labor force as their subjects. Compensatory programs, however, are aimed at children in segments of the society which either do not participate in the labor force or do so in a marginal way. Even if we had shown that there is room at the top and that education is the high road to mobility, this would not hold automatically for the poor or for blacks. The problem is particularly acute for Negro Americans. They are the principal target group of Title I programs in the larger uban areas, and they are identified nationally as the main object of compensatory treatment in the schools and elsewhere. Is there room at the top for Negroes? Does education "work" for them in the same fashion as it does for whites?

Merely to put the questions suggest the answer. Although summary measures of discrimination are not easy to come by, there is an enormous difference in the distribution of occupations for black and white Americans. Most studies suggest that roughly two thirds of these gross differences cannot be accounted for by such "objective" measures of qualification as education or training. The remaining differences are presumed to be due to discrimination. Moreover, the most sophisticated study on this point (Blau and Duncan, 1967) found that, even when whites and Negroes in the same regions and with similar social and economic backgrounds are compared, blacks attain much lower levels in the occupational structure. The differences are due chiefly to discrimination. Most important, however, is whether schooling is the solution to this problem. On this point, the study concludes: "Negroes have less incentive than whites to acquire an education and to make the serious sacrifices that doing so entails for persons from the underprivileged socioeconomic classes . . . approximately the same amount of educational investment yields considerably less return in the form of superior occupational status or mobility to nonwhites than to whites" (Blau and Duncan, 1967, p. 212). Under these circumstances it is hard to see the special relevance of compensatory-education programs for blacks; attacks on job discrimination, and programs of income maintenance, work training, and job creation would seem to be more appropriate.

It would be a mistake to conclude from this that schooling bears no relation to mobility among social and occupational classes. It does suggest however that—although there is some association between length of schooling and adult status—schooling is probably not related to adult status in the ways most compensatory programs assume—through improved performance on standardized tests of IQ of achievement.

It goes almost without saying that the findings to date offer little support for the ideas underlying compensatory programs. But the problem does not end here. As mentioned earlier, all the projects supported by Title I assume that the schools can affect those attributes typically thought to be the agents of later achievement: test scores, self-concept, school retention, and the like. Yet these assumptions were sharply challenged shortly after Title I and Head Start had been set in motion. In 1966 the U.S. Office of Education published the *Equality of Educational Opportunity* report, which announced that differences among schools in resources and educational practices are not significantly related to differences among schools in the children's performance on standardized tests of achievement or verbal ability. The only differences that have an important impact on test performance involve the students' social inheritance; children from advantaged homes enter school with an enormous lead on disadvantaged students (in terms of test scores), and they maintain or increase this lead through the twelve years of school (Coleman, 1966).

This news was not received with wild enthusiasm by either the Office of Education or the various professions it represents. The report was treated as though it were some species of important leper; it could hardly be ignored, but then neither could it be welcomed with open arms. Educators and bureaucrats alike contented themselves with either attacking it (on the grounds that it was methodologically faulty or that it measured the wrong things) or suggesting that since it was concerned only with the *existing* differences among schools, one could hardly make inferences about the effect of new remedial programs, which went beyond these differences.

The really remarkable element in the report's reception, however, was neither the pain nor the anger with which it was greeted—it was the surprise. The entire affair would have given an innocent observer the impression that the survey's findings ran counter to the results of decades of research on the effects of schooling—when the fact is that the EEOS report's conclusions were almost perfectly consistent with the results of this earlier work.

The previous studies were hardly exhaustive. They were mainly small studies involving a few classrooms, several schools, or at most a few school systems. But they did focus on many of the gross relationships usually assumed to make a difference to students' school performance: per-pupil expenditures, class and school size, teachers' qualifications, and the content of curricula. With very few exceptions, the results showed that the school-to-school differences in these characteristics are unrelated to differences in students' test performance. As Stephens (1968) has pointed out in a review of these studies, the consistently negative results became so well known among researchers that it was commonplace to refer to the findings without even so much as a cursory citation.

One could, of course, always argue that small studies of a few classrooms or schools would inevitably turn up small differences, since the schools and classrooms were almost always adjacent and therefore probably quite similar. This objection, however, cannot be sustained in the case of results from Project Talent, a massive national study of American high schools underwritten by the U.S. Office of Education in the early 1960s. The Talent survey collected a great deal of information on student background and achievement, as well as schools' characteristics, programs, and facilities. Students were tested at grade 9 and then again when they reached grade 12, which made it possible for later researchers to ascertain the impact of differences in school resources on differences in what students learned during the four years of high school.

Shaycoft (1967) undertook just such an investigation, with two principal results. First, she found that the simple correlations (corrected for attenuation) between students' ninth-grade and twelfth-grade performance on tests of such basic skills as reading comprehension and abstract reasoning ranged between .85 and .95. This means that between 70 and 90 per cent of the variation of students' twelfth-grade performance was explained by variations in their ninth-grade performance. As things stood in the early 1960s, then, the student "output" of high schools was little different from their student "input." In four years American high schools had done almost nothing to change the relative ordering of achievement with which the students began. Such findings provide little encouragement for the notion that schools differentially affect achievement.

The second part of Shaycoft's investigation only confirmed this dismal result. Having shown that for the most part student perfor-

mance on tests of basic skills is quite invariate over the high school
years, she sought to determine whether school characteristics have any
impact on the remaining 10 or 20 per cent of the variance. She concluded that the results "were inconclusive"; apparently none of the
school characteristics measured in Project Talent had any consistent
association with the residual achievement differences. This result
(which was published at about the same time as the EEOS) accorded
perfectly with an earlier cross-sectional analysis of the ninth-grade
scores (Thomas, 1962).

While these results would discourage most advocates of compensatory schooling, they would come as no surprise to students of human
development. In a study published in 1964, Benjamin Bloom reviewed
the results of all extant research on the stability of individual intelligence over time. The simple correlation between IQ at age eleven and
age seventeen (for the same individuals) was always found to be on
the order of .90. This is perfectly consistent with the results from
Project Talent. In fact, had any other result appeared in the Talent
data it would have been astonishingly inconsistent with everything
previously known about the relative stability of IQ.

Thus, were one to formulate reasonable inferences from the
pre-EEOS research on the effects of schooling, the two chief results
would be as follows: (1) The differences among schools which people usually suppose to be important—size of school, amount of budget,
teachers' qualifications, and curriculum content—are not related to
students' test performances. (2) Achievement and IQ test scores are
a relatively invariate human characteristic (at least when the tests are
well made), and they are highly related to indices of social inheritance
and family background. Now, none of this meant that schools could
not "make a difference" to student achievement. All it meant was
that the *gross differences among schools usually thought to be important* have no educationally significant impact on test scores.

The analyses reported in the EEOS—and the results of subsequent reanalysis of the data at Harvard—confirm this conclusion.
Although the survey measured school resources and practices in much
more detailed fashion than either Project Talent or the earlier studies,
there was no effort to go much beyond the gross characteristics measured in previous work. Chiefly as a result of the great haste with
which the original report was prepared, its analyses were flawed in
several respects. But reanalyses carried out at Harvard (Mosteller and
Moynihan, 1970–71), which corrected some of the methodological
flaws, only strengthened the original findings. These results show, for
example, no relationship between teachers' qualifications or experience

and student achievement. Nor are there achievement differences associated with variations in per-pupil expenditures, class or school size, or curriculum or grouping policies. Indeed, none of these school attributes had more than a small zero-order correlation with achievement scores; and once school-to-school variations in students' social inheritance were removed, the associations vanished completely.

Much the same results can be produced with no reference to the school-resource measures but simply by examining the relation between school "input" and "output" in the EEOS. Among the Northern urban schools, the correlation between average achievement at first grade and sixth grade is in excess of .8; the same correlations between ninth-grade and tenth-grade achievement are in excess of .95. These confirm Shaycoft's work: most of the differences in "output" of elementary or senior high schools are accounted for by differences in their "inputs." Of course, this relationship is not carved in stone; if schools were different, the correlations might be smaller. But the important point is that as things presently stand, the output of schools is very little different from their input. Schools do little to change the relative ordering of ability with which they begin.

Thus, the EEOS results reinforce and solidify the pattern apparent in earlier research. The survey confirms the similarity between schools' input and output, and the fact that gross differences among school resources and practices have no impact upon differences in student achievement. As the evidence stood in the mid 1960s, there was no empirical encouragement for the notion that schools could have much differential effect on students' achievement.

Program Content

The obvious—and by 1966 well-worn—reply was that the existing differences among schools are either too small or too crude to affect achievement. Although this argument has the advantage of being applicable to negative findings of any sort or size (and is therefore indefinitely useful), it is not entirely persuasive. After all, the existing differences among schools cannot simply be brushed aside; they are differences among schools attended by the nonpoor—the differences that most Americans have been concerned about during the past four or five decades. If they are too small or too crude to affect achievement, what have the arguments been about all these years? To argue that the existing differences among school resources and practices are too gross or crude to affect achievement is implicitly to agree that most of the educational "progress" of the last forty or fifty years is a hoax.

Although most advocates of compensatory schooling probably would not agree to that formulation, the programs do assume that the existing differences in education for poor and for advantaged children are too small to affect achievement, and their results might reasonably be taken as a rough test of this notion. The overwhelming majority of them, for example, seem to assume that the main difference between the educational needs of advantaged and disadvantaged children is quantitative—the latter group is presumed to need more. These programs are all aimed at achievement (mostly reading), and they regard compensatory schooling as a substitute for cognitive stimulation presumed to be absent in deprived home and neighborhood environments.

The results of these efforts, however, are hugely unconvincing. Part of the problem is that most of the evaluations obscure any clear idea of what happened. A recent review of exemplary programs, for example, found that the overwhelming majority of programs were evaluated by comparing test scores to national norms rather than to the scores of a comparison or control group. Consequently, it is impossible to tell whether the program had any impact (McLaughlin, 1971). Another difficulty is that many programs diffuse funds so widely as to add little to expenditures on any given pupil. But even if we confine ourselves to projects that concentrate substantial amounts of money on disadvantaged children, most of the results are discouraging. This was demonstrated on a grand scale by the More Effective Schools Program in New York City. Per-pupil expenditures were doubled or tripled, and the ratio of teachers to students was at least doubled; but there was no clear or consistent gain (over expectations) in students' achievement. The evaluation attributed this result to the fact that the conditions of instruction had changed (each student was exposed to much more educational resources) but the character of the resources had not changed (Fox, 1969, p. 63). Teachers were still doing the same things with fifteen children that they previously had done with thirty.

A few programs funded by Title I do seem to reveal achievement gains, although the evaluations are all questionable. Efforts to discern similarities among them turned up some similarities (continuity in staff and program over several years, for example) but none at the curricular or instructional level. The most important problem, however, is that most of the gains appear to have been clustered in the lowest quartile of the test distribution—suggesting that the gains may be nothing more than regression toward the mean.

Thus, although the reviews of Title I programs do not produce a totally bleak picture, they reveal no consistent evidence that the mere concentration of standard educational resources improves achievement. Most of the programs that take this approach produce no discernible gains, and among those that display gains there is serious doubt that the effects are genuine. If we simply took the universe of resource-concentration programs and calculated the changes that any given program would succeed on the basis of the percentage that already have, the resulting probability would be extremely low. The results from these programs, then, are consistent with earlier research: gross differences among schools have little impact on achievement.

Alternative Approaches

But achievement is not the only possible outcome of schooling, and resource concentration is not the only imaginable way to affect test scores. Although Title I programs present several alternative outcomes (absenteeism, vandalism, self-concept), the alternatives are either unmeasurable, unmeasured, or trivial. Title I program evaluations are not the best place to search for alternative models of successful strategies.

How might such approaches be identified?

One useful way is to begin with the unsuccessful programs. Their most impressive and consistent characteristic is the global quality of both the program aims and the diagnosis of children's problems. Most assume an undifferentiated lack of cognitive stimulation in children and propose enrichment with standard (or slightly modified) curriculum materials and teaching techniques. Yet there is little evidence that the tests usually employed to measure IQ assess an undifferentiated range of cognitive skills, nor is there any evidence that undifferentiated enrichment (in the typical classroom sense of the phrase) is related to cognitive growth. Indeed, all the experimental evidence runs in just the other direction. The only preschool programs with decent evidence of success in raising IQ for disadvantaged children in classroom settings are those that focus narrowly on verbal and linguistic abilities. The aims of these programs are narrow, and their techniques (rigid classroom drill and specially designed curriculum materials requiring fairly intensive teacher retraining) are carefully fitted to the aims.

Bissell (1970a) has surveyed the available evidence on these programs and reanalyzed the evaluation results. She contrasted the effects of two kinds of programs: (1) highly structured programs concentrating on language development and (2) more permissive programs focusing on the traditional range of goals, especially enrichment. Her conclusions are worth quoting:

> *Preschool programs with general objectives of fostering cognitive growth, with specific emphasis on language development, and with teacher-directed strategies that provide highly structured experiences for disadvantaged children are more effective in producing cognitive gains than programs lacking these characteristics. Preschool programs high on the dimension of quality control, having well-trained staff, a high degree of supervision, and a low pupil-teacher ratio, are the most effective programs in producing cognitive gains [p. 28].*

The results from this research clearly demonstrate that substantial IQ gains are possible with classroom programs. Although the results are ambiguous in some respects—the effects of the programs declined over the succeeding two years—they do show that schools can improve test performance. There is no reason to believe that these results could not be replicated in the primary grades.

These findings suggest that specific attacks on learning differences associated with variations in class culture and child rearing can succeed. That notion is confirmed by the results of other experiments in which aspects of parents' behavior were changed. In one case parents of preschool children were trained to be more effective in a range of school-related activities, including teaching their children to read and helping with schoolwork; in another, this training in school-related activities was augmented with general competency training in home management and related skills (Bissell, 1970a). In both cases the children showed marked improvement on IQ tests over otherwise similar nonexperimental preschoolers.

The underlying difficulty with these programs, however, is the same as with the compensatory programs: they assume that IQ influences the probability of success after schooling is completed, and this notion rests on an extraordinarily unsubstantial empirical foundation. It may be that raising IQ in the early school years increases the probability that students will complete more years of school—either because there is some intrinsic relationship between the two or because the students' successful participation in the program changes the expectations of all parties concerned. It also may be that nothing will change but the students' IQs. Unfortunately, we will never know the answers from the existing experiments. They are too small, and the conditions of the students' subsequent experiences too diverse in place and quality for follow-up studies to be helpful. Experimentation on a much larger and longer scale would be needed to find out whether changes in early IQ have any social significance.

Another approach to finding promising strategies is to identify potentially important educational outcomes and try to devise ways to redistribute them. College matriculation is one obvious example. Although in one sense most standard remedial programs are aimed in this direction, they apply undifferentiated enrichment in an undifferentiated fashion to an undifferentiated group of students; increasing their achievement is presumed to increase their chances of matriculation. Another reasonable approach is that of the Upward Bound program. In these projects the most promising (and motivated) students are identified fairly late in high school and are told that completion of the program is nearly a guarantee of college matriculation (nearly eight out of ten who complete these programs gain admission to college). The students are provided with a variety of formal instruction: some is remedial, some is designed to familiarize them with university work, and some seems to be aimed simply at their morale and expectations. Upward Bound graduates have a much higher rate of college entrance than would otherwise be expected, and they seem to drop out less frequently than average.

Another educational outcome of possible importance is high school completion; it is not hard to imagine analogous ways to increase its likelihood for disadvantaged students, and in fact there appear to be several types of successful dropout recovery programs (Millsap, 1969). Some are aimed at bright but disaffected students and seem to consist of nothing more than providing a more interesting and unusual academic fare than can be found at the typical high school. Others are aimed at students with minimal academic skills, in which case the crucial element appears to be a remedial program that is integrated with a job. While these programs come nowhere near the scale of Upward Bound, they do seem to succeed.

These programs do not present precisely the same problems as the preschool projects. It is true almost by definition that a work-study program for dropouts which provides both a high school diploma and a job has a positive effect on the adult outcomes of schooling. The same thing can be said of the Upward Bound programs. The really important question is why. Is it because changes in the objective probabilities of success alter expectations and therefore behavior? If this were the case, presumably a program like Upward Bound would have roughly the same effect on less able students. An analogous experiment would be to identify promising students at the end of elementary school and enter them in the academic curriculum of high school, rather than allowing them to slip into some other track. Or is it because both types of programs are highly selective and simply offer an opportunity to students who—were all else equal—would achieve the same end through the usual channels? The only way this idea could be tested (and then only in part) would again be to offer an opportunity like Upward Bound to students of a wide variety of ability. In either event, the questions underscore our ignorance about the process of schooling. We simply do not know whether educational attainment (clearing the certification hurdles) is chiefly a function of inherited status and the attendant differences in both objective assistance and expectations it generates, or whether the selection system does involve intellectual and psychological criteria which are at least in part independent of social inheritance, and which do have some genuine relationship to performance later in life. Some of these questions could be explored if a somewhat more experimental approach to a program such as Upward Bound were adopted, but there is little evidence that this will occur.

Conclusions

Has compensatory education failed? In the most narrow sense, it has. Most Title I programs which seek to improve achievement have no discernible effect—apparently because the programs seek to provide for disadvantaged students more of the school resources which have never been found to affect the achievement of advantaged students. On the other hand, compensatory programs need not fail; highly structured preschool programs aimed at language development produce impressive short-run IQ gains. The most important difference between these experiments and most Title I programs (or, for that matter, most other preschool programs) is that the successful experiments were aimed narrowly at skills clearly related to what tests of IQ and verbal ability happen to measure. That is, the programs rest on a body of knowledge which at least approximates a model of the learning measured by the tests. Given the relative plasticity of IQ prior to age ten or twelve, there is every reason to believe that similar programs at the primary level would yield similar results.

In addition, there are other models of what might be called compensatory education; at least their object is to redistribute educational outcomes and to improve the life chances of children from disadvantaged circumstances. These programs, however, focus on more distant outcomes of schooling—college entrance and high school

graduation. They differ from the preschool and compensatory programs because they seek to affect these outcomes directly, by visibly
altering the objective probabilities of success, rather than indirectly,
by raising achievement or IQ.

The difficulty with both approaches is that they rest on extremely limited evidence about the process of schooling. We have no
evidence that IQ affects life chances, though if it does cause longer
school attendance, it may. Nor do we understand why programs like
Upward Bound succeed. Is it because they simply select students who
would have done well anyway (were it not for the consequences of
discrimination) or because, within the "normal" range of human
ability, anyone who has the opportunity can succeed? If the first is
true, it might be argued that the school selection system rests on
criteria which bear some intrinsic relation to later achievement. If the
second is true, it could be argued that the school selection system rests
on a series of arbitrary conventions, which work to the advantage of
those who could expect success anyway. Without a good deal more
evidence, it is difficult to know which account is more likely and, for
that reason, impossible to arrive at firmly grounded compensatory
strategies.

Thus, while most standard compensatory programs have failed
to affect achievement, there was never any evidence that much else
could have been expected. Nor is there any evidence that the life
chances of poor children would be different if the programs had
succeeded. Although it is easy to imagine the experimentation and
research on the process of schooling which would illuminate these
issues, there is litle evidence that either will be undertaken. Instead,
the majority of compensatory programs will probably continue to
"fail" at a task whose significance is unknown; and other programs,
like Upward Bound, will succeed for reasons no one understands.

References

BISSELL, J. S. "The Cognitive Effects of Pre-School Programs for Disadvantaged Children." Unpublished paper, National Institute of
Child Health and Development, 1970. (a)

BISSELL, J. S. "The Cognitive Effects of Pre-School Programs for Disadvantaged Children." Unpublished Ph.D. dissertation, Harvard
Graduate School of Education, 1970. (b)

BLAU, P., AND DUNCAN, O. D. The American Occupational Structure. New
York: Wiley, 1967.

BLOOM, B. S. *Stability and Change in Human Characteristics.* New York: Wiley, 1964.

COHEN, D. "Politics and Research: The Evaluation of Social Action Programs in Education." *Review of Educational Research,* 1970, *40*(2), 213–238.

COLEMAN, J. S., et al. *Equality of Educational Opportunity.* Washington, D.C.: U.S. Office of Health, Education, and Welfare, 1966.

DUNCAN, O. D. "Ability and Achievement." *Eugenics Quarterly,* 1968, *15,* 1–11. (a)

DUNCAN, O. D. *Socioeconomic Status and Occupational Achievement.* Ann Arbor, Michigan: University of Michigan Population Study Center, 1968. (b)

FOX, D. *Expansion of the More Effective Schools Program.* New York: Center for Urban Education, 1969.

MC LAUGHLIN, M. "Parent Involvement in Compensatory Education Programs: A Review." Unpublished qualifying paper, School of Education, Harvard University, 1971.

MILLSAP, M. A. "An Evaluation of Dropout Prevention and Dropout Recovery Programs." Unpublished paper, Office of Program Planning and Evaluation, U.S. Office of Education, 1969.

MOSTELLER, F., AND MOYNIHAN, D. P. (Eds.) *Equality of Educational Opportunity.* New York: Random House, 1972.

SHAYCOFT, M. *The High School Years: Growth in Cognitive Skills.* Pittsburgh: American Institute for Research, 1967.

STEPHENS, J. M. *The Process of Schooling.* New York: Holt, Rinehart and Winston, 1968.

THOMAS, J. A. *Efficiency in Education: A Study of the Relationship between Selected Inputs and Test Scores in a Sample of Senior High Schools.* Unpublished Ph.D. dissertation, School of Education, Stanford University, 1962.

CHAPTER 14

Rethinking Urban Religious Education

Andrew M. Greeley

This chapter presumes with Clifford Geertz (1970) that religion is the quest for the real; it is the set of symbols that man uses to cope with the fundamental and primordial question of the meaning of life and the meaning of *his* life. But religion is different from other meaning systems—common sense, science, esthetics, history, and ideology—in that it answers the most fundamental of questions. The religious answers not only interpret reality; they guarantee the interpretability of reality. For if man cannot deal with the unexpected, the irrational, the tragic, the unjust, then the whole interpretability of the universe is called into question and man is forced to face the possibility of chaos.

In the Geertzian model the religious meaning system underpins and pervades, at least to some extent, the other meaning systems. Religion tells man what is the Really Real and thereby colors and

165

shapes his response to more peripheral phenomena. Religion is man's world view; it is the other side of the coin of his ethos, for world view of mythos tells man what is the nature of reality, and ethos or ethical system tells man how he must adjust to reality. The two sides of the coin define both reality and the good life. Even if man's world view does not presume a transcendent, even if it is devoid of most manifestations of the sacred, it is nonetheless a meaning system which underpins and reinforces all of man's other meaning systems. The pertinent question in the Geertzian framework is not "Is there a God?" but rather "Who is your God?"—that is to say, "What is your definition of the Real?" And the pertinent social science question is not whether man has a religion but what is the nature of his religion; that is to say, what are the symbols with which he copes with the ultimate and defines his ethics.

Thomas Luckmann (1967) argues that man's religious "interpretive scheme" is acquired in the act of "individuation"; that is, when man discovers he is separate and exists over against others, he is forced to reflect on the meaning of his existence. The answers that he comes up with are of course shaped by his culture, his family background, and his own biographical experience. But religion is as primal to man as the fact of individuation; for once he perceives himself as individuated, man needs an *explanation*.

In the perspective of writers like Geertz and Luckmann, the permanence of religion ceases to be a matter for question. Neither author would argue that all men are equally religious or that all men need religion at every moment of their lives. Their position is much more modest: All men need, at least occasionally, some answers to basic questions; and most men need such answers with some degree of frequency in the course of their lives.

One might even argue that from one viewpoint man's religious needs are more explicit in the modern Western world. For in most cultures in which men have lived, the "interpretive scheme" or the "template" is inherited from one's ancestors, not only at the same time one acquires language but with the same finality. One may be more or less enthusiastic, more or less devout, more or less unquestionably committed to the fundamental responses of one's milieu; but there are not too many alternative options available. The religious question is for the most part implicit. However, in the contemporary world, as Luckmann points out, religious interpretive schemes compete in an open marketplace. Men and women become to some extent "consumers," who shop in the supermarket of interpretive schemes. The range of choice is not infinite, and only a few people will settle for an interpretive scheme that is greatly different from that of their parents; nonetheless, the fact of the availability of options now makes the religious issue explicit. If one can, at least within some limitation, choose one's own religion, then one cannot escape the burden of some sort of choice. Perhaps the reason for much of the restlessness among upper-middle-class young people is that they are going through a difficult period of religious decision; they are trying to formulate for themselves a "mythos" and an ethos. They are much like the Indonesian and the Moroccan whom Geertz describes in the concluding pages of *Islam Observed:* engaged in a quest for the Real—much like Geertz himself, for that matter.

If religion is something primordial and pervasive in the human condition, one may very well wonder why there has been so little concern about religious education in American academic research. One might venture three explanations: First of all, many if not most American social scientists who are interested in research on education are themselves not religious or at least are ill at ease with their own religious heritage, to which they maintain some vestigial if puzzled loyalty. Under such circumstances, one can readily think of many other things to study besides religious education. (Professor Robert Havighurst, to whom this volume is dedicated, stands as a unique exception to this generalization, both among his own generation of scholars and also among the generation succeeding his.)

Second, American public education in the present stage of its development is irreligious. It is not permitted to engage in explicitly religious education; it is also under severe constraints to behave as though religion does not exist. There is, one must admit, precious little in the words of the Constitution, the early history of the public schools, or even the political and educational history of the United States to justify such a posture toward religion in the public schools. The "wall of separation" doctrine is a creation of contemporary secular jurists, and both the doctrine and its frequently absurd applications can hardly be justified in terms of the past. However, both religion and religious education are declared off limits to American public schools. Therefore, since "mainline" educational research is concerned with public schools (under the assumption that education and public education are practically the same thing), and since religious education cannot take place in public schools, mainline educational research is not to be concerned with religious education.

Finally, the principal institution that engages in religious education in a classroom context is the Roman Catholic Church. Until recently the Roman Church has not been all that interested in having its education researched and evaluated by professional scholars; and, to tell the truth, professional scholars were not all that interested in researching and evaluating Roman Catholic schools, at least in part because they were inclined to doubt whether the existence of such schools was a particularly good idea. In other words, if one had been tempted to do research on religious education, the most obvious place to begin would be the Catholic schools, and that thought itself was usually a sufficient barrier to any further consideration of the possibilities of evaluating religious education.

However, if the perspective of this chapter is correct, then religious education is an extremely important topic for research. It may also be a topic of considerable importance for those concerned about urban educational problems in American society.

We know that many leaders of the black movement in the past decade were ministers. We know that the black churches played in the past, and still play, an extremely important role in the lives of many people of the ghetto. What we do not know with any degree of precision is the role that religion plays in motivating the poor to move beyond the ghetto, or in persuading them to be content with their lot in the ghetto, or in leading them toward social action directed toward the elimination of the ghetto. The cheap and easy answer to such questions is to say that the principal function of religion in the black community has been to make the black man resigned to his fate; but this flies in the face of both the phenomenon of the vigorous religiousness of the upwardly mobile black and the fact that much of the militant black leadership has been and continues to be clerical.

Furthermore, there is still much to be learned about the function of religion in the lives of "Middle Americans"—hence, much to be learned about how these people pass on their mythos and ethos to their children. Anyone who has read the emergent literature on Middle Americans knows that they are deeply attached to their churches. But are these Middle Americans, in particular the white ethnic component, quite as insecure, threatened, and anxious as some of the publicists describing them would have us believe? Do they cling to their churches as pillars of stability and permanence in a time of confusion and change? Finally, are they as opposed to religious change as some observers argue? (Middle-American Catholics, for example, do not seem at all to be opposed to change in the birth-control teaching.) There is little doubt that at times Middle Americans are offended by the elitist rhetoric used by certain of their clergy, but it is at least plausible to argue that one can dislike certain of the clichés of the liberal elitist rhetoric and still not be opposed to social change (Greeley, 1971).

There are also acute religious problems in the affluent suburb. The whole literature of suburban *Angst,* which has appeared since the end of World War II, ought to leave us in no doubt about how plagued the upper-middle-class professional is about questions of meaning and belonging, even if he does not always ask them explicitly. But even if we do not agree with the Cheever-Updike view of American suburbia, we are forced to concede that those offspring of suburbia who inhabit the counterculture are profoundly concerned about religious questions; frequently, they are even bizarrely concerned. Whether, then, one is poor or struggling or affluent, one does not seem able to escape questions of meaning, and the answers to such questions are bound to affect the consideration of the problems and worries and opportunities of urban life.

The interested researcher would also want to know what the various religious traditions think of the city. A number of writers have argued that the American intellectual spirit has always been antagonistic toward the city, at least from the time of Nathaniel Hawthorne. As one young woman remarked to me, "If Hawthorne were alive today, he would never have come any closer to Chicago than La Grange." One could legitimately ask the various American religious traditions whether they are capable of generating a vision of urban life: of harmony amid diversity, of serenity amid excitement, of cultural challenge amid economic productivity, and the generation of urban values around which social reform might be directed. If the religious traditions—secular or sacred—are not able to produce a vision of the Good Urban Life, then where are such visions to come from?

Finally, the recent concern about physical environment has about it a certain religious aura and at least implies certain ideas about the nature of the Real. If the so-called "ecological movement" is to be more than a passing fancy among limited elite groups, it will have to be anchored in the fundamental interpretive scheme of average Americans. The researcher concerned with urban problems would want to know whether concern with the physical environment is compatible with the basic religious traditions of American society and whether in fact it might represent a return to forgotten insights of these religious traditions; or, on the contrary, it is possible—as some have argued—that Christianity is of its very nature indifferent to the physical environment (a position which is hard on St. Francis of

Assisi). In either case, it should be obvious that man's fundamental meaning systems are bound to have a deep effect on the attitudes toward the physical environment.

If researchers are concerned about these aspects of urban religion and about how the religious traditions are passed on from generation to generation, they will have to investigate the three basic educational institutions—family, church, and school—and parcel out the differing contributions of each. They will also, of course, want to evaluate these contributions as well as to delineate them. The question of the evaluation of the impact of religious education is important, it seems to me, for three reasons. First, it is of fascinating theoretical interest to learn what are the effective means of transmitting fundamental values and what are the ineffective means. Second, it seems appropriate to evaluate the contribution of religion to the improvement of the quality of urban life. Finally, from the point of view of the churches, or indeed from the point of view of any human institution concerned with the transmission of fundamental values, there is excellent reason to ask whether one institutional transmission is more effective than another or whether one set of techniques promises greater payoff than another set of techniques. Is religious education more effectively carried on by the family or the church or the school? More precisely, under what circumstances do which combinations of these three institutions seem to promise the greatest payoff? And within the classroom, or for that mater the Sunday school class or the family discussion group, what kinds of instructional methods are likely to be most effective?

Those who propose to evaluate religious education will encounter certain special problems. First of all, religious educators in some circumstances are sacred persons, and any criticism of religious education runs the risk of being taken as a criticism of the sacred. Furthermore, one is dealing not merely with sacred persons but with sacred doctrines, presumed to have a certain inherent effectiveness. If one exposes young people to these doctrines for a certain period of time, it is taken for granted that the doctrines will affect their attitudes and behavior. He who asserts, on the basis of evaluation research, that a given method of religious instruction or a given institution of religious instruction is having no effect runs the risk of being accused not merely of incompetent research but also of having no respect for sacred doctrine. For if he respected sacred doctrine, he ought to know that it most certainly has an effect on the students that hear it.

There is, of course, an extremely serious methodological problem in trying to evaluate the effect of either Sunday schools or parochial schools on the attitudes and behavior of the students who attend them. It is precisely those from the most religious families who are the most likely to participate in religious education. If one merely compares those who have had religious education with those who have not had such education, without holding constant the family religiousness, one has no way of knowing whether what one discovers is a family effect or a school effect.

Peter Rossi and I (1966) wrestled with this problem at great length. We came up with a methodology that still seems serviceable. The basic finding to emerge from our research was that the greatest payoff of religious education comes when the child of a religious family goes to a religious school. In other words, neither the school by itself nor the devout family by itself produces the same effect that can be obtained when the two are working in concert. It was also interesting to note that in the absence of the devout family background the school had relatively little effect on the attitudes and behavior of the parochial school graduate in adult life.

The evaluation of religious education, particularly urban religious education, then, is appropriate, interesting, feasible, difficult, and, at least in some sense, necessary. My own feeling is that this evaluation research will occur only in a context of close cooperation between university research scholars and church organizations. I am convinced that such evaluation research would be immensely profitable for both the churches and to the scholars and quite possibly also to the life of the city (though I am under no illusion as to how extensive one can expect the contribution of social research to be to the improvement of urban life). Robert Havighurst, of course, was a man who pioneered this sort of research a long, long time ago. There have been only a few to follow in his footsteps, and while cooperation between the churches and the universities in evaluating the impact of religious education wiuld be desirable, only the most optimistic would describe such cooperation as likely in the immediate future. It will require many more men like Robert Havighurst before such cooperation is taken as a matter of course.

References

GEERTZ, C. *Islam Observed*. New Haven, Conn.: Yale University Press, 1970.
GREELEY, A. M. "Political Attitudes among American White Ethnics."

Paper presented at meetings of the American Political Science Association, Chicago, September 10, 1971.

GREELEY, A. M. AND ROSSI, P. L. *The Education of Catholic Americans.* Chicago: Aldine, 1966.

LUCKMANN, T. *The Invisible Religion.* New York: Macmillan, 1967.

PART IV

Systems Perspectives

What are the kinds of schools found in metropolitan areas? What values do they embody? Can education be spread further over the life span? How can the processes of educational decision making and dissemination be made more effective? These are the kind of questions raised in Part Four.

Levine asks how schools can meet the diverse goals of social and cultural groups within urban areas. He distinguishes between two types of schools operating today: (1) "postmodern" schools for middle-class children—schools that focus on the meaning of life, self-identity, and new value systems; (2) "premodern" schools in slum and working-class areas of the city—schools that have not met the challenge of inculcating the rudimentary academic skills needed in our advanced industrial society. Employing systems-analysis concepts, he identifies several ways to incorporate vital reforms: overall internal differentiation, multiple feedback and facilitating mechanisms, and increasing goal specificity for subunits with the system.

Stein and Miller, using economic analysis, identify great inefficiency in the practice of requiring all formal education in the individual's preproductive years. They recommend "recurrent education," originally developed in Sweden; that is, education and train-

173

ing made available throughout the life cycle. Programs for recurrent education are not widely recognized, but they already constitute a healthy response to problems of urban education. They are represented in proprietary schools, manpower training, and other forms of continuing education. If well organized, they are likely to meet the needs of their special students: the disadvantaged, dropouts, reentrants to the job market, and those who wish to shift or upgrade their occupation.

Wynne discusses some ways of implementing the changes advocated by some of the other writers in this volume. Drawing on dissemination research in agriculture and pharmaceutical medicine, he argues that we need a new theoretical framework for understanding and improving the processes of communicating research findings and carrying out their implications in the schools. He lists thirteen characteristics of an effective dissemination system.

Chase asserts that research and development, even if integrated and systematic, will not bring about constructive changes in urban education unless adopting school systems continually assess local needs, involve all educational interest groups in decision-making, and specify objectives as well as alternative means for new programs. He describes an effort of this kind carried out by the Development Division of the Dallas Independent School District and concludes with some observations on what can help make such efforts successful in the future.

CHAPTER **15**

Effective Education in Metroplex School Systems

Daniel U. Levine

$\mathcal{B}$ecause metropolitan areas have
become increasingly stratified geographically by socioeconomic class,
schools in the metropolitan system of education can be classified according to whether the overriding educational needs of their students
are primarily those of premodern or postmodern settings, or somewhere in between. The predominantly working-class school—particularly the heavily lower-working-class school in the inner-city core—
can be considered "premodern" in the sense that many or most of its
pupils are not acquiring the rudimentary academic skills needed to
function adequately in an advanced industrial society. Academic
achievement in these schools is very low, truancy rates are very high,
and in general educators have not figured out how to deliver effective
education in the face of lower-working-class habits (particularly the
"street culture") associated with the transmission of poverty and
failure from one generation to the next. The predominantly middle-

class school—particularly the heavily upper-middle-class school in "exclusive" neighborhoods—can be considered "postmodern." That is, students in middle-class schools typically achieve well academically and can certainly maintain their social status or avoid downward mobility if they want to do so. Therefore, the major problems in educating students in postmodern schools involve such imperatives as the need to find meaning in life, the search for a stable and satisfying identity in a world abundant with options, and the construction of new value systems to replace those outdated by rapid change in the social and physical environment.

When students in postmodern schools discover—not necessarily as a matter of conscious volition—that the most important task in their lives is to come to grips with such problems, they tend to become alienated from the school, with its traditional premodern emphasis on academic achievement and vocational preparation. As they proceed through school, they then tend to invest less effort in reaching these goals. Consequently, it may seem that their main problem is with traditional subject matter; and millions of Americans apparently believe that somehow postmodern youth can be adequately educated if only teachers will require students to "knuckle under" and master the content of premodern curricula. Such a perspective, however, is not only regressive but tragically unrealistic, since it ignores the fact that alienation from traditional education in the postmodern school arises from problems in identity and meaning rather than from inability to handle traditional subject matter.

By this time it should be clear why the title of this chapter refers to a "metroplex" system of education. The metropolitan system of education includes a variety of schools which face differing problems (or, at least, mixtures of problems) and should have varying goals and programs. Not only will such variations continue to exist for the indefinite future, but they probably will become both more pronounced and more subtly compounded as urban society continues to grow more internally complex and specialized. Only a few of the differing types of school settings in the metropolitan area have been described in my typology of "postmodern," "neo-modern," and "premodern" schools, but these basic types are sufficient to make the point that differentiation within the metropolis should be a conditioning force in determining goals and programs for any given school. At the same time, the needs for certain kinds of pluralistic educational experience and for educational attention to racial and ethnic identity can be seen as common strands throughout the system, even though their meaning and importance also vary somewhat from one community or school to another. Complexity is thus an inherent if not defining characteristic of the metropolitan system of education.

If it is true that the educational programs developed and implemented in metropolitan schools not only should bear some relationship to the rapidly changing metropolitan society outside the school (which I assume is self-evident)' but also should vary in accordance with the major problems which urban development poses for a particular school's student body, then the most important task of decision makers in the metropolitan educational system is that of ensuring that schools identify and effectively implement appropriate programs.

Appropriate Educational Programs

My purpose in the remainder of this paper is to sketch out a few principles of organization and administration that policy makers and top-level administrators in metroplex school systems should observe in working to revise and implement educational programs appropriate for the metropolitan setting. For this purpose, a problem-solving focus—aimed at overcoming innumerable obstacles to implementation throughout the educational system—is necessary. In addition, implications for organizational functioning and administrative practice must be spelled out.

First of all, *the organization and administration of an effective and appropriate metroplex educational system require considerable internal differentiation.* That is, units or subsystems within the larger organization do not operate with identical or even similar structures and are not expected to follow standardized administrative approaches throughout the organization; instead, each unit is designed and operated explicitly in accordance with the nature of the tasks to be accomplished, the type of clientele it serves, the technology it is to utilize, and other particularistic aspects of its internal and external environment (Lawrence and Lorsch, 1969). For example, a unit that utilizes a stable technology to accomplish a narrowly defined range of clear-cut goals can and, other things being equal, should depend more on rules or regulations in coordinating resources and processing inputs than a unit in which a changing technology is used to achieve amorphous goals.

A perfect example of the wisdom of differentiation within metropolitan education can be delineated by comparing the somewhat different problems and goals of premodern schools in the inner city and postmodern schools in outlying parts of the city or the suburbs. As noted in the previous section, the primary challenge in the postmodern school is to help the young develop competence and wisdom in establishing a satisfying and productive identity and in learning to cope with freedom and choice in a postindustrial metropolitan society. But education for identity and freedom clearly is not the kind of highly specific and well-understood goal that can be attained by means of any presently available, established technology; hence, as Arnstine (1971) has pointed out, traditional bureaucratic organization exemplifying close supervision and coordination of resources is not a very suitable means for accomplishing these educational purposes: "A bureaucracy may promote efficiency, but a group has to know where it is going if it is to try to be efficient about it. If a group's goals are *not* clear-cut and definite—if the members of the group are in fact permitted the freedom and even encouraged to change those goals— then questions of efficiency become secondary. Indeed, efforts to be efficient will even interfere with attempts to create better or more appropriate goals."

By way of contrast, in a predominantly low-income school in the inner city the immediate and clear-cut goal of equipping students with basic academic skills must be accomplished before primary attention can be given to broader, less clearly definable goals—if only because both parents and students insist on it. Since the goal is specific and the means to achieve it are available, administrative and organizational approaches stressing close supervision and systematic coordination of existing resources have proved more successful than approaches that depart markedly from these aspects of rational bureaucracy. Following this reasoning, premodern schools in the inner city necessarily will be organized and administered somewhat differently from postmodern schools elsewhere in the metropolis.

This is not to say, however, that inner-city schools can be successful if their organizational patterns perpetuate the dysfunctional aspects of "rational" bureaucracy. For one thing, rational bureaucracy (that is, close and highly coordinated supervision and leadership) will not succeed in the inner city unless it is tempered by fundamental organizational modifications designed to locate responsibility and ensure accountability (Lonoff, 1971). Nor does it mean that simplistic efficiency criteria can be applied in designing organizational structures and determining how they are to function; for various reasons, it is as imperative to depart from traditional efficiency considerations in the inner city as in the middle-income school and to scrap whatever aspects of traditional bureaucracy obstruct the educational necessity for individualized instruction (Levine, 1971).

A second principle: *Effective delivery of appropriate education in a metroplex system of education requires multiple feedback and facilitating mechanisms for implementing programs in the schools.* If the emphasis in metropolitan schools is to be on solving a multitude of day-to-day, situation-specific problems that arise unpredictably in different parts of the system, organizational means must be invented and made available to ensure that problems first are identified and then actually are dealt with. Within a unit of the system, this necessitates new types of power relationships and decision-making arrangements as well as changes in reward practices to ensure that problems and interests as perceived by each group (parents, teachers, students) directly concerned with the unit are given serious attention rather than swept under the rug. From the perspective of the larger system, which is the main concern of this paper, the task of transforming individual school units into problem-solving organizations can be envisioned as one of establishing a variety of mechanisms to help identify and correct unit malfunctions. Such mechanisms can be classified under the broad headings "feedback" and "facilitating mechanisms."

Feedback mechanisms. Examples of mechanisms that would serve primarily to provide feedback at various levels in the metroplex education system or in the system as a whole include the following: First, *problem-assessment documents for each unit and for the system as a whole.* Serving a function analogous to the President's "State of the Union" message, problem-assessment documents should identify problems according to priority and should be presented to decision-making congresses, such as a teacher-parent-student cabinet, which have real power to take action to clear up the problems identified. Problem-assessment documents should be distributed as widely as possible, and a time schedule should be set up requiring administrators to make public reports on progress toward the solution of problems identified in the documents.

Second, *ombudsmen and inspectors.* The basic distinction between an ombudsman and an inspector, as the terms are used here, is that the ombudsman responds to complaints or reports of malfunctioning while the inspector takes initiative to identify malfunctions in the operation of units throughout the system.

Third, *information and evaluation subsystems.* Much excellent work has been done in the past few years to develop information-collection and evaluation approaches that are directly and practically useful in improving the delivery of educational services in the schools. The evaluation model currently under development at the UCLA Center for the Study of Evaluation, for example, clarifies the various steps (beginning with Needs Assessment and continuing through

Program Planning, Implementation Evaluation, Process Evaluation, and Outcome Evaluation) involved in establishing a comprehensive evaluation system (Klein, Fernstermacher, and Albin, 1971). Based on his experience as director of research in a large public school system, Mazur (1971) suggests a number of ways in which an information systems unit might work closely with an operating school unit to enhance the latter's capacity for achieving its particular set of goals. For instance, computer printouts prepared by the information system and returned to the schools might red-flag the students who are achieving in the lowest quartile, and principals might be asked to report every ten weeks to help improve performance for each student thus identified. Extensive analysis of individual test items and cluster of items might accompany the printouts in order to aid in identifying areas of strength and weakness in the instructional program.

Facilitating mechanisms. While a good deal of effort now is being invested in the development of feedback mechanisms, very little attention in theory and almost none in practice is being given to the possibilities of establishing mechanisms for directly helping individual school units become more effective in achieving their goals. The following possibilities might be of great value in this regard:

First, *expediters and facilitators.* The position of expediter or facilitator as envisioned here would be equivalent to that of a roving troubleshooter with definite authority to circumvent bureaucratic impediments to the attainment of organizational goals. For example, a Deputy Superintendent for Facilitation might have the authority to sign requisitions and obtain delivery of supplies for schools where requests have become clogged in normal channels for processing, approval, and distribution of materials. Similarly, a Facilitator for Staffing might be given power to provide temporary authorization for hiring personnel whose applications for certification are unduly delayed in the normal process of personnel selection and placement. A position such as facilitator or expediter would provide more definite authority to correct organizational malfunctions than does an ombudsman position as customarily defined. A good example of a new facilitator role is that of the "catalytic" coordinator—a position developed in the Corning Glass Works Company and used with apparent success. A catalytic agent differs from the typical consultant in that he is a permanent employee of the organization and thus is in a position to supply information and advice related to internal affairs of the organization which an outside consultant could not be expected to have at hand. His task is to work with each member of a project team and the team as a whole "to ensure that all data are brought to light and properly evaluated. . . . Stated in its simplest terms, his task is twofold . . . he must act as information collector, or at least catalyze the collection of missing information; [and] where all the available information has been collected, he must assist the team in using it to reach the best possible strategy for the project" (Chambers, Mulbick, and Goodman, 1971). A somewhat similar position is that of the "integrator" (Lawrence and Lorsch, 1967).

Second, *school-support units.* School districts frequently use outside consultants for a variety of purposes, but much more valuable in the long run would be the establishment of support units to work with school faculties more intensively and on a more long-range basis than is now the case with respect to outside consultants or even in-service training or staff development departments where they do exist. A school faculty, after all, is similar to what Landau (1971) calls a "traditional society" inasmuch as schools are social systems "not prone to change. . . . When change agents are introduced here, novelty is even more threatening. For new roles defy those of sacred tradition, new decision criteria appear as heresy, and new systems of organization challenge the gods. Planning out, directing, and engineering a developmental program assaults the foundations of such societies." When one attempts to introduce change into a traditional (formerly closed)' system, a member of that society tends to lose "confidence in the validity of his habitual responses, in his whole unquestioned scheme for interpreting life. . . . With the probability structure of the old system disrupted, 'typicality' or 'normality' has been lost, but new modalities have not been gained." Landau argues that "intermediate" or "mediating" institutions are necessary to "close the acknowledged gap between administrator and community," to "pair more effectively with indigenous systems," and to provide "closer coupling . . . [in generating] the normative relations and action patterns that open a closed set." This is precisely the function that school-support units should perform in implementing change within the metroplex system of education. To discharge this function successfully, a school-support unit should be small and flexible and should have access to resources allowing it to expand rapidly as needed in working with an individual school. It should not be required to do very much fixed, comprehensive planning in advance of staff development activities initiated in the field.

Third, *efforts to improve the schools of the metropolis should follow a focused, school-by-school approach to change.* This principle follows directly from the preceding discussion concerning the desirability of establishing school-support units to work intensively with

individual schools. As long as resources for school reform are not unlimited, available resources should be focused on reforming whatever
number of schools can be really changed—a single school if necessary
—rather than diluting them ineffectually in an attempt to help too
many schools at once. It would be better to err in the direction of
overconcentration (waste) of resources and at least learn what works
and what does not work in a particular type of school than to take the
chance that school-reform efforts will fail because they are under-
financed.

In this regard it must be admitted that we simply do not know
whether focused-change programs at the secondary level can work,
no matter how well supported and carried out. At the elementary
level, there is considerable evidence that, given proper leadership
and support, faculty attitudes and behaviors in metropolitan area
schools can undergo a rather thorough transformation. To my knowledge, however, no one has yet demonstrated that this can be done at
the secondary level without first removing at least half the faculty in a
school and replacing them with personnel who are oriented toward
change and do not share the typical secondary teacher's preoccupation
with subject-matter learnings.

The focused-change principle fits well with studies that Platt
(1970) has conducted to determine how change pervasive enough to
affect a large, complex system generally takes place. Platt points out
that rapid transitions ("hierarchical restructuring") in such systems
occur in "quantum jumps," which can be detected in phenomena as
diverse as biological evolution and scientific revolutions and which in
human affairs are characterized by a "sudden collective change of
awareness or flash of understanding." Although "it is not at all clear
whether self-structuring hierarchical jumps of this kind can be to any
appreciable degree anticipated or guided," any restructuring that does
occur "has to be built around the largest well-functioning subsystems."
Thus, even though it is not certain that we can engineer a sudden
transformation throughout a metroplex system of education, which is
composed of many malfunctioning or conflicting subsystems, such
transformation will be most likely to occur if focused change first is
brought about in a critical number of its component units. This point
of view in no way justifies running so-called "pilot projects" to avoid
making major changes in the system as a whole; on the contrary, it
suggests that real change throughout the larger system requires a
combination of focused change in a manageable number of units with
an overall plan for concomitant encouragement and introduction of
change in other parts of the system.

Fourth, *if metropolitan schools are to implement suitable educational programs effectively, policy makers can never forget that personnel and leadership are more important than the most advanced administrative approaches and the finest plans for change.* Differentiation in administrative and organizational approaches within the larger system can make it possible to deal intelligently with diversity, but freedom to mold school structures and programs in accordance with the nature of the task to be accomplished is meaningless unless an administrator uses it wisely and courageously in a particular situation. A multitude of feedback and facilitating mechanisms are necessary to identify and correct malfunctions in any part of a system or the system as a whole, but ultimately even the most comprehensive and praiseworthy set of mechanisms to accomplish these purposes is useless without widespread determination to use them successfully.

Fifth, *complexity should be avoided within operating units of the metroplex educational system.* Educators long have been aware of the dangers of overcapitalization in technology. When a large number of resources are used to purchase a particular system of expensive materials and equipment, commitments thereby incurred may make it politically if not pragmatically impossible to adopt alternate materials and methods for many years to come. Introducing complex administrative and organizational techniques often will have analogous results, even though such overinvestment in complex structures is less visible than is elaborate equipment that provides a tangible monument to organizational folly. Just as some school districts have been boxed into a corner by overcommitting their resources to an expensive technology, so others are likely to run off the track by investing in a complicated information system without first making sure that personnel throughout the district have the knowledge, incentive, and commitment to use it effectively.

Recognizing that metropolitan systems of education necessarily will be exceedingly complex and internally differentiated is not the same as saying that a particular unit should be any more complex in its structure than is absolutely necessary to obtain its goals successfully. Just the opposite. A good rule of thumb would be to strive for as much simplicity as possible in the organizational approach used in any given unit.

For example, complicated modular scheduling techniques introduced in many high schools have generated overwhelming problems for administrators, teachers, and students; but recent experience in several newer schools (John Adams High in Portland, Oregon; Northwest High in Shawnee Mission, Kansas) has shown that the same goals can be achieved without or with only a skeletal version of modular organization. Similarly, elementary educators seldom have been able to succeed in implementing nongraded forms of organization (which are deceptively simple in concept but actually require complex internal reorganization and structuring); current efforts to implement the multi-unit form of organization are demonstrating that the same goals are attainable without complex schemes to eliminate graded structures.

Particularly when it is kept in mind that changes in one aspect or segment of organizational structure or practice are unlikely to work unless concomitant and compatible changes are made in all other major aspects and segments (Heathers, 1971; Janowitz, 1970), the importance of striving for as much simplicity as possible becomes immediately apparent. Unnecessary complexity in the design of the structure or program for a school increases the number of points at which malfunctions can occur, multiplies the difficulties of dealing with malfunctions when they do occur, and exponentially expands the task of taking account of all segments in a well-planned proposal for systemic change. In addition, it is easy to become so immersed in the complications (not to say the pseudo-scientific terminology) of a "grand design" for change or improvement that one all but loses touch with reality in the schools. Beware the hawkers of plans that entail the accomplishment of simultaneous change in countless aspects of organizational structure and practice, as much as those who propose segmental change only.

References

ARNSTINE, D. "Freedom and Bureaucracy in the Schools." In V. F. Haubrich (Ed.), *Freedom, Bureaucracy and Schooling*. Washington, D.C.: ASCD, 1971.

CHAMBERS, J. C., MULBICK, S. K., AND GOODMAN, D. A. "Catalytic Agent for Effective Planning." *Harvard Business Review*, 1971, *49*(2), 111–115.

HEATHERS, G. "Guidelines for Reorganizing the School and the Classroom." In M. Hillson and R. T. Higman (Eds.), *Change and Innovation in Elementary and Secondary Organization*. New York: Holt, Rinehart, and Winston, 1971. Pp. 252–255.

JANOWITZ, M. *Institution Building in Urban Organization*. New York: Russell Sage Foundation, 1970.

KLEIN, S., FERNSTERMACHER, G., AND ALBIN, M. C. "The Center's Changing Evaluation Model." *Evaluation Comment,* 1971, *2,* 9–12.

LANDAU, M. "Linkage, Coding, and Intermediacy. A Strategy for Institution-Building." *Journal of Comparative Administration,* 1971, *1,* 1419–1423.

LAWRENCE, P. R., AND LORSCH, J. W. "New Management Job: The Integrator." *Harvard Business Review,* 1967, *45*(6), 142–151.

LAWRENCE, P. R., AND LORSCH, J. W. *Organization and Environment.* Homewood, Ill.: Irwin, 1969.

LEVINE, D. U. "Concepts of Bureaucracy in Urban School Reform." *Phi Delta Kappan,* 1971, *52,* 329–333.

LONOFF, R. "Supervisory Practices That Promote Academic Achievement in a New York City School." *Phi Delta Kappan,* 1971, *52*(6), 338–340.

MAZUR, J. L. "Operationalizing Accountability in the School System." Paper presented at the 1971 Annual Meeting of the American Education Research Association, New York City, February 5, 1971.

PLATT, J. "Hierarchical Restructuring." *Ekistics,* 1970, *30,* 272–275.

CHAPTER **16**

Recurrent Education

Bruno Stein and S. M. Miller

𝕮𝕮𝕮 𝕮𝕮𝕮 𝕮𝕮𝕮 𝕮𝕮𝕮 𝕮𝕮𝕮 𝕮𝕮𝕮 𝕮𝕮𝕮 𝕮𝕮𝕮

There is increasing dissatisfaction with the way in which education is acquired. Traditionally, education takes place during an individual's early years, after which—for most people—it stops. Tradition, however, is a poor excuse for maintaining a system that increasingly fails to cope with the needs of an urban and technologically oriented society. Such a society requires flexibility from its members—an ability to adapt to rapid change. The traditional mode of education, with its once-and-for-all preparation for life, strengthens rigidity. It also has other undesirable social and economic consequences.

In the standard economic model of the life cycle, education is treated as an input of human capital that generally takes place during an individual's reproductive years. This may be called the front-end-load model. Investment decisions are made on the schoolchild's behalf, out of funds provided by parents and by the taxpayers. When the child reaches his teens, full-time work becomes an alternative to school, thus altering the cost of the investment, which now expands to include the cost of the forgone work opportunity. At this stage, the model

186

assumes that the child is a choice maker who surveys his alternatives and "rationally" decides whether or not to continue school and, if the former, what kind of schooling to pursue. To be sure, the choices are made under a set of genetic, social, and economic constraints. More to the point, they are made under the conditions of uncertainty, ignorance, and emotional turmoil that characterize adolescence. Later in life, the dissatisfied individual can blame himself and his parents for a wrong decision. As each incremental education step becomes "higher" and more specialized, the cost of reversing erroneous choices rises exponentially. At some point, it approaches infinity. What is done cannot be undone. The summation of a series of choices (whether or not to complete high school, whether or not to go to college, what to major in, whether or not to complete college, and so on) constitutes a lifetime commitment.

The economic reasoning found in the standard model is popular with policy makers. It does not require any reexamination of basic educational modes and institutions. This makes it easier to plan and to sell the plans to the body politic. The prejudice in its favor is confirmed by conclusions drawn from the usual popular and simplistic benefit-cost analysis. In the analysis, benefits are measured as the present value of the estimated earnings attributable to the added education. At any relevant rate of discount, benefits measured in this fashion are greater from a dollar added to early school programs than from a dollar added to adult education, since younger people have a longer remaining work life than those who are in mid-career. A better and broader measure of benefits would yield different results, but no such measure has yet been developed. In the meantime, hard-nosed planners will have us believe that a bad measure is better than no measure at all.

Inequities and Inefficiencies of Traditional Education

The in-school front-end learning process has many functions aside from the transmission of knowledge. It is an aging vat for young people prior to their entry into the labor market. It allocates educational capital, and therefore income, in a way that largely preserves the existing income distribution. It gives youngsters a tolerance for tedium that is useful for boring jobs. It provides credentials that do not necessarily reflect the possession of a set of abilities for any particular job. However, the standard model of the front-end educational load operates in ways that are socially inequitable and economically inefficient.

The social inequity is both vertical (along the socioeconomic scale) and horizontal (among people of the same socioeconomic status). The vertical inequity is obvious and has been amply documented by data from Project Talent. There, it was found that high-ability students of low socioeconomic status are less likely to go to college than low-ability students of high socioeconomic status. The inequity is compounded by racial and ethnic discrimination. It would be a mistake, however, to consider the inequity as principally a race issue, as is frequently done, since, within racial and ethnic categories, it operates along social-class lines.

Horizontal inequity, the unequal treatment of equals, may seem to be a less pressing problem, but the magnitude of this problem is really not well known. The labor market operates in mysterious ways, so that of three young men of roughly equal social class, race, mechanical aptitude, intelligence, and education, one might easily become a well-paid construction worker, the second a medium-paid auto worker, and the last an unemployed coal miner. Fortuitous as well as economic circumstances are likely to determine these occupational paths. To call them "fate" is to leave more to happenstance than is either necessary or desirable.

The economic inefficiency of the front-end-load model comes from its waste of human resources. This simple proposition can manifest itself in rather sophisticated forms—in structural unemployment, for example, which is found when a poorly trained labor force coexists with job vacancies, or, stemming from this, in the existence of a poor trade-off between price stability and unemployment. The latter means that inflation occurs while unemployment is relatively high. Since price stability has a high priority in the minds of fiscal and monetary policy makers, unemployment rates in the 5–6 per cent range may easily become permanent minima rather than temporary economic phenomena connected with recessions.

Although educational reforms are not offered as a panacea for our economic and social ills, it should be clear that the standard educational model is a poor way to do business.

Alternative Models

Alternatives already exist to the front-end-load model. They are a response to private and social needs and are brought into being by both the political and the market mechanism. Thus, high school equivalence examinations are available to the ambitious dropout. Night schools offer collegiate education, some even as far as the Ph.D. (although high-status schools *take pride* in their refusal to do this).

Proprietary (profit-making)' schools offer training in a large number of technical skills. Employers have training programs, both formal and informal, and some sponsor educational programs not only for executives but also for workers. Manpower-training programs have become a major government activity in the past decade and are widely touted as the remedy for poverty and excessive welfare payments. Clearly, alternative models of education are in great use (although exact information on this is imperfect). However, they suffer by invidious comparison with the front-end load. As the exception rather than the rule, they evoke images of the *Education of H*Y*M*A*N K*A*P*L*A*N* or of specialized (and often stigmatized) social programs for the needy.

Adult education and training is usually viewed as a one-shot corrective for some particular problem rather than as a process that can be repeated as someone develops and encounters new opportunities as well as new needs. This characteristic is especially true of the publicly sponsored programs. For example, we have basic education courses for functional illiterates; but these courses are usually independent of any next step. Similarly, we have retraining programs to meet various employment crises; clients are expected to enroll in whatever may be available, without reference to advancement or to the next technological change that can disemploy them again. The retraining, often as not, is for another dead-end job to replace the earlier one that disappeared. As more and more people and their employers think in terms of career ladders, the need for educational ladders becomes greater. Change may be nearer than many might think.

The existing delivery system in adult education is hopelessly chaotic. The potential student who has some need or yearning for more education finds the educational marketplace full of unconnected bits and pieces. The best he can hope for is a program here or a program there. Despite the vast amount of education that is available, there is little by way of linkage.

The term "recurrent education" can be used to denote a system that makes education and training available, in various doses, to individuals over their lifetimes. The concept, developed in Sweden and refined by the Center for Educational Reform and Innovation of the Organization for European Cooperational Development, presents an alternative to conventional education. On the one hand, it treats adult education as a system of services that provide a variety of educational paths. On the other hand, it differs from the usual concept of adult education in that it treats the education of an individual as a process that is not necessarily completed during youth but may *recur* during the person's life.

A system of recurrent education can provide the element of flexibility needed to overcome the inequity and inefficiency inherent in the dominant position of the front-end-load model. The beneficiaries would be not merely the system's clients but also the entire community, whose stock of human resources would be enlarged and improved.

Recurrent education, the policy suggestion that we advocate, is not a projection for the distant future. In fact, it may already be emerging from the chaos of continuing education, peripheral education, and the other parts of the alternative educational near-system. Only within the last few years have social-policy analysts discovered this area of activity. Attempts to measure its extent have foundered, however, on the difficulty of formulating a commonly accepted definition (Moses, 1970, p. 22). Moreover, data are not easily available because most adult education activities are peripheral to the main purpose of the organizations engaged in this activity (U.S. Office of Education, 1970b, p. iii.). It is not surprising that estimates of the number of students in adult education range from 13 million to 44 million, with an intermediate estimate of 25 million by the National Opinion Research Center (Cortright, 1971; Moses, 1970; Johnstone and Rivera, 1965, pp. 1–2). A British scholar who surveyed university adult education in New York commented with despair on the statistical confusion that marks the topic, and her task was, after all, a relatively narrow one (Ellwood, 1967, p. 2).

Nevertheless, it is useful to present a summary of existing measurements of adult education. One reason is to stimulate further research. Most data count the number of students, and do this imperfectly. The most comprehensive of such studies, the Office of Education's *Participation Survey,* has not been published yet. It is a household survey, attached to the May 1969 *Current Population Survey* (repeated in 1972). Preliminary information indicates that it may have undercounted students by a very serious margin of error. There is no complete establishment survey from which to get information on the delivery system itself, its costs, and other data that would be needed for planning purposes.

A more important reason is to show that the basis for a vast recurrent-education system already exists. It would not have to be built from scratch but could make use of ongoing activities.

In effect, a third-tier educational program has been evolving. It is neither the first tier of locally run, local and state-financed (with recent increases in federal funds) public education nor the second tier of private and parochial education. The two tiers constitute "the core educational institutions" with which Moses (1970) has been concerned. The third tier, with many components but few connections, is built of long-standing activities and new programs like the federally sponsored manpower programs. Because of its diversity, the similarities in purpose and the enormity of numbers have been obscured. There has been a failure consequently to recognize the contemporary significance of third-tier or recurrent education and to move rapidly toward a system.

We have adapted Moses' categories for the purpose of grouping data on numbers of students on some consistent basis. Our eight categories include organizational programs, proprietary programs, manpower and antipoverty programs, correspondence schools, educational television programs, continuing education at the college level, adult education below the college level, and "other" programs.

Organizational programs. This category refers to programs conducted by private business, labor unions, government, and the military to train and upgrade their employees and members. Moses estimates that in 1965 approximately 14.5 million adults were involved in organizational education programs in the United States. Yet this is, at best, a minimum estimate (aside from its outdatedness). In the case of business, the researcher soon discovers that the relevant figures may be subsumed under categories other than education and cannot easily be abstracted from company reports and similar sources. As for labor unions, one cannot even hazard a guess as to the size of this sector, since not even the AFL-CIO keeps statistics on labor educational activity.

Governments engage in considerable education and training of employees. In the fiscal year ending June 1969, the federal government spent at least 104 million dollars to train slightly more than one million civil servants (U.S. Civil Service Commission, 1970, pp. 95, 124–126). No aggregate figures are available for state and local governments.

"Join the army and learn a trade" is an old slogan. Excluding the professional schools, service academies, and ROTC programs, the Department of Defense reports 367,858 servicemen registered as students with the United States Armed Forces Institute, where general education at the high school and college levels is made available to servicemen in their off-duty hours through correspondence courses (Ducey, 1971). An additional 240,875 servicemen are registered in other off-duty educational programs (Ducey, 1971). Here, the reader will note the definitional problem and its data-gathering consequences.

The Armed Forces Institute spans four of our categories: organizational, correspondence, continuing education at the college level, and adult education below college level. This kind of overlapping plagues the subject, and considerable disaggregation is needed to disentangle the figures in order to avoid double counting.

Technical-training programs in the armed forces are also very significant, but we were able to locate figures only for the army. These show that 380,000 soldiers received technical noncombat training in fiscal year 1971—in programs ranging from six to eight weeks to more than a year, depending on the complexity of the skill involved (Quigley, 1971). With the rest of the armed forces included, the real figure must be over a half million.

A general problem in locating appropriate figures is that data on numbers of servicemen receiving training are derived from cost figures. The Department of Defense accounting system does not, by and large, break down such costs by combat and noncombat skills. Accordingly, ordinary published data from the Department of Defense must be used with care by those like us who are not interested in adult education for combat.

Proprietary schools. These are private schools, usually run for profit, which administer programs outside of the educational "core." One order of magnitude of this activity is found in Table 1, from a study conducted by Harvey Belitsky of the Upjohn Institute for Employment Research (Belitsky, 1969, p. 9)'.

Table 1. ESTIMATED ATTENDANCE AT PROPRIETARY SCHOOLS, 1966

Type of School	No. of Schools	No. of Students
Trade and Technical	3,000	835,710
Business	1,300	439,500
Cosmetology	2,477	272,470
Barber	294	15,876
Total	7,071	1,563,556

The above numbers may be an understatement. Conversation with relevant trade associations leads us to believe that the number of trade and technical schools is closer to 7,000, with enrollments of about two million per year (P. Taylor, 1971)'. Similarly, 600,000 may be a better estimate for business school attendance. For whatever it is worth, an estimate three times as great as the above 2.6 million is given by Moses (1970, p. 22)', who calculates the number of students at 7.8 million in 1965.

Economically, proprietary schools constitute quite a lively industry. These enterprises have met the test of the marketplace; in some fashion, good or ill, they satisfy demand at prices above the cost of production, often competing with university-based continuing education programs. The profitability of the industry has attracted investment from corporations such as Bell & Howell, RCA, ITT, Time-Life, and Control Data Corporation. The willingness of customers to pay shows that there is a strong need for the services rendered by these schools, even though the industry is constantly plagued by charlatans.

Manpower and antipoverty programs. This rubric covers the entire range of federal programs operated or sponsored by the Department of Labor and the Department of Health, Education, and Welfare (exclusive of apprenticeship). Most of these were developed during the Kennedy-Johnson years and operate on the proposition that manpower training is a proper antidote to unemployment, poverty, and welfare dependency. In 1969, according to the Bureau of National Affairs (1970), some eight million people took part in these programs, at a cost of 1.7 billion dollars. In practice, some of the programs are disguised forms of income transfer payments. In many cases this was unintended; and it is the hope of their operators that the clients might become employed upon graduation. In a few cases, welfare departments put relief clients into the program in order to shift the relief payment from a federal-state account to an all-federal one. The summer program of the Neighborhood Youth Corps, however, is clearly designed to "cool" hot-temperature rioting. Expenditures display a seasonality that is unrelated to any conceivable educational or training need.

Considering their size and cost, antipoverty manpower programs have been disappointing. The confusion of purpose may be a factor, but we believe that the problem lies in the very nature of the programs: short-term, narrowly vocational programs conducted to deal with immediate crises and, in the case of the poverty population, aimed at students with more than the usual difficulty with study. A manpower-training program aimed at a broader clientele would do a better job for its entire student body. A broader clientele would include workers, both employed and unemployed, above and below the poverty line; their reasons for participation would include desire for advancement, higher income, and more satisfying work.

Correspondence schools. Learning-by-mail programs are conducted by a great variety of organizations, such as universities, government, and business and industry. Accordingly, data on correspondence education overlap with data on other types of education. The interested researcher must take care to factor them out in order to avoid double counting.

The best source of data is the National Home Study Council. A 1969 survey by that organization estimated a total home-study student body of 4.9 million, half of which consisted of students in federal and military schools (R. Taylor, 1971). Members of the National Home Study Council accounted for 1.6 million students, and nonmember private schools reported another 161,000. The remainder consisted of students in correspondence courses given by universities, religious groups, businesses, and miscellaneous organizations. Students taking courses in more than one school sometimes are counted twice, so that these data, like others, need a closer look before they can be considered additive with other educational statistics.

Television programs. Moses (1970) estimates that approximately five million adults were involved in televised "programs of instruction which are presented in a systematic manner and which allow for formal contact between the learner and the program." This does not include documentary or other special educational programs. The medium has, of course, great potential in the form of the Open University and other approaches to schools without walls. In California, for example, a group of engineers are pursuing further studies in their employer's quarters through television lectures provided by a university that is a considerable distance away.

Continuing education at the college level. A bewildering variety of courses and activities—ranging from courses in "Art Styles through the Ages" and "Sales Brokerage Practices and Techniques" to degree programs that compete with community colleges (New York University, 1971)—are included in this category. In 1969, an estimated 3.5 million adults were enrolled in this growing form of educational activity (U.S. Office of Education, 1970b). Many were taking the classic types of extension courses: foreign languages, art appreciation, and modern literature. Others were in packaged programs that lead to specific skills and certificates, such as in practical nursing, secretarial skills, bookkeeping, factory-supervision techniques, and even industrial relations. These are the same types of programs that are found in the proprietary schools. Still others were involved in courses for credit, many leading to college degrees.

Degree study for adults is available at community colleges, where the associate degree is offered, as well as at many regular colleges and universities (particularly urban ones), where degree possibilities include the associate, bachelor's, master's, and even doctorates. The availability of part-time study at any given school may be a historical accident, often having arisen from a need to fill empty buildings in the evening (the same or similar economics of overhead cost that led to the creation of many university extension divisions). Elite universities do not as a rule engage in such activity. Thus, no one can work his way through Yale Law School at night; the adult businessmen who attend Harvard Business School are on leave—usually paid leave—from their firms. Unfortunately, other universities and their subdivisions, seeking to improve their public images, have imitated the elite universities by abolishing their night schools. Alas, the simple act of excluding students in and of itself is not likely to improve either the quality or the reputation of a school, except in the eyes of its president and trustees.

Adult education below the college level. Here is an activity that enrolls four million adults (Cortright, 1971), including a half million who are learning adult basic education (U.S. Office of Education, 1970a, p. 1). We have not estimated the number of credentials and diplomas that result from all these efforts. We know, however, that a few employers are beginning to look upon the night school diploma in a new light. They are beginning to appreciate the students' energies and enterprise and to realize that the standard high school diploma proves little about the ability or even the literacy of a graduate.

The distribution (availability) of opportunities to attend night school is only partially related to the demand and need for such opportunities. The tradition of having night schools was developed in our central cities several decades ago, at a time when secondary education was far from universal, and night schools served upwardly mobile central city dwellers who sought to upgrade themselves. Suburban and other outer-city areas are far less likely to provide night-school services, even if tuition charges can be levied. It should be noted that adult basic education is most needed in the lowest income brackets. Therefore, it is not likely to be provided by local governments that have little or no commitment to adult education or by the private sector if, indeed, the potential students are too poor to make it profitable. Adult basic education is commonly associated with welfare programs. While this association enables it to get federal subsidies, it also suffers from the stigma attached to public assistance.

Other programs. Inevitably, we wind up with a category called "other." This includes the education activities of libraries, museums, YMCAs, religious groups, and various community organizations. If some of this activity seems trivial, much of it is not. And in all cases, the students are people who are making an effort to grow, to develop, to do something with themselves and their lives. They operate, here and in other categories, in a chaotic market for education and usually without information about alternatives. Nowhere does one even find a complete directory of available courses. The cost of collecting information is great in time and effort. Impulse buying, therefore, replaces informed choice; it is as wasteful in education as it is in consumer goods.

Potential Students

Obviously, it would be very useful to parallel the previous section on the institutional sponsorship of continuing education programs with an accounting of who are the students (age, sex, previous education, and work experience) in each of these programs. At this point, the best that we can do is to try to characterize in broad strokes the kinds of students involved. The four overlapping categories we employ are the disadvantaged, the college dropouts, the reentrants, and the job shifters and upgraders.

The disadvantaged. The poor and the black (the educationally deprived) have had particular trouble with schools. Consequently, their occupational and income potentials have been severely blunted. In the 1960s, many entered programs, whether labeled educational or not, in order to improve their competitive position in the labor market. With the strong emphasis on equality of opportunity and social mobility and with the continuing difficulties of schools in working effectively with the disadvantaged, they are a large body of clients for recurrent-education programs. Recurrent education is especially important to this group.

College dropouts. Many youths are dropping out of college. Continuing education programs provide later opportunities for them to get a degree or to move into more specialized training without a degree but with the chance for higher income. A twenty-four-year-old or a thirty-four-year-old student completing college or getting specialized training is different from an eighteen-year-old student in a similar position. New institutions have been developing to respond to these new needs.

Reentrants. A surprising number of people do not work continuously from school leaving to retirement. When they reenter the labor market, they frequently need to be "refreshed" or "retooled." Obviously, this situation applies to a growing number of women who reenter the labor market after their children are three or six or eighteen. Less obviously, there are many people in institutions (prisons, hospitals) who reenter the work sphere and need training (while in the institution or later) to facilitate their employment. And perhaps we should begin to think of counterculture youth who may age into returning to the "straight" world and are occupationally disadvantaged if they do not have training and education available to them.

Shifters and upgraders. Technological changes and unemployment may lead many to learn new skills. Many employed blue-collar as well as white-collar workers engage in additional training in order to be upgraded into better-paid jobs. Indeed, the upgrading of blue-collar workers may be one of the most important uses of recurrent education in the next years. (France now has extensive plans for the retraining of already working blue-collar workers.) The notion is spreading that there should not be dead-end people; that better-paid, more interesting jobs should be available to many, rather than restricted to those who received higher education when young and began on the job-promotion ladder rather than the low-ceiling route. In the future, a new group is likely to become important: people who want to shift jobs just to get variety. Thus, horizontal mobility as well as vertical mobility desires may engender considerable retraining efforts for an older generation.

Shortcomings of Current Alternative Programs

The alternatives to traditional education, as presently structured, suffer from a variety of faults: promises that will not be kept ("train at home to earn $10,000 in your spare time"), foolish demands for educational credentials (Miller and Riessman, 1968; Berg, 1970), and, far too frequently, tragically low-caliber training. Therefore, we believe that these diverse activities have promise *only* if viewed as one system. A one-system approach seems to us desirable for the following reasons:

First, the absence of a notion of a full system encourages a *low degree of comprehensiveness* in programming. The individual may not be able to find in his locale all the components needed for development.

Second, an emphasis on training by particular employers is likely to lead to the development of skills with *low transferability.* Where the program is oriented to the trainee's employer or prospective employer, the skills developed are likely to be narrow and specific, with limited capacity to be useful in other employment situations. What is needed are useful, highly transferable skills which at the same time meet a specific employer's needs.

Third, an atomistic system limits the development of a long-run program for the individual; what is required is the meshing of educational and training facilities with the needs of individuals as they emerge over time.

Fourth, the absence of a system makes it difficult to impose quality controls over programs and to connect them effectively with each other.

Fifth, when programs are discrete, disconnected activities, they may become narrowly vocationalized, so that broader considerations of developing the social competence of individuals get little attention.

Problems of Recurrent Education

What are some principal questions in the development of a system of recurrent education?

First, can we achieve systematization without stifling the innovative energies that are now inherent in the unorganized adult educational system? Its very haphazard quality may, as some argue, be a source of strength rather than weakness.

Second, how can the rigidities and faddism of public education be overcome? After Sputnik we spent billions to expand higher education for the young—the front-end load. Now we have sent men to the moon, and we have a surplus of college graduates and Ph.D.s (but not of nurses or M.D.s). Are we prepared to allocate education expenditures differently with less emphasis on the front-end and more on continuing education? We are close to guaranteeing all children fourteen to sixteen years of education. Need it be confined to children, and must it be all at once? How should funds be allocated between front-end and continuing education?

Third, will the possibility of regaining educational opportunities later in life encourage young people to be even less interested in school and lower their ability later to utilize educational possibilities? At the same time, will the core schools feel less pressure to change and improve if those in difficulty with these institutions quietly depart with everyone's confidence that somehow they will manage in the future to compensate for their present educational deprivation? Could a general result be that credentialism would be even more emphasized, since education would still play an important role and would be seemingly available to all persons at some point?

Fourth, recurrent education is expensive because of the lost time from work (opportunity costs) for adults going full time and is burdensome for those working full time and also going to school. Are there special adaptations like work sabbaticals (secured by the United Steelworkers' Union in collective bargaining) which can overcome these difficulties?

Fifth, what is a desirable administrative arrangement for the recurrent-education approach? To what extent should there be state-local control and finance, as is true of much of public education today? Should federal financing and influence be much more important than in contemporary public education? Since the students are adults and the emphasis is less on a set curriculum, should there not be high student involvement in decisions?

These are difficult questions. They make us aware that recurrent education is not an easy panacea and that it will be difficult to build on a systematic basis. On the other hand, they do not shake our confidence that recurrent education should play a significant role. One evidence of its vitality is the variety of activity occurring.

New proposals for organizing and financing the continuing education of those in the labor market are emerging with increased frequency: the open university for nonresidential, part-time students; a federally financed training allowance that individuals can offer employers; collective-bargaining provisions for educational subsidies to workers; the redesigning of job ladders and job training to promote greater mobility; the upgrading of programs, including the utilization of the fifth day as an education-training segment in firms with a four-day week. These proposals reflect an assumption that training and education need not be a once-in-a-lifetime activity and offer ways of developing recurrent education.

References

BELITSKY, A. H. *Private Vocational Schools and Their Students.* Cambridge: Schenkmann, 1969.

BERG, I. *Education and Jobs: The Great Training Robbery.* New York: Praeger, 1970.

Bureau of National Affairs, Manpower Information Service. *Reference File.* Washington, D.C., 1970.

CORTRIGHT, R. C. (Asst. Director, Division of Adult Education of the National Education Association). Personal correspondence, April 9, 1971.

DUCEY, C. A. (Captain, Office of Asst. to the Secretary of Defense for Education.) Personal communication, April 13, 1971.

ELLWOOD, C. *Survey of University Adult Education in the Metropolitan Area.* New York: New York University School of Continuing Education, 1967.

JOHNSTONE, J. W. C., AND RIVERA, R. J. *Volunteers in Learning.* Chicago: Aldine, 1965.

MILLER, S. M., AND RIESSMAN, F. *Social Class and Social Policy.* New York: Basic Books, 1968.

MOSES, S. *The Learning Force: An Approach to the Politics of Education.* Syracuse, New York: Syracuse University Research Corporation, 1970.

New York University, School of Continuing Education and Extension Services. *Bulletin,* Spring 1971.

QUIGLEY, D. B. (Captain, Deputy Director for Enlisted Manpower Management Systems, Department of Defense). Personal correspondence, April 21, 1971.

TAYLOR, P. (National Association of Trade and Technical Schools). Personal communication, April 13, 1971.

TAYLOR, R. (National Homes Study Council). Personal communication, April 13, 1971.

United Business Schools Association. Personal Communication, April 13, 1971.

U.S. Civil Service Commission, Bureau of Training. *Employee Training in the Federal Service.* Washington, D.C.: U.S. Government Printing Office, 1970.

U.S. Office of Education. *Adult Basic Education Program Statistics.* Washington, D.C.: U.S. Government Printing Office, 1970. (a)

U.S. Office of Education. *Noncredit Activities for Institutions of Higher Education, 1967–68.* Washington, D.C.: U.S. Government Printing Office, 1970. (b)

CHAPTER 17

New Dissemination Systems

Edward Wynne

$$\text{ (decorative ornamental border)}$$

If we want to improve urban education, one of our first concerns must be with *how* to give broader circulation to constructive ideas for improvement. It is axiomatic that a key step in any change effort is to get new information to the persons who will bring change about. In other words, change means different conduct; such new conduct is the product of new information, or of seeing old events in a changed perspective. The "changed perspective" is, in effect, new insights; that is, new information. But we cannot assume that useful new information will automatically be circulated when it is discovered.

If we accept these principles, and want to facilitate change, then we must study the ways in which change-producing information is disseminated. This topic has been the subject of many studies and analyses (see, for instance, Burchinal, 1968, Appendix B). Some of these have focused on the overall field of information dissemination.

Others have been directed at specific sectors of society: education, agriculture, medicine. The studies have had a practical effect on policy makers; they have influenced budgetary and planning decisions about information-dissemination systems. Some of these decisions are governing dissemination policies in urban education today.

I contend that change-oriented persons have given insufficient attention to the theoretical framework to be applied to dissemination to improve urban education. Since our current framework misinterprets the pertinent research on dissemination, a more productive theoretical framework should be evolved. Such a new framework would in the long run generally revise the character and increase the productivity of urban education and urban-education research.

This chapter compares the dissemination arrangements in agriculture and pharmaceutical medicine with the existing arrangements for education. Most dissemination analyses focus on appropriate techniques to follow. I touch on this aspect but also consider (1) the motives of the person receiving change-promoting information—is he likely to be for, against, or neutral toward change (see Sieber, 1968); and (2) since the number of changes that can be proposed is infinite, what changes are most "profitable." Finally, the chapter proposes improved dissemination policies for urban education.

General Principles

Dissemination research has analyzed how change-producing ideas have been adopted by ultimate users: housewives who adopt better canning methods, farmers who accept new farming practices, doctors who prescribe new drugs, school administrators who revise school practices. There have been over 1,100 studies of such activities in the past forty years. According to Rogers (1970), individuals confronting an innovative idea follow a five-step process: awareness that something new or different exists; curiosity or interest in the innovation; assessment of the potential of the innovation; actual trial of the innovation; and adoption or rejection of the innovation. These factors interact in complex ways at each stage of the decision process to determine the likelihood of adoption and the rate at which an innovation will diffuse throughout a system.

Studies have determined that there is a typical pattern of dispersion for widely adopted innovations. The studies characterize the process as an S curve. Over some period of time, there are typically only scattered adoptions of an innovation; then, if the innovation does become widespread, there are a large number of adoptions in a comparatively short time; finally, the few remaining nonadopters are picked up, die off, or fail. The length of time for dissemination will vary, but the basic S curve holds true (Rogers, 1962). A better dissemination system can be defined as one that lessens the time span for the S curve and improves the ideas adopted.

Essential factors in determining the rate of adoption are the information-dissemination channels in operation at the various stages in the five-step process (Rogers, 1962, 1968; Coleman, Katz, and Menzel, 1966; Brickell, 1962).

Mass communication (an ad, a newspaper article, or a note in a professional journal) is important to make the adopter aware an innovation exists or that an accepted practice is unsatisfactory. Awareness alerts the adopter to the existence of the innovation; perhaps it also gives the idea a degree of legitimacy.

Once awareness is attained, the idea will die unless some event (an idea-stimulating person or a stimulating method of presentation) stimulates the adopter's interest. Our minds hold an enormous body of information at the awareness level; we have evolved techniques to shield ourselves from the overstimulation we would face if all these data were analyzed. To lift information above the awareness level, we require a stimulus that makes the information significant. Such stimuli (1) reassure us by coupling the idea to persons or institutions we put confidence in or (2) involve especially stimulating methods of presentation. Idea-stimulating persons may be strangers we meet and talk with, or they may be friends, neighbors, or fellow professionals we hold in regard. The presentation may be a conversation, a demonstration, a movie, a conference, or an effective book.

After interest is stimulated, the potential adopter wants evaluative information before he tries a new endeavor or abandons an accepted practice. The evaluation need not satisfy rigid formal criteria, and an intuitive element may play a role. The most significant evaluators are the adopter's peers. Their circumstances and problems are the same as his own; if the idea works for them, it may work for him too.

Once he decides that the idea has possibilities, the adopter wants to try it himself. He will naturally prefer procedures that permit him to try the idea in a limited way: to apply it to one class at a time, or to just a portion of a crop, or in weaker doses with his patients. At this stage the adopter is very interested in practical how-to-do-it information: therefore, salesmen or other idea promoters often play in important role at this point.

Finally, the adopter will weigh the evidence and conclude whether the innovation should become a part of his normal operations.

This typology can be applied only in general terms. Steps may be merged, abbreviated, or skipped. However, the more significant or expensive the change, the greater the likelihood that adopters will pass through all stages in appropriate order. Therefore, anyone interested in a far-reaching change should give sensitive attention to these information and analysis patterns.

The innovation's characteristics also affect the adoptive process. Is it susceptible to fractional trial—so that adopters may more easily pass through the trial stage? Whose personal or institutional interests may be advanced or diminished by implementation of the innovation? Can it be easily communicated—so that awareness and interest may be stimulated without great expense? Can it be adopted by one person (or by a segment of an institution), or does adoption require the acceptance and/or engagement of an entire institution? Is it susceptible to objective evaluation—so that interest and evaluation may be accelerated?

Personalities loom large in determining the success of the dissemination system. The task of interesting often conservative persons and institutions in new ideas requires a special tact and perception. In many dissemination systems, this role is filled by change agents—persons who are not the adopter's peers, who are sympathetic to the adoption process, and who can win the confidence of the potential adopter and supply him with information not available through his peer group. The change agent may be a salesman, a minor bureaucrat, or a consultant. In large organizations the change agent may even be an employee of the adopter. Regardless of his job title, he is a person sympathetic to change but able to relate to the adopter.

The design and management of a disseminating system can determine the prospects for adoption. How is the decision made about what innovations to promote? For example, even giving *equal* weight to all ideas reflects the decision that none are better than any others. What persons decide such priorities, and to what tune do they march? For instance, who decides the scope of distribution of a negative evaluation of a program—which can be a kind of change-producing information? What persons or institutions pay for dissemination? Also, regardless of where the dollars ultimately come from (that is, the taxpayer), what administrators decide whether and how to spend money?

Considering the matter technically, is there coordination between dissemination and the research and development elements of the enterprise—so that items are researched that reflect the needs of the adopting system, and development packages are prepared that lend themselves to dissemination? Can the disseminating system foster demonstrations? Does it have access to mass media? Has it a cadre of change agents? Does it have the funds to disseminate complicated ideas to large systems? Is its budget flexible, so it can spend money on the rather esoteric costs involved in dissemination—publishing costs, conferences, speeches, all sorts of "hand-holding" enterprises?

The adopter's organizational structure is significant. Must innovations be accepted by a total institution (a school or a school district), or can they be applied by a subdistrict (an individual teacher or farmer)? Does the subdistrict have the necessary independence? The answers depend on the structure of the adopting system and the nature of the innovation. Different adopting frameworks may be desirable during the life of a particular innovation. In the early stages, it may be desirable to have the innovation tried on a small scale by individual units. At a later time, it may be feasible to "sell" the innovation to persons who can commit a large enterprise. Unfortunately, neither adopting systems nor innovations can always be reshaped so easily.

The last element in our overview is probably the most critical —though it is often not explicitly treated in most adoption studies. *What are the real values of the adopting system and its employees vis-à-vis the goals the innovation seeks to promote?* Do farmers want more corn? Do doctors want patients to get better faster? What persons associated with schools aggressively want children to learn better? Significant innovation inevitably requires adaptation for the adopters; this means tension. As a minimum, they will need to learn new techniques and habits or abandon existing ones. This means effort and inconvenience. In the long run all of this may be warranted if the adoption succeeds, but innovation does require special motivation—especially for the first triers, who lack the reassurance of a convenient peer example.

Innovation not only requires new learning; it may diminish the prestige or power of a person or subsystem associated with the old way. Then it may have to overcome active hostility. Again, many innovations simply are bad ideas. Against this backdrop, adopters must feel important rewards are offered for successful innovation, to justify being first in the water. The most restraining combination is an environment in which there is reluctance to change *plus* very minor rewards for those who conduct successful change. So the final issue is —How are the employees in the system trained, hired, given raises, promoted, transferred, or fired?

Characteristics of Two Systems

An effective system has been developed for the dissemination of information to doctors about proprietary medicines—prescription drugs. The system is partly maintained and managed by federal planning and expenditures (for instance, the National Library of Medicine, which produces the *Index Medicus,* is federally financed). Still, most of the dissemination costs and structures are managed by private drug companies. Such companies make large profits from the sale of drugs under trade names. However, since the key link in this chain is a doctor's prescription, specifying the drug by its trade name, the doctor must be informed of the potential of the drug and made familiar with the trade name (Harris, 1964; May, 1961).

The dissemination system of the drug companies is extremely impressive: In 1966, drug manufacturers spent an estimated six to eight hundred million dollars a year (or an average of three thousand dollars per doctor in private practice) in promotional expenses (Goddard, 1966). In 1958, fifteen thousand drug salesmen made over twenty million calls on doctors, hospitals, and pharmacists (Harris, 1964, p. 89). In the same year drug companies bought 3,790,908,000 pages of paid journal advertising, plus 741,213,700 direct-mail impressions (Harris, 1964, p. 18). One study disclosed that the average doctor received three visits from drug salesmen (or detail men) per week (Coleman, Katz, and Menzel, 1966, p. 180). One doctor received 1,825 direct-mail ads and notices in one year; many were multicolor, glossy-paper, top-quality jobs (Olsen, 1964, p. 240).

Clearly, this enormous dissemination expenditure may seriously warp the judgment of physicians. There have been severe criticisms of the quality of information transmitted over this network (Harris, 1964; Goddard, 1966). Despite the criticisms, we must recognize the industry has a complex problem, with 54,000 drug stores and 4,500 hospitals also to be covered (Olsen, 1964). The doctors work under notorious pressures. The task of getting current, accurate, and fairly complex information about new developments to them is bound to be costly.

What are the effects of these massive efforts on the average doctor's adoption process? An important study of the adoption of a new drug by doctors is reassuring. First, it emphasized the importance of the industry's dissemination system. That system was usually responsible for first bringing the drug to doctors' attention: 80 per cent of the doctors first heard of the drug from drug house advertising; 57 per cent from the detail man; 18 per cent from direct-mail ads; and 5 per cent from periodical ads (Coleman, Katz, and Menzel, 1966, p. 53). Unquestionably, the dissemination system also played a significant part in stimulating the doctor's interest in the new drug. *However, once awareness-interest thresholds were passed, the doctor's peers played the major role in his determining whether to evaluate, try, and adopt the drug.* Each doctor had a network of colleagues to whom he turned for counsel. It was the opinions and experiences of his network that determined his final decision. Different doctors had different networks. "First adopters" had contacts outside their geographic areas that made them more likely to act early. In addition, the first adopters were most informed on current professional literature, and thus received information independent of drug company sources. The industry's dissemination system "lubricated" the adoption process, but the final decisions still rested on personal confirmation.

The system for disseminating innovation to farmers is, to a significant degree, publicly financed. The system is the Cooperative Extension Service, jointly financed by federal and state governments. The service uses a wide range of dissemination techniques. Newsletters, press releases, television and radio interviews are all tools for local extension agents. (There is an extension agent in every county in America.) Offices are maintained to answer inquiries. Demonstration projects are conducted. Every effort is made to relate the agent's concerns to those of local farmers. In many areas, local farmers play an important part in shaping extension hiring and policy decisions. Field trips are encouraged, to bring farmers in close touch with peers who have tried new ideas. The service consciously tries to develop strategies about innovations to be promoted. A close interrelation is maintained between research, development, and dissemination.

The growth of the productivity of farmers serviced by this system has been extraordinary: The number of persons supplied farm products by one farm worker increased from 10.69 in 1940 to 25.85 in 1960 to 37.02 in 1965 (U.S. Department of Agriculture, 1967); the annual budget of the Cooperative Extension Service increased from 33.5 million dollars in 1940 to 142.3 million dollars in 1960. Agriculture averages one dollar on dissemination for every two dollars on research. One might hypothesize that this extraordinary growth in productivity has been significantly related to the efficiency of its innovation-dissemination system.

Dissemination Systems in Education

Many dissemination studies, most of them dealing with elementary and secondary education, have considered how new ideas are adopted in education (Brickell, 1962; Carlson, 1965; Marsh, 1964). Much of the dissemination is the product of informal, semisocial exchanges. For the moment, however, let us conceive of a dissemination subsystem called the *explicit dissemination subsystem:* a system designed and financed with a view to putting out change-producing information. This restricted definition permits us to focus on certain types of education dissemination.

Agriculture and pharmaceuticals both have substantial explicit dissemination systems. The systems use mass media as tools and include persons whose formal job is just to talk—to visit people and get new ideas and information to them. These visitors implement a conscious "selling" strategy and relate their tasks to the activities of the other parts of the innovation network—the research, development, and mass-dissemination efforts.

The explicit dissemination systems in education are harder to identify. Textbook publishers have extensive machinery for bringing their wares to the attention of school systems and coordinate their efforts with mass media campaigns. Equivalent efforts are planned by developers of audio-visual equipment and other educational hardware. However, these subsystems cover only a small fraction of the activities of the education system; over 60 per cent of the expenditures in education are for instructional personnel. Only 2 per cent goes for textbooks (Research and Policy Committee, 1968). The subsystems for textbooks and hardware just do not supply the dissemination needed for many of the important ideas that must affect education.

There are other explicit subsystems. The U.S. Office of Education sponsors the Educational Resources Information Center (ERIC). ERIC collects, digests, and indexes significant materials about educational innovations and arranges for the dissemination of these materials, generally to persons who subscribe to or query its system (Burchinal and Haswell, 1966; Burchinal, 1968b). ERIC's long-range goal is to "supply researchers, writers, curriculum specialists, and dissemination agents with quick responses to their information needs" (Burchinal, 1968b, p. 2). ERIC's annual budget from USOE is about five million dollars a year.

The explicit dissemination subsystems of the Office of Education are the regional laboratories. The term "laboratory" is a misnomer, since the laboratories do not conduct experiments; instead, their objective is to develop and demonstrate educational innovations. In fiscal year 1971, twenty-five million dollars was expended for the laboratories (Hanna, 1970). This sum totals about .07 per cent of national annual expenses in elementary and secondary education for a year. The office also supports a certain number of research and development centers, each focusing on a particular topic. The 1971 funding level for these centers was nine million dollars. The proposed National Institute for Education may eventually take over many of the responsibilities of the existing USOE dissemination and demonstration systems. However, while the NIE does envisage a significant enlargement of these activities, its dissemination will probably be conducted in much the same way as dissemination is now conducted by the USOE (Levien, 1971).

The teacher-training programs funded by the Office of Education may also be considered, in part, as explicit dissemination enterprises—since the materials taught should include change-producing information. Unfortunately, these programs are conducted under certain constraints. For instance, when the Education Professions Development Act was passed in 1967, an effort was made to permit funds to be used to finance college training programs for school board members. This provision was deleted from the draft act, apparently because of the resistance of the various education professions. Evidently new ideas should be circulated (or strained) by the professions. What comes through the strainer?

Incidentally, analysts have observed that a major factor affecting the decision to innovate in education is the ability of the adopter to see the innovation in operation in circumstances approximately similar to his own. The demonstration element is especially important (it is alleged) because educational evaluation is notoriously subjective. Potential adopters want first-hand evidence before they put their reputation on the line. In addition, the adopter must be convinced that the demonstration has been conducted with the same level of resources that are available to him in his school. Demonstrations that succeed because of extraordinary efforts or resources only discourage emulation (Brickell, 1962, p. 63). From this we can sense that the planning and conducting of demonstrations is an important and highly demanding task.

There are two federally assisted dissemination activities that rate special mention: the varied attempts to engage private contractors in school-related pay-by-results schemes (some financed by the U.S. Office of Education) and the education voucher experiments that the Office of Economic Opportunity is attempting. At this moment, no school district has a voucher plan in operation, though some contracting-out arrangements are underway. Both of these efforts have attracted considerable attention and controversy (Welch, 1970, 1971).

Each state department of education is also, in effect, the base for an explicit dissemination system. The state, in meeting its responsibility to oversee education in its schools, is naturally situated to act as a center for the dissemination of new ideas. In Great Britain,

"school inspectors," with responsibilities equivalent to those administered by the states, are credited with being important change agents in
advancing the British infant school movement (Featherstone, 1967).
Unfortunately, the record of state action in America has not been
encouraging. In some cases, the states have had noble aspirations but
have not been able to amass the resources to put theory into practice
(Brickell, 1962). In other cases, informed critics have concluded, excessive emphasis on "professionalism" has hampered the state education departments in fostering change (Sanford, 1967).

There are also innumerable *informal dissemination structures*
throughout education. The structures include various professional
associations (of administrators, curriculum specialists, researchers,
classroom teachers for various age groups), with their patterns of conferences and publications. These associations, however, are inhibited as
disseminators because their responsibilities as protectors of disciplines
and professions are in conflict with the obsolescence that change often
creates; because many productive innovations cannot easily fit into
the professional patterns; because the substantial costs of effective dissemination cannot be easily borne by membership dues; and because
a professsional organization is not naturally composed largely of a
group of "first-wave" adopters and consequently is not an ideal base
for the launching of a substantial innovation.

We should also recognize that numerous (in absolute numbers)
change agents exist throughout the entire education system, though
their jobs are not formally identified as such: employees of state education agencies, faculties of schools of education, various consultants,
some staff members in larger school districts. The federal programs
have probably greatly increased such jobs. Unfortunately, the geographical mobility of these persons is often limited; hence, we have a
dissemination pattern that clusters innovations around sites where
something new has begun—a development that a wider geographic
network would diminish. Without laboring the point, we may conclude that these persons have not adequately made up for the lack of
a more rational informal dissemination system.

Finally, we should consider *independent dissemination systems*
for education—systems that are not financed or managed by professional educators or their "allies." These systems have a low level of
financing, a modest access to education research, and (comparatively)
large influence. The systems are diverse. For example, they include the
periodic education issue of the *Saturday Review* (the previous "Education America" section of the *Review* was financed by the Kettering
Foundation), the education specialists maintained by the various civil

rights organizations (and by some citizens groups), the U.S. Commission on Civil Rights, the Office of Economic Opportunity, the education committee of the Committee on Economic Development, popular writers (often of an excessively romantic vein) who write on education problems, and education reporters associated with the media. Sometimes, the sophistication of these sources is modest; but "In the kingdom of the blind, the man with one eye is king." Usually, the writers and their sponsors are at least removed from the crippling effect of the existing motivation system in education.

Motivation to Change

As many commentators have observed, our educational system is one in which, despite all the rhetoric, change and the major goal of change—teaching more children better—are subordinate values. This proposition has nothing to do with the morals, abilities, or intelligence of teachers or administrators. The fact is that the goal structures for educational professionals are not as sympathetic to effective innovation as the goal structures in farming or even in medicine. Any farmer who fails to grow more corn per acre this year than last year is out of business; that is what the decrease in farming operators means. The consequences are not quite so clear when a doctor is comparatively unsuccessful; but patients do shop around, and hospitals and professional associations maintain a degree of quality control, and very effective doctors get significantly higher incomes. But what educator ever got a raise for teaching more students better? Or what educator was dismissed or school closed because students were not learning?

In sum, the existing hiring and reward systems in education do not give educators incentives to accept the risks associated with genuine innovation. Why should they risk fostering on-the-job change without the possibility of real reward? Farmers may innovate from compulsion; the genuinely innovating educator is acting in an apparently irrational fashion. In a way, his suspicious colleagues are right to question his motives. What is "wrong" with a man who risks his job (and thus his family's support) to promote an unnecessary change? Of course, we hear a great deal about innovation in education, but the word has come to mean an apparent, relatively painless change—a change that involves no harm or risk.

A Better Dissemination System

First, it will reach laymen and lay institutions as well as educators. In education, the most important "changes result as a response

to the demands of the suprasystem" (Griffiths, 1967, p. 178). For
example, consider school decentralization, desegregation, education of
the disadvantaged, voucher and contracting-out systems, and revisions
of college student governance. These moves bring to mind the civil
rights movement, the Supreme Court, Congress, the Office of Economic Opportunity, economist Milton Friedman, the Ford Foundation, Mayor John Lindsey of New York City, Students for a Democratic Society, the *New York Times,* the Ku Klux Klan, Lyndon
Johnson, and so on. These people and institutions were counseled by
educators (as well as by those in other professions). But in the main,
the key dissemination systems were those that reached these lay figures
and their various constituencies (Wynne, 1972, pp. 101–124). Major
education change cannot take place without winning the public, as
well as the technicians, and many productive major changes cannot
occur without laymen overriding the opposition of professionals, who
are constrained by the present antichange goal structure.

    Financing of such dissemination will prove tricky; institutions
and professionals will be reluctant to promote such expenditures—
"don't wash our dirty linen in public." But perhaps foundations (the
Bundy Report, issued by the Ford Foundation) and noneducational
government agencies (the United States Commission on Civil Rights
has been active in desegregation dissemination) may be used. Another
form of financing such dissemination is the public purchase of books
on how to improve education. Unfortunately, such purchases are in-
spired by the sensationalist impact of such books and do not always
provide the base for continuing constructive lay involvement. But the
concept of the public's buying its own information—just as it buys
business analyses, newspapers, race tips, travel guides—is eminently
constructive.

    Second, *it will be especially concerned to disseminate innova-
tions that aim at structural changes.* Many "innovations" are susceptible to the charge of faddism. In assessing innovations in New York
State, Bricknell (1962, p. 19) says, "Few innovations took place in the
kind of people employed, in the way they were organized to work
together, in the types of instructional materials they used, or in the
times and places at which they taught. *In short, schools as structured
institutions remained the same."* The existing dissemination system can
share some (small) responsibility for this fault, and we must develop
a system that is able to transmit more serious innovations.

    But the problem is not largely a "technical" one (that is, the
ability of the system to transmit the information). The issue is, first,
the *will* of the system to get the word around. Important school inno-

vations often offend existing professional interests as well as some laymen. The resistance of professionals (who usually have considerable influence on the existing dissemination system) is a major handicap. This is largely why influences apart from the existing formal dissemination system have been prominently identified with so many major changes. Therefore, the dissemination system must be interested in identifying "serious innovations" that rate some priority; and it must have the will to push them. A few examples of such innovations: proposals to use programmed-instruction techniques (as proposed by Bereiter and Englemann) to teach reading and other cognitive skills (Pines, 1967); attempts to increase consumer choice and school accountability by contracting-out and voucher arrangements (Welch, 1970, 1971); school-decentralization efforts, where genuine authority is given to neighborhood groups; the large-scale introduction of program-budgeting techniques in school districts (Rappaport, 1967); proposals to involve school board members and parents in the process of school evaluation and productivity rating, in order to move toward greater accountability (Wynne, 1972); a proposal to restructure schools so that the teachers function mainly as resource persons and the bulk of the teaching of subjects is done for lower-grade students by students from upper classes (Melaragno, 1971); the strivings toward the freer and more open classroom—if accompanied by some structuring or evaluative framework (Wynne, 1971).

All these proposals (except perhaps the programmed-instruction proposal) assume continuing the existing cost level of schools. To a considerable degree, they aim at impacting organizational values or at least committing school systems to finite, definable goals. The dissemination system should be able to handle proposals such as these.

Third, *it must assume that, in the intermediate run, the existing goals and motivation patterns of schools will radically change.* Promoting real change, in the current system, is like trying to push cooked spaghetti through a keyhole. School interest in serious, radical innovation is modest, to say the most. However, the rate of innovation in New York State schools doubled within eighteen months after the appearance of Sputnik (Bricknell, 1962). Did their dissemination system improve during the period? The Cooperative Extension Service does an adequate job, but how hard is it to interest farmers in growing two ears of corn where one is now growing? Farmers "pull" information from the service. Since the benefits from new drugs are not always apparent, the pharmaceutical dissemination system has information-pushing (as well as pulling) components. The push components are essentially the reason for the great cost of the pharmaceutical dissemination enterprise: in 1960, whereas Cooperative Extension cost 142 million dollars for 1.7 million farmers, the pharmaceutical system cost 700 million dollars for 157,000 doctors. If we hope to promote education innovation, we cannot possibly afford the cost of a system that must effectively advise *and* exhort. Therefore, education dissemination must assume that schools want improvement; at the same time, it must promote a revised motivation structure.

Fourth, *it will stimulate new priorities for education research.* If the new system focuses on changing the motivation of professional educators, it will inevitably seek research about how this can be done. Accountability? Decentralization? New means of measuring output? Different systems of hiring, promotion, allocating raises, and defining responsibilities? These are all researchable topics—though they are not necessarily current research priorities.

In addition, it will do the following: (1) It must assume that large parts of the cost (and management) of the dissemination system will be borne by states, local school districts, and citizens. (2) It will be an evolutionary product. (3) It will contain numerous subsystems. (4) It will place great reliance on change agents and informal communications. (5) It must be capable of conducting realistic demonstrations. (6) Where dissemination resources are limited, as they usually will be, the system will be targeted on change-oriented persons. (7) It would cost a lot more to operate than the present system. (8) This more efficient system will be no more of a threat to our free society than our current inefficient system. (9) It will enable us to educate more children, more effectively, with our current level of resources.

References

BRICKELL, H. M. *Organizing New York State for Educational Change.* Albany: University of the State of New York, 1962.

BURCHINAL, L. G. "Research Reports and On-Going Projects on the Change Process." *Articulation of Resources for Research Utilization.* Bethesda, Md.: ERIC, ED-013-971, 1968. (a)

BURCHINAL, L. G. "Information Retrieval for Education and Training." Paper presented at the Fourth Annual Conference and Exposition on Education and Training, August 1968. (b)

BURCHINAL, L. G., AND HASWELL, H. "How to Put 2½ Tons of Education into One Handy Little Box." *American Education,* 1966, *2*(2), 23–25.

CARLSON, R. O. *Adoption of Educational Innovations.* Eugene: Center for Advanced Study of Educational Administration, University of Oregon, 1965.

COLEMAN, J. S., KATZ, E., AND MENZEL, H. *Medical Innovation, A Diffusion Study.* New York: Bobbs-Merrill, 1966.

FEATHERSTONE, J. "Schools for Children: What's Happening in British Classrooms." *New Republic,* 1967, *157,* 17–21.

GIDEONSE, H. D. "Educational Laboratories." *Phi Delta Kappan,* 1965, *47,* 130–133.

GODDARD, J. L. (Commissioner, U.S. Food and Drug Administration). Testimony before the House Intergovernmental Relations Subcommittee, May 25, 1966.

GRIFFITHS, D. E. "System Theory and School Districts." In P. A. Sexton (Ed.), *Readings on the School in Society.* Englewood Cliffs, N.J.: Prentice-Hall, 1967. Pp. 170–187.

HANNA, G. "1972 Appropriations." *Educational Researcher,* Sept. 1970, *11.*

HARRIS, R. *The Real Voice.* New York: Macmillan, 1964.

LEVIEN, R. E. *National Institute of Education: A Preliminary Plan for the Proposed Institute.* Santa Monica, California: Rand, 1971.

MARSH, P. E. "Wellsprings of Strategy Considerations Affecting Innovations by the PSSC." In M. Miles (Ed.), *Innovation in Education.* New York: Teachers College, Columbia University, 1964. Pp. 211–241.

MAY, C. D. "Selling Drugs by Educating Physicians." *Journal of Medical Education,* 1961, *36,* 1–23.

MELARAGNO, R., AND NEWMARK, G. "The Tutorial Community Concept." In J. W. Guthrie and E. Wynne (Eds.), *New Models for American Education.* Englewood Cliffs, N.J.: Prentice-Hall, 1971. Pp. 98–113.

MORT, P. R. *American Schools in Transition.* New York: Teachers College, Columbia University, 1941.

OLSEN, P. C. *Marketing Drug Products.* New York: Topics Publishing Co., 1964.

PINES, M. *Revolution in Learning.* New York: Harper & Row, 1967.

RAPPAPORT, D. "New Approaches in Education." *The Price Waterhouse Review,* Winter 1967, 3–8.

Research and Policy Committee. *Innovation in Education: New Directions for the American School.* New York: Committee for Economic Development, 1968.

ROGERS, E. M. *The Diffusion of Innovations.* New York: Free Press, 1962.

ROGERS, E. M. "The Communication of Innovations in a Complex Institution." *Educational Record,* 1970, *49,* 68–71.

SANFORD, T. *Storm over the States*. New York: McGraw-Hill, 1967.

SEIBER, S. D. "Organizational Influences on Innovation Roles." In T. L. Eidell and J. M. Kitchell (Eds.), *Knowledge Production and Utilization in Educational Administration*. Eugene, Ore.: University of Oregon, 1968. Pp. 120–142.

United States Department of Agriculture. *Agricultural Statistics*. Washington, D.C., 1967.

United States Department of Health, Education, and Welfare. *1967 Annual Report*. Washington, D.C., 1967.

United States Senate, 90th Congress, 1st Session. "Notes and Working Papers Concerning the Administration of Programs Authorized Under Title III of the Elementary and Secondary Education Act." Prepared for the Subcommittee on Education, Senate Committee on Labor and Public Welfare, 1967.

WELCH, J. "Perspectives on Performance Contracting." *Educational Researcher*, Oct. 1970, *21*, 1.

WELCH, J. "Perspectives: The OEO and the Vouchers." *Educational Researcher*, June 1971, *23*, 5.

WYNNE, E. "Heart and Mind Together." *Education and Urban Society*, 1971, *3*(3), 351–360.

WYNNE, E. *The Politics of School Accountability*. Berkeley: McCutchan, 1972.

CHAPTER **18**

Research and Development

Francis S. Chase

What is implied by the term "research and development" as applied to the achievement of educational goals? Without becoming involved in niceties of definition, I would designate as research all activities undertaken primarily for the discovery or closer mapping of knowledge—whether the motivation is curiosity, social utility, or attainment of other objectives. I would include under development all activities consciously directed toward a formulation or construction designed to perform specified functions. In education this usually implies a product, such as sets of instructional materials intended to further stated objectives, accompanied usually by recommended conditions of use.

As used by me and other observers and participants, the combined term "research and development" signifies more than some research and some development. It employs an ordered series of steps—

217

typically, through the use of systems analysis—to identify and solve problems and verify solutions: first, objectives are derived from analyses of needs; then, carefully selected means of achieving the objectives are welded into a consistent system; and finally, the performance of the system is monitored to strengthen its elements until performance criteria are met.

It is my conviction, however, that the refinement and extension of research, development, and implementation strategies and processes hold greater promise for the improvement of education than any of the products now available or under development. Effective systems of product development are being worked out through the efforts of the federally funded research and development organizations; but significant impact on education will be felt only when state and local education agencies incorporate the essence of systematic problem solving in their own planning, management, and operations.

Even the most carefully developed innovations are unlikely to produce the desired effects in the adopting system unless the following conditions are met: (1) The school, school district, or other agency is engaged in a systematic and continuing assessment of the needs for education among the populations it serves. (2) Students, parents, and others in the community served, as well as teachers and other educational personnel, are involved in the definition of needs and in decisions concerning the specific changes desired. (3) Alternative means of closing the gaps between desired and current performance in meeting educational needs are analyzed carefully. (4) The objectives of proposed programs and adaptations are specified, so that progress toward achievement can be evaluated reliably. (5) Provision is made for staff and community development in order to facilitate the assumption of new roles and modifications in behaviors. (6) Systematic evaluation and feedback from those affected serve as the basis for continuing improvement of programs and procedures and for the introduction of new strategies and products (Chase, 1971, pp. 11–12).

The evidence on the extent to which these conditions are met in urban school districts is scanty; but the indications are that most of them as yet are exemplified to only a slight degree in most cities. In an effort to find out what happens when a serious attempt is made to incorporate the essence of research and development operations in a large city school system, I spent several days in June 1971 exploring the work of the Development Division of the Dallas Independent School District. Dallas was chosen for two reasons: first, because in the past two years Dallas is reputed to have pioneered in making systematic research and development a foundation for educational improvement; and second, because it was readily accessible to me.

The Development Division of the Dallas Independent School District is directed by Rogers Barton, Associate Superintendent, who reports directly to the General Superintendent, Nolan Estes. The functions of the Development Division are shared by four assistant superintendents who are responsible respectively for curriculum development, multicultural program development, accountability and personnel development, and planning, research, and evaluation.

The budget for the total Development Division rose from $1,600,000 in 1969–70 to $3,400,000 for 1970–71; and the budget for 1971–72 was slightly in excess of $4,000,000. Local funds allocated to the Development Division rose from $385,000 in 1969–70 to $1,279,000 in 1970–71 and was expected to exceed $1,000,000 again in 1971–72. In 1969, 1970, and 1971 private foundation funds supported the division by yearly grants of over $750,000. (In addition, the Texas Education Agency provides some financial and a great deal of moral and professional support.) Federal funds accounted for $1,333,-759 or nearly 40 per cent of the 1970–71 budget and for over $2,000,-000 or approximately 50 per cent in the 1971–72 budget. The increased proportion of federal funds in the requested 1971–72 budget was accounted for by the new allocation of $1,280,000 in federal support for Targeted Achievement in Reading.

Development projects consumed more than three fourths of the budget allocations for 1970–71 and were expected to use nearly three fourths of the 1971–72 budget. The remainder of the budget supports the central office functions of planning, research, and evaluation; curriculum development; multicultural program development, information systems development; and personnel development.

The largest development projects in terms of budget allocations are the Paul L. Dunbar Community Learning Center, with a budget in excess of $500,000 each for 1969, 1970, and 1971; the Career Education Program Development, to which $576,000 was allocated in 1970–71 (its first year) and for which $400,000 was budgeted for 1971–72; the High School Performance Contract, with a budget of $500,000 starting in 1970–71 (its first year beyond the planning stage); and the Targeted Achievement in Reading, which was allocated $150,000 in 1969–70, $200,000 in 1970–71, and $1,280,000 for 1971–72. The Bilingual Education Center and the Turnkey OEO Performance Contract were each slated for budgets of $250,000 in 1971–72.

In an unpublished document dated February 27, 1970, the long-range goals of research and development in the Dallas Independent School District were stated as follows:

> *(1) Stimulate the development and implementation of strategies and plans to facilitate desirable changes within the institution and among selected cooperating institutions.*
> *(2) Stimulate the systematic evaluation and the continuous assessment of the school district's programs and services.*
> *(3) Develop internal capability to utilize information from basic and applied research in the solution of priority educational problems.*
> *(4) Provide usable information along with alternatives and criteria for informing policy and management decisions concerning long- and short-range planning of programs and services of the school district.*
> *(5) Stimulate the development of innovative programs and services which are in response to the priority needs of the school district.*
> *(6) Provide technical assistance and service to operation departments.*

Subsequently, the goals were reexamined and restated with reference to a division of responsibilities among the four departments and the several branches in the Development Division. This process is illustrated by the Department of Planning, Research, and Evaluation's "Goals and Budget Presentation" dated June 2, 1971. Seven goals are given for the department, with a number of subgoals under each. Long-Range Goal I, to "provide technical assistance to operational and support department of the school district as they plan, implement, and evaluate their products," is followed by six subgoals, with specific activities for each. For example, Subgoal A covers research and evaluation services to the Paul L. Dunbar School in the development, refining, and implementation of seven evaluation designs and two hundred hours of curriculum development and revision consultation. Subgoal B specifies the design and analysis of evaluation procedures and data for ten "Penny for Innovation" projects in several different schools; and Subgoal E calls for definition of the staffing requirements for the evaluation component at the Skyline Career Development Program and four man weeks of recruiting and orienting research and evaluation staff.

There are three subgoals under Long-Range Goal II, one of which is "to provide technical assistance . . . to the Department of

Instruction in planning the longitudinal evaluation of ongoing programs, including Early Childhood Education and selected schools." Other activities of this department (selected from a long list) include participating in the Ohio State University Consortium for training evaluators; developing an evaluation design for the Drug Abuse Education program; and conducting staff development seminars relative to behavioral objectives, curriculum development, process evaluation, and test construction.

Specific goals and activities are also listed for the Planning Systems Group and the Information Systems Group. Among the 1971–72 activities listed for the former group are the following: to conduct ten "plan-making" training sessions for district middle-management personnel; to program and implement (in cooperation with the Council of Great City Schools) Program Management Information Systems on the computer facility of the Dallas Independent School District; and to implement an Educational Resources Management System in at least one department of the district other than the Planning, Research, and Evaluation Department.

Among the numerous activities of the Information Systems Group for 1971–72 are the following: to maintain and modify computer programs to provide services required by the district; to facilitate planning decisions relating new procedures to stated system goals and to develop a "Basic Resource Actuating Information Network"; and to conduct staff development programs on system design and instruct personnel in the use of information-processing equipment. Perhaps the thrust of this group is best illustrated, however, by two of its long-range goals: to develop a totally integrated information system and to develop a student-oriented computer learning system.

The Accountability Department lists three long-range goals: (1) To increase the academic achievement and skill development of students who are educationally deficient. (2) To increase the student-retention power of the participating schools in the Dallas Independent School District. (3) To increase the cost effectiveness of instruction in mathematics, communications, and certain occupational skills throughout the target grade levels, target populations, and target schools.

In 1970–71, targeted achievement programs were implemented for 300 students in reading and 300 students in mathematics in grades 1, 2, and 3; for 300 students in reading and 300 students in mathematics in grades 7, 8, and 9; for 625 students in reading and 625 students in mathematics in five inner-city high schools; and for 50 boys in automotive mechanics, 50 boys in machine metals, and 50 girls in drafting in three inner-city high schools. A program of achievement motivation was installed for 625 students in five inner-city high schools; and a program of management-support services to provide the district with cost-effectiveness evaluation data and a management information system was put into operation. For 1971–72, the Accountability Department set itself eleven tasks, including an extension of the targeted achievement and motivation programs to additional schools and programs and a larger number of students.

Curriculum-development activities include a cluster of programs being worked out at the Paul L. Dunbar Community Learning Center; more than twenty career programs being developed at the Skyline Career Development Center; and a great variety of "innovative learning" programs, now being tried out in elementary grades and with children ages three to five.

The Paul L. Dunbar Community Learning Center in 1969–70 started with the critiquing of programs and materials developed elsewhere and the subsequent selection of several programs which appeared well adapted to the identified needs of Dallas children. The Center operates in accordance with the following basic ideas: (1) The design and development of materials and other facilities for learning are conducted on-site; that is, in a school, with a staff of specialists working directly with the regular staff of the school. (2) The development staff is trained through participating in analysis of needs and the several steps in program design and development. (3) On the basis of the experience at Dunbar, and after the required level of competence has been attained, programs are extended to other schools and other groups of teachers. (4) After further refinement and evaluation, the staff development procedures will be packaged for widespread dissemination. (5) Evaluation is directed to determine the cost effectiveness per unit of achievement gained, and the budget is designed to separate development from operating costs.

The principal of the Dunbar School is also the project director of the development programs and the coordinator of staff development. Working closely with the principal are the coordinators of curriculum design, staff development, parent involvement, research and evaluation, and pupil personnel. There are curriculum-development centers for work in science, art, early childhood, mathematics, social studies, communication skills, physical education, and music.

Each of the specialized centers serves as a developmental laboratory. The social studies center, for example, is exploring ways to learn about man and his interaction with his environment. The basic materials used up to this time have been those developed by Del Felder at the Southwest Educational Development Laboratory and the strategies developed by the late Hilda Taba. In both cases, training sessions are provided for teachers; and the facilities, materials, and equipment are made available to both teachers and students.

The multicultural social studies program, from the Austin Laboratory, was pilot tested in the Dunbar School in 1969–70 with 350 students and six teachers in grades 1 and 2. The success of the program, with students achieving 88 per cent mastery of program objectives, led to its extension into four other Dallas schools in 1970–71. In that year the first-year program was used with 474 students and nineteen classrooms, and the second-year program was used with 480 students in nineteen classrooms. The third-year program served 175 students in six classes. Analysis of the test results for the second year showed that 82 per cent of the children had attained 82 per cent of the program objectives.

Another program under development at Dunbar is the cognitive-curriculum program, which incorporates strategies based on Piaget's theories and developed by David Weikart. This program has now gone through the second year of pilot testing in a kindergarten class of twenty-five students, and the results so far have been distinctly encouraging. There is also a communication-skills program, which was developed by the Southwest Regional Educational Laboratory and has now been pilot tested in four kindergartens, three multi-age, and fifteen first-grade classes in six schools during the 1970–71 school year. The goal is that 80 per cent of the children will achieve 80 per cent of the program objectives as measured by criterion test items. A second-year communication-skills program, designed to develop the reading skills of first-grade children, was initiated in February 1971 with 354 children.

Other programs being used by the development teams at Dunbar include the individually prescribed instruction in mathematics developed by the Learning Research and Development Center at the University of Pittsburgh and Research for Better Schools, the AAAS process-learning approach in science, and the Suzuki and Kodaly music programs.

Conversations with the development specialists reveal that they are well acquainted with curriculum developments throughout the country and have visited a number of the sites where the most significant developments in their particular fields are occurring.

The Dunbar Center has an extensive parental-involvement program, the aim of which is to create an atmosphere in which parents and children can learn together. The program involves parents and other community volunteers in continuing learning activities and helps them to discover how to encourage their children to learn. A large number and variety of activities are designed to expand the educational program from the classroom to every home in the area by creating leadership roles for community members, promoting understanding about learning, and involving parents in the learning-teaching processes of the school.

A variety of cooperative learning programs are offered so that parents can observe their children at school and learn along with them. A mother may learn about homemaking while helping her daughter develop table etiquette; or a father may learn how to play the violin with his son in one of the Suzuki music classes. Parents may choose to work in the classroom helping a teacher with the lesson, serve in the cafeteria during lunch, or work in the office of the resource center to see the operation of the school plant at first hand. Parent advisory committees serve the school in planning the educational and community programs. A variety of classes are offered for parents, including sewing, typing, special seminars on drug abuse, income taxes, and safety programs. Summer programs provide both education and recreation for parents and children. A parental package, which is being pilot tested at Dunbar, will be refined for use in other schools and other communities.

Among the products produced in this program are a school paper, a parent-participation handbook, an early childhood handbook for parents, and a parental-involvement brochure. There is a home and family life education course taught through the use of work units, home visitations, and conferences. The aim of this program is to aid people in coping with the daily problems of living. The interest in the program is indicated by the attendance, which ranges between 70 and 92 per cent of those enrolled. Among the results of this program is that social welfare has been extended through it to thirty-nine families and fifty-seven jobs have been found for students. Other results are increased parental involvement in school programs, more parent visits to the school, improved school attendance, and increased volunteer service by parents. The Dunbar Center has employed sociologists from the inception of the program to make social surveys, accumulate demographic data, and serve as consultants to the staff regarding sociological implications of particular events and situations.

The Career Development Program of the Skyline Center is developing several clusters of career programs, with each cluster offering many specific career options. Twenty-three career programs are now being developed, eleven through a performance contract with RCA and twelve by the staff from the Dallas Independent School District.

The students for the Skyline Career Development Center are drawn from all high schools in the district and are chosen on the basis of motivation, past achievement, emotional maturity, self-discipline, and intellectual potential. Attendance is on a flexible basis; students may attend full time, half time, or for only a few hours each day. A shuttle bus system provides transportation to and from each school in the district at any hour of the day.

The Career Development Center is staffed by carefully selected teachers, and supplementary instruction is provided by businessmen, professors, and visiting experts. The aim is to provide a balance of academic and career education leading to a high school diploma with the assurance of skills for immediate employment or adequate preparation for college or technical school. The clusters of careers include business and management technology, study of man and his environment, computer technology, horticulture, the world of construction, electronic sciences, aeronautics, transportation services, plastics technology, aesthetics and dramatic arts, food management, child- and youth-related professions, health, and medical and dental technologies.

The Department of Planning, Research, and Evaluation takes great pains in designing evaluation for its several programs. In addition to the programs described under curriculum development, the department is engaged in evaluation of other programs and operations. For example, a complex longitudinal design has been developed to provide information regarding points on which the Dallas Independent School District should concentrate its drug-abuse program. Other instruments and procedures have been designed to evaluate, over a period of at least two years, the effects on teacher behavior of the Educator's Self-Appraisal and to identify the conditions that appear necessary to enable teachers to make appropriate changes in their behaviors. Another example of an evaluation design is the design for evaluation of performance contracts to determine the effects on attitudes and school success produced by achievement-motivation training as well as changes in mathematics or other subjects. The design for evaluation of occupational training seeks to discover the concomitants of success in each of the occupational-training programs and the differential effects produced, as well as the direct effects on employability and the longitudinal effects of the occupational-training program.

Attention is also being given to assessing the effects of programs on dropouts, absenteeism, and vandalism. During the 1970–71 school year, the department conducted an educational-product audit, the purpose of which is to furnish information to all those interested in the education of Dallas youth regarding their educational achievement. In deciding the educational objectives to which the audit is directed, teachers, subject-area consultants, members of the staff of the Department of Planning, Research, and Evaluation, and outside consultants were closely involved. Prototype exercises were constructed for each of the major objectives chosen. The selection of tests and the arrangements for sampling and for data analysis were given close attention. Plans for reporting were developed in such a way as to avoid comparison between individuals, classrooms, or schools and to publish data only on large groups located within five previously specified major geographical areas of the city. The reports will go to the teachers and to subject-matter consultants, curriculum specialists, school administrators, and interested adults, including members of the board of education and concerned parents.

Undoubtedly, the reach of the Dallas program, which is now in its third year, still exceeds its grasp; but the accomplishments to date, the evidence of staff capabilities, and the constant effort to improve operations generate confidence in continuing contributions to the improvement of education in Dallas. The Dallas research and development operation may be characterized as experimental and problem solving. It links the functions of planinng, research, development (both curriculum and personnel), and evaluation in a tightly managed operation under the direction of the Associate Superintendent for Development. It is based on a continuing assessment of educational needs in Dallas and a corresponding assessment of the performance of the school system, with a persistent search for strategies and products that will help close the gap between needs and performance.

The development staff carefully scrutinizes materials and procedures developed elsewhere and selects those that seem best adapted to local needs or to the needs of particular cultural and ethnic groups. It utilizes a combination of "borrowed" ideas and materials (which are refitted as necessary to the needs in Dallas) and of "home-grown" programs, which are designed to meet special needs and situations in the city of Dallas. It also employs performance contracting with a number of firms in an attempt to satisfy needs that lie beyond existing tested materials and the developmental capabilities of the Dallas Independent School District.

All of the experimental programs incorporate carefully worked-out systems of evaluation to determine the extent to which program objectives are met and to identify desirable and undesirable side effects. Because of its emphasis on evaluation, the Dallas Independent School District is a member of a consortium which, under the leadership of the Ohio State University Center for Evaluation, is now developing a model training program for evaluation specialists and managers. Planning, research, and evaluation together constitute one of seven priority goals for the 1970s, chosen by the board of education to facilitate widespread improvements in schools. The other high-priority goals are individualization of instruction, early-childhood education, career education, staff development, fiscal accountability, and community relations. Thus, the staff of the Department of Planning, Research, and Evaluation is directly responsible for one of the board's seven priority goals and also is charged with provision of special services to each of the other six priority areas.

In carrying out its responsibilities the Department of Planning, Research, and Evaluation has developed a capable technical staff and has provided training in educational research and development for over two hundred staff members in the district. The board of education expects the administration through this department to develop systematic plans for projects and programs; to install, monitor, and report to the board of the progress of projects and programs; and to present empirical evidence of the outcome of projects and programs. Accordingly, systematic planning and evaluation activities constitute an integral part of all major projects developed.

Because of the range of activities, the acceptance of the concept of accountability, the attention to personnel as well as curriculum development, the systematic attention to development to facilitate desirable educational changes, the emphasis on evaluation, and the imaginative interrelationship of functions within a unified structure, Dallas probably comes as close as any city to presenting an exemplary model for educational research and development. It also seems to realize to a high degree the conditions previously listed as essential for the success of innovations in any educational system. To achieve its purposes, it reaches out to the research and development centers, the regional educational laboratories, and other nonprofit organizations supported by the federal government for educational research and development. At the same time, it avails itself of the services of commercial publishers and other firms that have capabilities in educational technology or other aspects of educational development. The reaching out to other agencies, however, is preceded by a careful assessment of local needs and accompanied by a careful nurturing of ideas developed within the school district and by systematic attempts to enlarge the research and development capabilities of personnel employed by the district.

In trying to improve education in our cities and elsewhere, we are wise to make full use of all that science and engineering can offer and to employ the talents of planners, systems analysts, social scientists, and curriculum specialists. At the same time, we shall do well to act as if each individual has within him or her the capacity to become to some extent the architect of his own education and to remember that other persons—parents, teachers, friends, persons in authority, and persons encountered in work and play—have important roles in shaping educative experiences, including the quality of interaction with abstract ideas and materials. This suggests that in developing systems for education we might try to build in options which may be exercised by adopting authorities, by teachers, by families, and by individual learners. The choices, however, should be guided by as much information as can be supplied on the probable effects of departures from recommended modes of use.

Reference

CHASE, F. S. "Educational Research and Development in the Sixties: The Mixed Report Card." Background paper submitted to the Select Subcommittee on Education, U.S. House of Representatives, April 1971.

PART V

Historical Perspectives

In this part, historians furnish a frame of reference for educational concerns by posing questions like these: What has been the role of centralization and standardization in the development of the American public school? To what extent have these movements impeded reform in urban education? How has the struggle for power in school governance affected educational efficacy? In the process of transition, what problems arise when institutions of higher learning become multifaceted universities?

Tyack traces the struggle for centralization, coordination, and standardization in urban school systems from 1880 to the present. In the evolutionary process of reform, power has increasingly been transferred from the community and laymen to professional schoolmen, who perceive "one best system" for all urban schools. Tyack sees a return to more community control as a way to incorporate diversity and pluralism so desperately needed in our disparate urban neighborhoods.

McCaul, in a history of governance of the Chicago schools from 1835, describes the struggle for power among several offices and groups: the board of education, the mayor, the superintendent and administrative hierarchy, and citizen leagues. He identifies several favorable trends to improve governance: involvement of a consultative panel of university experts for advice to the board of education on the complex issues it faces; changes in the composition of, and appointment procedures to, the board; and an organized system for citizen participation on neighborhood and area councils. Also, the new principle of equality of educational opportunity suggests that state boards of education are likely to have an increasingly greater voice in determining policies of all schools.

Houle, in a retrospective account of an imaginary West Dakota A. and M. University, describes its transformation from a land-grant school, serving the largely agricultural needs of the state, to an urban university. His account of the use of federal and state funds, university consortia, and collaboration with urban groups makes clear the kinds of changes required to marshal the special capabilities of the university to help solve our pressing urban problems.

CHAPTER **19**

The "One Best System": A Historical Analysis

David Tyack

$$\textcircled{a}\textcircled{a}\ \textcircled{a}\textcircled{a}\ \textcircled{a}\textcircled{a}\ \textcircled{a}\textcircled{a}\ \textcircled{a}\textcircled{a}\ \textcircled{a}\textcircled{a}\ \textcircled{a}\textcircled{a}\ \textcircled{a}\textcircled{a}$$

"**N**o doubt excessive decentralization of administration has been one of the chief obstacles to improvement in every department of our free school system." This was John Philbrick's conclusion after surveying American city school systems in the 1880s. In his own lifetime Philbrick had seen village schools slowly transformed into large educational systems. As a grammar schoolmaster in Boston in 1847, he had introduced one of the most significant innovations in the history of American education, the graded classroom. From 1856 to 1878 he had served as superintendent of the Boston Public Schools. Like many other leading schoolmen of the time, he believed that there is "one best way" to run urban schools and that the administrator must discover the right patterns and imple-

This chapter is adopted from a talk delivered at the De Paul University colloquium on urban education and is based on research sponsored by a grant from the Carnegie Corporation.

231

ment them (Bunker, 1916, Ch. 3; Krug, 1966, pp. 72–75; Philbrick, 1885, p. 19).

Decentralized school politics and lay administration made this piecemeal bureaucratization difficult. Communities were often reluctant to transfer control of schools to the new managers. From the superintendents' perspective, the lay school boards of the nineteenth century were too large and inefficient; they represented pluralistic local interests; they meddled far too much in educational administration; and, at worst, they treated schools as a source of patronage and graft. What John Philbrick and his colleagues wanted was more power for the professional expert. What they often encountered was frustration: sabotage by their own subordinates; carping by armchair critics; refusal of board members to relinquish control over jobs and contracts; and the thrust of "extraneous" considerations—like party loyalty, ethnicity, and religion—into what should have been purely "professional" decisions. In short, the schools were "political," whereas the managers wished them to be hierarchical in structure, guided by objective rules, meritocratic, consistent, and rational (Anderson, 1968; Gilland, 1935, Ch. 6; Katz, 1968).

As a result of these frustrations, a number of leading schoolmen would later join forces with influential laymen to reshape urban education. At the turn of the century they would campaign to centralize control of schools in small "nonpolitical" boards, whose chief function was to legitimize the decisions of the superintendents. They would argue that the school board, far from being a political forum, should operate like a corporate board of directors. An hour a week should be sufficient time for a board to transact its work: "there is no more need for oratory in the conduct of a school system than there would be in the conduct of a national bank." Only if schools were "taken out of politics" could the professionals properly serve the clients. And with this centralization of control would come large bureaucracies transforming urban education into a virtually closed system of politics and decision making (Cubberley, 1914, p. 92; see also Cronin, 1965; Iannacone, 1967).

Need for Order

The central features of the urban educational landscape are so familiar today that it is hard to realize that earlier structures of schooling were far different. Picture, for example, the Boston Public Schools in 1850. If you were one of the 11,000 children attending a primary school, you would have gone to one of the 161 one-room, one-teacher, ungraded schools scattered across the city, each organized much like a rural school. It you then became a grammar school student, you would have found yourself most likely in a large room with perhaps 200 pupils taught by a reading or writing master who had assistant teachers to help him in hearing recitations. Only 261 students attended the two high schools. There was no superintendent of schools, no professional supervision. Instead, 97 school committeemen chose textbooks, examined students and teachers, and supervised the schools. As a result, education was heterogeneous, more a collection of village schoolhouses than a coherent system.

This lack of system bothered school reformers. The charismatic Horace Mann strove to awaken his countrymen and to channel their generalized faith in education into support of the common school. The very names given the public school movement—"crusade," "revival" —underlined its evangelical origins (Katz, 1968, pp. 157–171). The next generation of schoolmen, more bureaucrats than evangelists, believed that if public education were to fulfill its high mandate it must be unified and standardized. Philbrick spoke for these leaders when he declared in 1885 that the chief task of the new educational statesman was the "perfecting of the system itself. With this end in view, he always has some project in hand: the establishment of a training school for teachers, an evening school, or an industrial school; the adoption of a better method of examining and certificating teachers . . . an improvement in the plan of constructing schoolhouses; the devising of a more rational program and a more rational system of school examinations." This was the key: the *rational* system, the "one best way." Philbrick (1885) scorned those "amateur educational reformers" who argued that the school "machine is already too perfect" (p. 58), that administrators were putting organization before education. "The best is the best everywhere" (p. 57), he argued. "If America devised the best school desk, it must go to the ends of the civilized world" (p. 58).

And so we find that, during the latter half of the nineteenth century, schoolmen across the nation sought to bureaucratize urban education. In part, they paid attention to organization because they had to cope with vast numbers of children. The superintendent of schools in Brooklyn reported in 1893 that there were 377 classes with enrollments over sixty, and 130 with enrollments over seventy (Penniman, 1895, p. 289). Reformers thought it utopian to push class sizes much below fifty children per teacher. "Organization becomes necessary in the crowded school in congested districts," wrote the superintendent of the Worcester schools, "just as hard pavements cover the city street" (Marble, 1894, p. 166).

As part of this daily task of dealing with masses of pupils, schools needed to provide the socialization necessary for urban life. In 1874, seventy-four leading educators, including many city superintendents, signed a statement written primarily by William T. Harris and explaining the "Theory of Education in the United States": "The commercial tone prevalent in the city tends to develop in its schools quick, alert habits and readiness to combine with others in their tasks. Great stress is laid upon (1) punctuality, (2) regularity, (3) attention, and (4) silence, as habits necessary in an industrial and commercial civilization." Further, they argued, the new forms of corporate organization "make such a demand upon the community for directive intelligence that it may be said that the modern industrial community cannot exist without free popular education carried out in a system of schools ascending from the primary grades to the university" (Doty and Harris, 1874, pp. 12–16). The bureaucratization of schools, then, was considered essential to the whole process of modernization.

In justifying the new positions of superintendents and supervisors, the specialization of functions, and the creation of hierarchical structures, schoolmen often found it useful to compare schools with factories, with railroads, and even with the army. During the nineteenth century, such comparisons were rarely more than casual analogies, useful for public relations in an age when businessmen had great influence and prestige. In contrast with factories or large mercantile organizations, schools remained relatively simple in internal structure, their hierarchy based on relative power more than on minute division of labor, and their "product" difficult to define in precise, nonnormative terms. In addition, the pattern of political control of schools—the intersection between the lay community and the schoolmen—remained pluralistic; the lines between "policy" and "administration" were fuzzy and ever changing, the delegation of responsibility to superintendents ambiguous. Not until the turn of the century, with the campaign to centralize control of schools and to "take them out of politics," did schoolmen consciously try to use business corporations as a blueprint for urban school systems (Katz, 1968; see also Callahan, 1962).

Process of Standardization

For a bureaucratic system to work, it was obviously first necessary to get the children to school—and on time. To some schoolmen this task might have been onerous, but to the City Superintendent of the Portland Public Schools (1876) it was pure poetry: "A school with an enrollment of fifty, daily attendance fifty and none tardy is a grand sight to behold in the morning and afternoon" (pp. 8–9). Cities vied with each other in reporting rates of attendance and punctuality, sometimes computing them to the third decimal point. This spurred Philbrick (1885) to comment: "when we see 98 or 99 per cent of attendance reported, we know that this must be either, on the one hand, simply the result of a particular manner of keeping the records or, on the other, of a pressure equally powerful and harmful brought to bear upon the pupils" (p. 191). Some teachers had so "overdrawn the evils of tardiness" that children hid all day to avoid coming into class late; others used more positive methods, such as keeping honor rolls for those who had perfect attendance (Tyack, 1967, pp. 483–484).

It soon became clear, however, that voluntary schooling would simply not attract all the children, especially those who presumably needed education most. Thus, compulsory schooling became a prime goal of some urban administrators. Horace Mann had questioned whether rearing children "in a state of ignorance" is "one of the inalienable rights of a republican," and later schoolmen echoed his thought. "Would you have a policeman drag your children to school?" a superintendent asked rhetorically. "Yes, if it will prevent his dragging them to a jail a few years later" (Philbrick, 1885, pp. 185, 188). In 1866 Massachusetts passed a law decreeing that truant children be taken from their parents and put in public institutions. Only slowly did the idea of coercive attendance gain acceptance, however; in New York, truant officers had to go into the slums in pairs to avoid being beaten by irate parents and neighbors. And even in urban slums, where parents wanted their children to go to school, often there were not enough seats in the classrooms. Until well into the twentieth century, universal education was more a hope than an actuality. (See Rubenstein, 1969, pp. 50–51; Stambler, 1968, pp. 202–205.)

Crucial to educational bureaucracy was the objective and efficient classification of pupils. Reformers attacked the customary village pattern of grouping children of diverse ages and attainments in one-room neighborhood schools. They also questioned the efficiency of teaching the older children in grammar school classes of two or three hundred. Emulating German practice as described by Horace Mann, Philbrick introduced the first "egg-crate school" in Boston in 1847. Instead of having two large halls, his Quincy Grammar School was divided into twelve rooms, in which students were grouped according to academic achievement. In time, the scattered primary schools became consolidated into buildings which also contained several grades in separate classrooms. In 1856 Philbrick announced his "one best system" of classifying pupils:

> *Suppose we have six hundred scholars, of all ages, residing within a reasonable distance from a central point, and suppose we erect for their accommodation a union schoolhouse, containing twelve rooms, each room capable of accommodating fifty scholars. Now, after an examination, let these six hundred scholars be distributed in these twelve rooms, according to their advancement. . . . Let all in the same class attend to precisely the same branches of study. Let the principal or superintendent have the general supervision or control of the whole, and let him have one male assistant or subprincipal, and ten female assistants, one for each room [p. 263].*

And thus was stamped on mid-nineteenth-century American education not only the graded school but also the pedagogical harem —the male principal and his "female assistants." This system rapidly spread to the muddy plains of Chicago and to the city of Portland, set among the fir forests of Oregon. Capping the graded arch of classrooms was the public high school. Observers at the time noted that the uniform classification of pupils and the specialization of function among teachers were but instances of a division of labor, which represented "the universal law of progress. The teacher's time and talents being concentrated upon certain work, it becomes easier by repetition and therefore is likely to be performed more efficiently" (Shearer, 1898, p. 18; see also Goodlad and Anderson, 1963, pp. 44–49).

Proper classification of students made possible a uniform curriculum. "A good program for one city would be, in its substance, a good program for every other city" (Philbrick, 1885). Here again the search for the "one best system" led schoolmen to emulate one another and to prescribe the teachers' work through close supervision and regular examination of the children's progress. The criteria for judging the teacher were clear: Did she adhere to the course of study? Did the pupils learn what was listed there? Each step of the educational ladder was carefully calibrated; a child could advance to the next rung only when he passed his test. "System, order, dispatch, and promptness have characterized the examinations," wrote the Portland superintendent in 1874. "Next to a New England climate, these examinations necessitate industry, foster promptness, and encourage pupils to do the right thing at the right time" (Report for 1876, pp. 8–9).

Division of labor and programming of instruction required coordination. In the stratified world of the urban school, coordination implied supervision—a man in control, a superintendent. To the ambitious bureaucrats who attended the meetings of the Department of Superintendence of the National Education Association, it was clear that lay school boards were incompetent to oversee the schools. The professional superintendent should be to urban education what the captain of industry was to business: "It is common with educators, when urging the substitution of supervision by superintendents for that by local committees, to direct the attention of the people to the analogy of all cooperative occupations of importance, such as railroads, cotton mills, banks, insurance companies, and the like; and to argue that . . . it would be the height of folly for the directors to distribute the duties among themselves. . . . This is a pointed and timely home thrust" (Harrington, 1872, p. 250).

Other schoolmen spoke of the superintendent as the conductor of an educational railroad or the inspector general of the classroom army, and it was the boast of more than one that he could sit in his office and tell by the clock what each child was studying at that hour. Along with the grandiose rhetoric of the superintendents ran an undercurrent of disdain for the boards they nominally served, a fear that their own powers were shaky, a prickly rejection of criticism (Tyack, 1967).

"Amateur Educational Reformers"

In the 1870s and 1880s a growing group of critics claimed that the very standardization the schoolmen had achieved represented not progress but regression. A great variety of people—businessmen, newspapermen, professors, even a few renegade school bureaucrats—joined in the attack on "the school machine." The editor of the Portland *Oregonian* declared in 1880 that the professionals had gained far too much power: "In nearly every city there has been growing up during the last ten years an elaborate public school machinery, largely managed and directed by those whom it supports. Nominally it is controlled by the taxpayers of the districts, but in reality by associations of persons who live as professionals upon the public school system."

A professor in Ohio warned: "There is no place where a crotchety, a bumptious, or tyrannical man can do more harm than at the head of the public schools of a large city. For a generation our schoolmasters have gone on developing the system, the public supporting them with abundant money and influence; and now, when the work is called perfect, and we are called on to fall down and worship . . . it is seen by the discerning that the Graded School is only an appliance, that it leaves education to brain and heart where it was before, and that the new system has become inflexible and tyrannous" (Hinsdale, 1878, pp. 30, 32).

A former teacher, Mary Abigail Dodge (1880), sniped at the captains of education: "The tendency is not to put more brains inside the schoolroom, but more offices outside. . . . The thing which a school ought not to be, the thing which our system of supervision is strenuously trying to make the school into, is a factory, with the superintendents for overseers and the teachers for workmen." All that supervision accomplished was to destroy "the life of the schools by making them a round and routine of uniformity and mechanical drill; taking from the teacher freedom, ambition, and influence, and sacrificing the pupil to a showy and sonorous 'system.'" No form of degradation more harassed the teacher than the unceasing demand for statistics, the endless blanks to fill out to please some superior:

> 'Twas Saturday night, and a teacher sat
> Alone, her task pursuing;
> She averaged this and she averaged that
> of all her class were doing [Hinsdale, 1878, p. 40].

Some critics of the urban school bureaucracies argued that the complex machinery of the schools crushed intellectual curiosity, initiative, and individuality. "My children learn little in the Public Schools but the rules," commented an Ohio lawyer. A professor described the "graded-school idea" thus: "to set the children of a town or city in a solid framework, containing twelve compartments from front to rear, and then to shove the whole forward at a uniform velocity, without regard to the surface of the ground or the length of the children's legs" (Hinsdale, 1878, pp. 28–29).

Patronage and Pluralism

Angrily, school administrators replied to the armchair critics of the school machine (Philbrick's "amateur educational reformers"). But the most powerful threat to their program of bureaucratization came from lay school board members. To the bureaucrats, ethnic or religious or party loyalties were aberrations irrelevant to the unified systems they were attempting to create. They wished to build meritocratic organizations insulated from political patronage, structures which would contain career ladders for themselves and other professional educators. They sought to subject all children to the "one best system" in the same way, regardless of social background; distinctions in classification of pupils or in instruction were to be made solely on educational grounds, free of "extraneous" community influences (Cubberley, 1914).

Throughout the nineteenth century, local politics in many large cities frustrated these bureaucratic designs. This was in part what Philbrick meant by "excessive decentralization of administration." L. H. Jones (1896), Superintendent of Schools in Cleveland, complained: "The unscrupulous politician is the greatest enemy that we now have to contend with in public education." When cities expanded, school boards generally grew larger, since new wards gained representation on the central committee. In 1885, in ten representative cities listed by Philbrick, the size of the central boards varied from eighteen to fifty, with a majority of members elected by wards. In New York, Philadelphia, and Pittsburgh, hundreds of ward committeemen shared the responsibility of running the schools. These central and local boards, a carryover from village patterns of district school trustees, often retained effective control over jobs and money. In a few urban systems, influential superintendents were able to select textbooks and teachers, assign contracts, and control the schools, subject only to the rubber stamp of an acquiescent board; but in most cities laymen refused to abandon their traditional powers. As a result, a common complaint of school administrators was that they could examine teachers but not hire them, write a course of study but not choose textbooks, write tracts on school architecture but not decide who would construct buildings. In short, there was "political" control of schools, often on a decentralized ward basis, as contrasted with the ideal of a centralized professional bureaucracy. (See Cronin, 1965; Rice, 1893.)

Here, then, was the origin of persistent conflict between school managers desiring professional autonomy and citizens reluctant to relinquish control. Here, also, was the source of their conflicting perceptions of power—those who saw a menacing "school ring" of bureaucrats setting up tyrannical "machines" versus superintendents who protested that they had responsibility without real authority. Superintendent Maxwell of Brooklyn was a case in point. He knew that his success depended largely on informal political skill, not formal power: "He knew Boss Hugh McLoughlin well and so, whenever Maxwell needed something, he knew where to get it. He went to the Boss on Willoughby St., and if, perchance, the Boss was whittling or absorbed in deep thought, Maxwell adapted himself to circumstances. He studied the whims and foibles of the leaders and played on their vanity to attain his ends." When he became superintendent of the unified boroughs of New York in 1898, "he was expressly forbidden by the city charter to interfere in the management of any school in the city" (Abelow, 1934, p. 104; see also Palmer, 1905).

Maxwell faced a problem common to city superintendents of the time: Since principals and teachers usually owed their jobs to the lay school board members, subordinates were frequently able to sabotage the plans of the managers. In Philadelphia, Superintendent McAllister did not even visit many of his schools, since he knew that he would be unwelcome (Rice, 1893). In Boston, teachers told visitors that they felt free to ignore the course of study (Katz, 1968, pp. 177–179)'. The Los Angeles superintendent complained in 1870 that the schools were "conducted on a sort of guerrilla system," by which he meant that the troops did not want a commander. In other cities administrators said that principals regarded their schools as "feudal baronies" (Tyack, 1967, pp. 481–482).

In 1896 the *Atlantic Monthly* published anonymous "confessions" of teachers who admitted that church membership, political partisanship, and personal claims on board members were prime reasons for employment. In commenting on this, L. H. Jones (1896) wrote: "It is difficult to decide which is the more startling, the innocent acceptance of the situation by teachers and superintendents or the depth of cupidity and cold-blooded selfishness manifested by the partisan politicians, and even by members of school boards." At the turn of the century, when reformers attempted to create objective criteria for hiring and supervising, teachers actively fought the concentration of power in the central office. They feared the possible autocracy of "one-man rule" and believed that their own interests were better served by a more pluralistic power structure in education. Almost universally, school employees fought the abolition of the ward boards in New York in 1896. Margaret Haley, the spirited Irish head of the Chicago Teachers' Federation, opposed giving the superintendent greater authority. And in Baltimore, teachers joined forces with politicians to oust reform superintendent Van Sickle (Hammack, 1969, Ch. 3; Strayer, 1911, pp. 330–31).

The schools were big business for politicians and an avenue of social mobility for politically astute immigrant groups. When the Immigration Commission (U.S. Congress, 1911, pp. 48–55) surveyed thirty-seven cities in 1908, it discovered that 42.8 per cent of the public school teachers were children of foreign-born parents and 5.8 per cent were born abroad (17.8 per cent were of Irish origin, 8 per cent German)'. In some cities, such as Philadelphia, the political machines required dues from the teachers for whom they had secured jobs. Control of school boards also gave businessmen and politicians other sources of graft and influence: sales of textbooks—a major scandal of the time, contracts for supplies and buildings, preferential tax assessments, and extortion (Salmon, 1908).

But patronage and graft were not the only stakes in control of schools. Symbolic issues were often more important to the great mass of the citizens. Most bureaucrats accepted WASP values and saw schools as a form of social control and homogenization. Ethnicity and religious diversity were irrelevant distractions. But to the polyglot residents of the large cities these were vital educational matters, and the lay boards often recognized them as such. Local ward boards, in particular, served as mediators between urban ethnic villagers and the larger society represented by the school system. A New Yorker observed in 1896: "The varied character of our population, and the concentration of special classes of our people in certain districts, makes it desirable that these people be represented in school matters, and this will only be possible by the appointment of local officials with necessary powers of action, who are acquainted with the distinctive characteristics (national, racial, . . . and religious) of the several neighborhoods" (Hammack, 1969, p. 114).

While school administrators generally accepted Horace Mann's version of a pan-Protestant "nonsectarian" religion, many urban Catholics and Jews found this form of religious teaching objectionable. Thus, local or central school boards often found themselves adjusting religious practices in schools to the wishes of the community.

Likewise, a number of immigrant groups wanted their children to study their native language in bilingual public schools. Germans effectively pressured school boards in Cincinnati, Baltimore, St. Louis, Chicago, and Milwaukee to teach German in elementary schools in those cities. San Francisco instituted "cosmopolitan schools," in which children of immigrant parents could study French and German (*Twenty-Second Annual Report,* 1875, pp. 144–148). In Milwaukee, as late as 1915, 30,368 out of 44,733 elementary school children were studying German, 3,102 Polish, and 811 Italian (*Proceedings,* 1915, p. 434).

During the latter half of the nineteenth century, superintendents were trapped between their vision of "the one best system" of school bureaucracy and the political realities of their positions. Even those who had served long and devotedly were often unceremoniously fired. For many, the job was a revolving door; the average tenure of office in San Francisco and Los Angeles was two years; Omaha, Buffalo,

Rochester, and Milwaukee, three years, Cincinnati and Indianapolis, five years. Aaron Gove (1909), for many years head of the Denver schools, observed that of the hundreds who served as superintendents, "most have left it for another prospect." Those who stayed with the profession, like Gove, struggled, piece by piece, to create bureaucratic foundations on which the future would build.

Centralization of Control

At the turn of the century a major wave of change came in urban education. This was hardly a grass-roots movement. Instead, it was reform from the top down, initiated by an interlocking directorate of leading businessmen and professional men, college presidents and professors, and school superintendents. They sought to reshape the governing political structure and to delegate major administrative decisions to the professional superintendent. In place of large school boards elected by wards, they wanted small ones chosen at large. Instead of proliferating lay committees to administer the schools, they built centralized bureaucratic staffs. In keeping with the rhetoric of elite progressivism, they claimed that such reforms would "keep the schools out of politics," but they really wanted more power for *their* people. Day-to-day influence shifted to the superintendent. Adopting the corporate board of directors as a model for the school committee, schoolmen sought—and largely obtained—greater authority for the manager. The common result of these reforms in urban education was to restrict public participation in decisions. Today, as new groups reach for power, as individuals seek a greater control over their destiny, as dispossessed people try to rebuild community, we live with the consequences of that reform (Tyack, 1972).

Implications Today

Now there is a crisis of authority in urban education that has called into question familiar articles of faith and institutional arrangements. Future historians will probably see the decade of the 1970s as a time of great ideological and structural change in American public education. Increasingly, citizens are doubting that progress will come from giving more power to professional leaders to reform the schools from the top down. Many doubt that experts will be able to devise a "one best system" of urban education that will serve all children equally well. New calls for reform—vouchers, performance contracting, community control—would profoundly shift the balance of power and thereby threaten vested interests and deep convictions of educators. It is a time of trial.

In a time of trial it is tempting to defend vested interests and old rationales without considering whether they have become dysfunctional. Goal displacement is a common phenomenon in large and old organizations—preserving jobs and familiar practices and outlooks without regard to the purposes of the institution. Free education has increasingly become a monopoly of public bureaucracies, and those who have felt excluded from a "closed system" of school politics have rebelled. Unless school systems find ways to become more responsive to these disenfranchised people, endless and bitter conflict lies ahead.

When one examines the origins of urban education, one finds patterns of "community control" not unlike those demanded by minorities today. The process of "reform" in the last hundred years has transferred power from laymen to professionals and has standardized education according to criteria devised by schoolmen. If one analyzes the two ambiguous words "community" and "control," one discovers that often the advocates of "community control" want access to jobs and affirmation of group identity in the classroom. People who have felt powerless and despised demand alternatives to what they label "educational genocide."

Generating alternative forms of education within urban public schools today will demand a new frame of mind. Many of our present failures stem from an inherited assumption that there is "one best system" of schooling (if only we could discover it) and that human variety is an inconvenience to be ignored as much as possible (unless it is "professionally relevant," like scores on IQ tests). Instead of regarding new patterns of schooling as a form of "deviance" from the norm—won through pressure politics or benevolent permission of bureaucrats—we should, I believe, invite and reward alternatives. Few would argue that the large high school is a humane environment, for example; yet the burden of proof often lies against those who would seek to create schools on a smaller, freer, more human scale.

Fortunately, there are signs today that urban educators are recognizing the need for pluralism. Of course, there are many obstructions: state education codes that prescribe innovation; administrators and teachers who sabotage the new because they fear it; alienated students who destroy even what they have helped to create; parents who oppose anything different from what they knew as pupils. But time and skill and patience can diminish such obstacles when the prime constituencies—the students, parents, and teachers—realize that they can together create meaningful choices.

A common temptation will always be to decree that this or that successful alternative should become the universal, one-best-system. That, of course, would undermine the whole principle of alternatives and choice. It is important to recognize that some may legitimately wish alternatives to the "right" of the present system, some to the "left." A group of teachers and parents may decide that firm discipline, individual desks bolted to the floor, and an old-fashioned curriculum suits their children best, while those in another "community" (not necessarily in one geographical area) may decide that they wish to run a Summerhillian school. In fact, genuine "communities" might well form from an initial commitment to a particular educational philosophy. Obviously not everything would be acceptable—Nazi indoctrination, or sectarian teaching, or a racially exclusive school; constitutional limitations alone bar much that would be unsound educationally and socially. (See Fantini, 1971, pp. 541–543.)

"No doubt excessive *centralization* of administration has been one of the chief obstacles to improvement in every department of our free school system." So might a Philbrick of 1985 write about our century. Centralization was an artifact, something that men constructed, in good faith and perhaps with wisdom in their time. Alternatives and decentralization we can create in our time, if we have the will.

References

ABELOW, S. P. *Dr. William H. Maxwell, the First Superintendent of the Schools of the City of New York*. Brooklyn: Schebo Publishing Company, 1934.

ANDERSON, J. G. *Bureaucracy in Education*. Baltimore: Johns Hopkins Press, 1968.

BUNKER, E. F. "Reorganization of the Public School System." U.S. Bureau of Education Bulletin No. 8, 1916. Washington, D.C.: U.S. Government Printing Office, 1916.

CALLAHAN, R. E. *Education and the Cult of Efficiency*. Chicago: University of Chicago Press, 1962.

City Superintendent of the Public Schools, Portland, Oregon. *Report for 1876*. Portland: Published by the Board, 1876.

CRONIN, J. M. "The Board of Education in the 'Great Cities,' 1890–1964." Unpublished doctoral dissertation, Stanford University, 1965. Rewritten as *Big City School Boards: Why and How Power Moved from the People to the Professionals in Urban Education, 1870–1970*. Unpublished manuscript.

CUBBERLEY, E. P. *Public School Administration.* Boston: Houghton Mifflin, 1914.

DODGE, M. A. *Our Common School System.* Boston: Estes and Lauriat, 1880.

DOTY, D., AND HARRIS, W. T. "A Statement of the Theory of Education in the United States as Approved by Many Leading Educators." Washington, D.C.: U.S. Government Printing Office, 1874.

FANTINI, M. "Options for Students, Parents and Teachers: Public Schools of Choice." *Phi Delta Kappan,* 1971, *52,* 541–543.

GILLAND, T. M. *The Origins and Development of the Powers and Duties of the City-School Superintendent.* Chicago: University of Chicago Press, 1935.

GOODLAD, J. I., AND ANDERSON, R. H. *The Non-Graded Elementary School.* (Rev. ed.) New York: Harcourt, Brace, Jovanovich, 1963.

GOVE, A. "Contributions to the History of Teaching." *Educational Review,* 1909, *38,* 493–500.

HAMMACK, D. C. "The Centralization of New York City's Public School System, 1896: A Social Analysis of a Decision." Unpublished M.S. thesis, Columbia University, 1969.

HARRINGTON, H. F. "The Extent, Methods and Value of Supervision in a System of Schools." *Addresses and Proceedings,* National Education Association. Boston: National Education Association, 1872.

HINSDALE, B. A. *Our Common Schools.* Cleveland: Published by author, 1878.

IANNACCONE, L. *Politics in Education.* New York: Center for Applied Research in Education, 1967.

JONES, L. H. "The Politician and the Public School: Indianapolis and Cleveland." *Atlantic Monthly,* 1896, *77,* 810–814.

KATZ, M. "The Emergence of Bureaucracy in Urban Education: The Boston Case, 1850–1884." *History of Education Quarterly,* 1968, *8,* 155–188.

KRUG, E. *Salient Dates in American Education, 1635–1964.* New York: Harper & Row, 1966.

MARBLE, A. P. "City School Administration." *Educational Review,* 1894, *8,* 163–169.

PALMER, A. E. *The New York Public Schools.* New York: Macmillan, 1905.

PENNIMAN, J. H. "The Criminal Overcrowding of Public Schools." *Forum,* 1895, *19,* 289–294.

PHILBRICK, J. D. "Report of the Superintendent of Common Schools to the General Assembly." *American Journal of Education,* 1856, *6,* 263.

PHILBRICK, J. D. "City School Systems in the United States." U.S. Bureau of Education, Circular of Information, No. 1. Washington, D.C.: U.S. Government Printing Office, 1885.

Portland *Oregonian,* February 9, 1880.

Proceedings. Board of School Directors. Milwaukee: Published by the Board, 1915.

RICE, J. M. *The Public School System of the United States.* New York: Century Company, 1893.

RUBENSTEIN, D. *School Attendance in London, 1870–1904: A Social History.* New York: August M. Kelley, 1969.

SALMON, L. M. *Patronage in the Public Schools.* Boston: Massachusetts Service Reform Association, 1908.

SHEARER, W. J. *The Grading of Schools.* New York: H. P. Smith Publishing Company, 1898.

STAMBLER, M. "The Effect of Compulsory Education and Child Labor Laws on High School Attendance in New York City, 1898–1917." *History of Education Quarterly,* 1968, *8,* 202–205.

STRAYER, G. "The Baltimore School Situation." *Educational Review,* 1911, *42,* 328–337.

Twenty-Ninth Semi-Annual Report of Superintendent of Public Schools of the City of Boston. Boston: Superintendent of Schools, 1874.

Twenty-Second Annual Report. San Francisco Public Schools. San Francisco: Spaulding and Barto, 1875.

TYACK, D. "Bureaucracy and the Common School: The Example of Portland, Oregon, 1851–1913." *American Quarterly,* 1967, *19,* 474–498.

TYACK, D. "Centralization of Control in City Schools at the Turn of the Century." In J. Israel (Ed.), *The Organizational Society.* Chicago: Quadrangle Books, 1972.

U.S. Congress, Senate. *Abstracts of Reports of the Immigration Commission.* Vol. 2. Senate Document 747, 61st Congress, 3rd Session. Washington, D.C.: U.S. Government Printing Office, 1911. Pp. 48–55.

CHAPTER **20**

History of an Urban System of School Governance

Robert L. McCaul

𝕮𝕮 𝕮𝕮 𝕮𝕮 𝕮𝕮 𝕮𝕮 𝕮𝕮 𝕮𝕮 𝕮𝕮

There are, of course, many ways of "explaining" the events of which the history of public school governance in Chicago is composed. These events may be seen as the results of actions by strong-willed men and women—by superintendents like E. Benjamin Andrews, Ella Flagg Young, or Benjamin C. Willis, or by presidents of the board of education like Graham H. Harris, Jacob M. Loeb, or James B. McCahey, or by mayors like Carter Harrison, William Hale Thompson, or Richard J. Daley. Or the structure of school governance may be seen as evolving in stages corresponding to the evolution of the structure of municipal government; or as moving from decentralization to centralization to decentralization to centraliza-

247

tion, sequentially through time, in response to intrainstitutional and extrainstitutional rhythms largely unknown. Or as a system subject to a kind of entropy that afflicts all human institutions and that as they enlarge and elaborate renders them more and more inefficient. Or as a system developing certain characteristics because the principles by which it is administered, organized, and financed have been borrowed from noneducational human enterprises. Or, to come at last to the approach of this paper, the events of which the history of Chicago public school governance is composed may be viewed as the consequences of a series of struggles on the part of various groups of persons and their allies for a share in the possession of the powers of governance or for participation in the exercise of these powers. (Although this paper is a case study of developments in Chicago school governance during the last century and a third, it will be obvious to anyone acquainted with urban school history that the Chicago experience is not altogether unique and that the data and discussion presented in this paper have relevance for other urban school systems.)

From 1835 to the present day various groups of persons, one after another, have attempted to make changes in public school governance, and other groups of persons have resisted change. The changes sought have been in the personnel possessing and exercising the powers of governance or in the mechanisms by which the powers have been possessed, allocated, and used. Certain groups have been actuated by some of the highest of motives—by love of their children or concern for the commonweal; other groups, by some of the lowest of motives —by prejudice or selfishness or by hope of graft and loot. Certain groups have sought to gain or retain powers for themselves because they hungered for the pleasures of dominance and authority or because they wished to protect pupils of their own ethnic, religious, or socioeconomic background or because they wanted security in their occupation or profession or because they genuinely believed that their individual knowledge and experience would enable them to improve the quality of policy making or policy execution within the system. Certain groups have sought to gain or retain powers not for themselves but for others, expecting that participation in governance by those others would bring the school system into closer accord with their ideals of democracy, civic virtue, effectiveness, or fiscal prudence. Certain of the groups engaging in struggles over the powers of school governance have consisted of persons within the school system itself— of members of the board of education, superintendents of schools and other administrators, teachers, nonteaching employees, and pupils. Certain groups have consisted of persons outside the system—of members of parent organizations or of the political, church, ethnic, business, or communications institutions of the city or of the agencies of state and federal governments.

Boards of Education

The first law dealing specifically with public education in Chicago was passed by the Illinois General Assembly in 1835 and approved by the governor on February 6. "An Act relating to Schools in Township thirty-nine North, Range fourteen East" provided for a decentralized structure of school government, with powers distributed among four sets of officials (the Cook County Commissioners, the County Commissioner of School Lands, a township board of common school inspectors, and district boards of common school trustees) and among the legal voters of the township and school districts. The most important of the powers held by the legal voters was that of electing the inspectors and trustees.

This structure lasted only two years and was then replaced by a centralized structure, with power of appointment of school inspectors and trustees vested in the city council. Sections 83 to 92 of the first city charter, March 4, 1837, and "An Act relating to Common Schools in the City of Chicago and for other purposes," approved March 1, 1839, transferred the powers of school governance to the Common Council of the City of Chicago. The members of the council were made "commissioners of common schools" and were to do "all acts and things in relation to said school funds which they may think proper to their safe preservation and efficient management." As commissioners, the councilors were given the power of raising by taxes sufficient money for building schoolhouses, supporting and maintaining public education, and paying teachers. They also received the powers needed to fix the salaries of teachers, prescribe the schoolbooks to be used and the studies to be taught, and "pass all such ordinances and by-laws as they from time to time deem necessary in relation to said schools and their government and management." Finally, the council was to appoint annually seven persons as inspectors of common schools and three persons in each district as common school trustees, the inspectors and trustees to have such powers and duties as might be prescribed by the council.

The provisions of the charter of 1837 and act of 1839 yielded marked advantages. The school and political territories of the city were made coextensive, and the city was freed from dependence on the county in school finances. Because the council had become the sole repository of the powers of school governance, coordinated action on school matters was facilitated and a "system" of public schools could be more readily organized. The new structure soon exhibited serious disadvantages, however. Very quickly the council found that it could not spare the time and attention needed for running the schools. It was saddled with responsibility not only for education but also for sanitation, police, fire, and other municipal services, all of which were proliferating as the city's population doubled, tripled, and quadrupled in the middle decades of the century. To lighten its burdens, the council gradually delegated the exercise of its school powers to the board of school inspectors. Besides, the revised city charter of February 16, 1857, abolished the position of district school trustee, imposing on the board of education (the new title of the old board of school inspectors) the business duties formerly transacted by the district trustees. Yet the board was still left in the awkward position of running the schools under a delegated authority.

The board chafed under its subservience to the council and under the uncertainty and inefficiency introduced into financing and managing the schools by the council's possession of statutory powers. In 1868 and in 1871 the presidents of the board requested the legislature to confer upon the board in law the powers delegated to it by the council. These pleas did not go unheeded by the Illinois General Assembly. Section 80 of "An Act to establish and maintain a System of Free Schools," approved April 1, 1872, contained paragraphs applying only to cities exceeding 100,000 in population; that is, only to Chicago. Of twenty-two powers of school governance listed in those paragraphs, sixteen were vested wholly in the board of education, three were vested in the board but could be exercised only with the concurrence of the council, one (the selling of school lands) was vested in the council but could be exercised only on written petition of the board, and one (the levying and collecting of school taxes) was vested wholly in the council and officers of city government. The act was explicit about the board's possession of the sixteen powers, stating that "no power given to the board shall be exercised by the city council."

Under the act the council was deprived of its power of appointing members of the board of education, this power now being committed to the mayor. No restrictions were put upon the mayor's right of appointment save that his nominations had to be by and with the advice and consent of the council and his nominees had to have been residents of the city for the preceding five years. The appointment of school board members has been a mayoral prerogative since 1872. Since councils have generally rubber-stamped the mayor's nominations and since residence, age, citizenship, and other formal requirements for eligibility have been merely circumstantial, the prerogative has been naked of legal safeguards that would prevent an unscrupulous or irresponsible mayor from appointing inferior people or worse to the board.

Section 80 of the act of April 1, 1872, brought to an end a period of council supremacy that had lasted a third of a century. It had taken the board thirty-three years to wrest from the city council the powers of governance centralized in the council by the charter of 1837 and the law of 1839. The board did not make a clean sweep, however; the council still held rights in the field of finance, and these rights were to be a source of friction between the council and the board for many years. Otherwise, the powers of school governance passed over to the board. Now these powers were as centralized in the board as they had been in the council, and the board proved as tenacious in its grip on them as the council had been. From 1872 on into our own day, and sure to continue beyond, battles have been waged to secure for the superintendents, the teachers, the nonteaching employees of the board, the pupils, and the people a share in the powers of school governance.

Superintendents of Schools

The ordinance of November 28, 1853, creating the office of Chicago Superintendent of Schools made the occupant completely menial to the board. He was to "act under the advice and direction" of the board in performing his duties, which the board would "from time to time direct." He had no authority over business and legal affairs; over the appointment, transfer, and promotion of teachers; or over the choice of textbooks or content of the curriculum. According to the ordinance, his only plenary power was to be that of granting pupils permission to enroll in the middle of semesters and attend schools outside of their home districts (Chicago Board of Education, 1880). Section 80 of the law of 1872 did not even mention the office of Superintendent of Schools, merely affirming that the board would have the entire superintendence and control of the schools.

Nor were the boards in the 1860s, 1870s, and 1880s disposed to delegate any fraction of their authority to the superintendent, although some boards were more relaxed on this score than others and some superintendents were more trusted and allowed more independence. Mostly the board acted as its own executive and ran the schools through standing committees of its own members. Yet all this while, from 1853 into the next century, the number of educational alternatives had augmented and the range of educational alternatives had expanded. A wise and appropriate selection among priorities and alternatives required familiarity with a specialized literature in psychology, sociology, and pedagogy that was becoming more extensive, technical, and recondite. Boards of education, composed of unpaid laymen with other responsibilities and other drains on their time, were being confronted with a multiplying volume of school business and a bewildering array of educational options. And civic, professional, and business groups were demanding higher standards of efficiency and honesty in the conduct of school affairs.

However resistant the board was to sharing its powers with the superintendent, it was not able to withstand forever the stimuli impinging upon it. In the 1890s some members began to realize that the board could not obtain the assistance it needed from the superintendent if it continued its "tyranny" over him (Chicago Board of Education, 1895, 1896; Chicago Educational Commission, 1899). Moreover, from 1898 to 1900 and from 1909 to 1915, Chicago had two superintendents, E. Benjamin Andrews and Ella Flagg Young, who were unwilling to wait docilely for the board to get around to conferring executive powers upon the office of superintendent. Andrews reached out for control of the hiring, promotion, and discharging of teachers, and Mrs. Young for control over the selection of textbooks and the program of courses. She also sided with the teachers in their efforts to extract from the board increases in salary and improvements in job security and teaching conditions. Although the board since 1895 had been talking about transferring executive powers to the superintendent in order to eliminate "pull" in hiring and promoting teachers and in order to achieve greater expertness in educational decisions, it took fright at Andrews' and Mrs. Young's aggressiveness and fought to keep them as powerless as preceding superintendents had been.

By 1916 wrangling and strife between the boards and superintendents and boards and teachers had pushed the school system to the brink of destruction, or so it seemed to the city council. The council ordered its committee on schools, fire, police, and civil service to investigate the disorganization of the schools, and the committee concluded that it was imperative to enact a new state law reserving to the board the right of making policy and giving to the superintendent power to organize and administer the system without interference from the board (Committee on Schools, Fire, Police, and Civil Service, 1916).

Such a law was enacted by the Illinois General Assembly at its next session. The Otis law (named after Ralph Chester Otis, the member of the Chicago board of education who had drawn it up)' was approved by the governor on April 20, 1917. Like the act of 1872, it provided for the mayoral appointment of school board members, with concurrence by the city council; and it stated explicitly that the powers vested in the board were not to be exercised by the council. Where the Otis law differed from the act of 1872 was in its assignment of specific powers to the superintendent of schools, business manager, and school attorney. The superintendent was to prescribe and control, subject to the approval of the board, the courses of study, textbooks, educational apparatus and equipment, and discipline in and conduct of the schools; and he was to perform such other duties as the board by rule might decide. *Only* upon recommendation of the superintendent (or by a two-thirds vote of all board members), was the board to make appointments, promotions, and transfers of teachers, principals, assistant and district superintendents, and all other teaching employees; select school sites; locate schoolhouses; and adopt and purchase textbooks and educational apparatus. Equivalent powers in the business and legal departments were allocated to the business manager and school attorney. All three officers were granted the right of attending board meetings and entering into its deliberations, but not the right to vote.

Just as the charter of 1837 and the act of March 1, 1839, had set the pattern of governance for the period from 1840 to 1871, and just as the act of April 1, 1872, set the pattern from 1872 to 1916, so has the Otis law set the pattern from 1917 to the present day.

This is not to imply that the Otis law and the procedures outlined in it have gone unaltered. The law kept the method of mayoral appointment without safeguards as it had been. A mayor could, if he wished, reach the superintendent through his appointees to the board, as Mayor Thompson had in maneuvering the ousting of Charles E. Chadsey and the impeachment of William E. McAndrew. A second flaw in the Otis law was that it made the superintendent, the business manager, and the school attorney coequals, each enjoying direct and independent access to the board. The superintendent did not have supervision over the planning of expenditures, nor did he have control over appropriations. In the depression, when finances became the most critical of all the elements involved in running the schools, Superintendents Bogan and Johnson were reduced to much the same state of powerlessness as superintendents had been prior to the Otis law. The president of the board, James B. McCahey, was able, on account of the troika administrative structure, to usurp the powers of the superintendent and business manager and act as the school system's top executive.

Groups of concerned citizens and teachers charged that the McCahey administration was destructive to teacher morale and the proper functioning of the schools. They also accused Mayor Kelly of using the system as a source of patronage for his political machine, and Superintendent Johnson of intimidating teachers and reaping personal profit from his position. Unable to prevail upon Kelly to appoint persons sympathetic to their views to the board, these groups succeeded in getting the North Central Association of Colleges and Secondary Schools to issue an ultimatum warning Kelly that accreditation would be withdrawn from Chicago public high schools unless administrative responsibility were centered in the office of Superintendent of Schools and a new superintendent and a new independent board of education installed. Kelly, alarmed at the prospect of blacklisting by the North Central Association, appointed a committee of five university presidents (of DePaul, Illinois Institute of Technology, Loyola, Northwestern, and University of Illinois) and the president of the North Central Association to consider the Association's decree and any other features of the school system the committee wished. Henry T. Heald, president of Illinois Institute of Technology, was elected chairman, and his committee published a report suggesting the formation of a Mayor's Advisory Commission on School Board Nominations and a revision of the Otis law to make the superintendent the chief administrative officer of the system (North Central Association, 1946; Committee of University Presidents, 1946). Kelly accepted these proposals and immediately established an advisory commission. The reform groups of the city, having failed to place persons of their choice on the board through the structure provided by the Otis law, had won their battle to add to that structure a mechanism that would, they anticipated, ensure the appointment of persons with ideals compatible with their own.

Since 1946 the Mayor's Advisory Commission on School Board Nominations, revamped by Mayor Daley in 1969, has submitted to the mayor slates of qualified candidates for the board. On the commission sit representatives from civic organizations and the universities, and their selection of candidates has reflected the upper-middle-class, professional orientation of the commission's membership. The commission is not a statutory body, and the mayors are not bound to confine themselves to its slates. Nevertheless, there is a movement underway in the legislature to enact a law that would legalize the commission and compel the mayor to appoint one of three candidates recommended to him by the commission for every vacancy on the board.

A second proposal of the Heald committee—that the Otis law be amended to eliminate the *troika* set of administrative officers at the head of the system—was carried out after Mayor Kennelly's election. On June 4, 1947, a law was enacted creating the office of General Superintendent of Schools, the incumbent to be "chief administrative officer of the board" and to "have charge and control, subject to the approval of the board, of all departments and of the employees therein of the public schools, except the law department." For reasons not altogether clear, the amendment left the school attorney still on the same plane as the superintendent, but it did straighten out the line of authority in the executive branch by subordinating the business manager to the superintendent.

Manifestly, since the 1890s there has been a trend toward involving the superintendent, as an "expert," more and more in policy making and policy execution by bestowing on him powers of initiative in certain phases of school governance and by making him the officer in the formal structure of governance to whom the responsibility of furnishing the board with information and counsel is entrusted. But the need for expertness has passed beyond the point where a board can safely rely on one expert or where a superintendent can act as a universal expert on all school matters. It is platitudinous to remark that school problems have become so complex that the task of framing appropriate solutions crosses many academic disciplines and fields of knowledge. Perhaps there would be some merit in attaching to the board a permanent consultative panel of professors from the departments of education, sociology, political science, and business of the local universities and an executive secretary and a small clerical and statistical staff. To this panel both the board and the superintendent could turn for counsel and for documentary and quantitative data focused on the particular problems confronting them.

The People

Various groupings of citizens—ethnic, economic, social, religious, and professional—have endeavored to obtain for themselves or for persons sympathetic to their needs, views, aspirations, or ideals some participation in school governance. These groups have begun by seeking to seat their own representatives, or representatives to their liking, on the board of education. If defeated, they have then tried to accomplish changes in the structure set forth in the charter of 1837 and the law of 1839 or in the law of 1872 or in the Otis law.

A frequent target of the "outs" has been the method of mayoral appointment. For example, as noted previously, the civic-reform groups who were outraged at what they thought was unethical, inefficient management of the schools by Kelly, McCahey, and Johnson were able to get the Mayor's Advisory Commission on School Board Nominations added to the procedural machinery. Other groups have attempted to divest the mayor wholly of his power of appointment. The substitute most commonly proposed has been election by the people at large or by areas or districts. Efforts to amend the school law so as to have an elected board were made in 1893, 1904, 1916, 1919, 1922, 1943, 1967, and 1971. All of these efforts have failed. The usual allegation brought against popular election is that it would introduce partisan politics into school affairs. How and why election should be more perniciously partisan and political than mayoral appointment is somewhat difficult to understand.

There is no denying that the method of mayoral appointment has left many groups in the city unrepresented on the board. Eventually Chicago may have a board, categorical in composition and blending appointees and electees, with some members appointed by the mayor from the city at large; with the superintendent of schools a member *ex officio;* and with a city counselor, a Chicago public school teacher, a nonteaching employee of the board, a Chicago public school pupil, and a citizen from each of the three areas of the city as members elected by their respective constituencies. All members of the board, including the superintendent, would have voting rights.

Another tactic pursued by groups excluded from the board has been that of agitating for the creation of additional agencies of school government at the area, district, and neighborhood levels to which they can have access. Typically, these groups have been the poor, the depressed, and the repressed of the city; but they have often found allies among more affluent, higher-status groups, who have argued on grounds of equity or efficiency that an all-city board should be balanced out by localized agencies of governance. The question of what kind of local agency would prove most effective was first debated in Chicago in the 1890s. Some persons believed that Chicago should follow New York's example and organize district school boards under the central board (*Chicago Tribune,* 1893). A less extreme remedy was proposed by Mayor Harrison's Educational Commission in 1899. It recommended that the mayor appoint for each school district a committee of six residents, who would visit the schools of their district and report their observations and recommendations to the board. The district resident commissioners were to serve three-year terms. Such a plan, the commission promised, would ward off two dangers: first, the danger of excessive conservatism produced by the administration of the schools by a superintendent and other "experts"; and second, the danger of rigidity and standardization produced by a structure in which only one agency, an all-city school board, makes policy for an entire, heterogeneous school system (Chicago Educational Commission, 1899).

The commission's bill was defeated in the state legislature, and the issue of centralism versus localism lay dormant until it was awakened in the 1960s by black and white militancy. The board then reacted by forming local school councils, principal-selection committees, school-area committees, and a subordinate school board in the Woodlawn area. The trouble with these area and neighborhood committees is that they are afflicted with weaknesses that may destroy their usefulness. Often they mix teachers and principals with parents and so are vulnerable to domination by the school administration; their lines of communication with the board and superintendent are uncertain; their opinions and suggestions need not be considered by the board and superintendent; their existence is at the pleasure of the board and superintendent and is not secured by statute or ordinance. Unless these defects are eliminated, more drastic forms of decentralization and local participation may become the objective of a crusade on the part of dissatisfied groups in the city. If they succeed, the consequences may be tragic (Havighurst, 1971).

Conclusion

Other groups than those already mentioned have come to share in school governance. For many years the teachers and their allies struggled to win for the teachers a say in school governance. In May 1967 they finally won their battle: the Chicago Teachers Union and the board signed a collective-bargaining agreement providing for "the first formalized participation of teachers at the city-wide level in the determination of board of education policy and in the administration of the schools" (Whiston, 1967). The pupils—through student councils, liaison committees, interschool councils, and places on faculty committees—may now express their grievances and their views on school policy. The custodians, clerks, and craftsmen employed by the board are civil service employees and unionized; therefore, the Civil

Service Commission and the unions, as well as the board, join in making decisions on working conditions, hiring, firing, and salaries. Some departments of the federal and state governments have forced certain patterns of teacher assignments and pupil enrollment and attendance upon the Chicago board.

As we have seen, the law of 1872 vested most of the powers of school governance in the board of education. During the century that followed, various groups sought to gain for themselves, or for others sympathetic to their ideals and views, a share in the possession and exercise of these powers. Their efforts resulted in an addition to the number of agencies and mechanisms of governance and a wider distribution of the powers of governance. The implications for educational change of these movements have been discussed toward the end of each section of this paper. In brief, the more significant of these are the following: (1) The movement to involve professionals like the superintendent and teachers in policy formulation and execution and the increase in the complexity of educational problems suggest the desirability of expanding the range of expert advice and information available to the board, perhaps by some such device as a permanent consultative panel. (2) The movement for broader representation on the board of education and the dissatisfaction with the method of mayoral appointment suggest that there will be a change in appointment procedures and the composition of the board, perhaps by the creation of a board blending appointees and electees and categorical in composition. (3) The movement to give parents and citizens a voice in school affairs at the local level will not cease unless the present neighborhood and area councils and committees are secured in their organization and regularized in their operation.

Changes of a higher and more far-reaching sort than those just mentioned are in the offing. There are now signs that we may be entering a new era, in which struggles over the powers of school governance in Chicago, in Illinois, and in other communities and states will be generated by a new ruling ideal—not the ideals of efficiency and participatory democracy characterizing previous eras, but the ruling ideal of equality of educational opportunity.

The reasoning behind this prediction may be roughly summarized in this manner. Since the middle of the twentieth century, it has been generally agreed that individual differences are in the main produced by variations in home and school environments. And variations in home and school environments—causing as they do differences in scholastic aptitude, aspirations, and training—instigate differences —that is, inequalities—in educational opportunity. To equalize educational opportunity, and equal educational opportunity is one of the traditional American ideals, it will be necessary to equalize school environments.

Cases involving these considerations have come into the courts, and verdicts have pronounced equal educational opportunity as one of the rights guaranteed citizens by the "equal-protection" clause of the Fourteenth Amendment. We may expect, therefore, that the ruling ideal of equal educational opportunity, backed by the might of the courts, will initiate a trend toward standardizing the means of education.

What effect will the trend toward uniformity have on the distribution of the powers of governance? Clearly, uniformity can be achieved only by an agency superior to the districts and possessing the powers needed for imposing uniform policies, practices, and conditions upon them. Such an agency must be at the state or federal levels in the hierarchy of government, though the possibility of its being a federal agency is remote. Thus, a struggle between state and local agencies of school governance is in immediate prospect. Very probably this struggle can have no other outcome than that state boards of education (or their equivalents) will emerge victorious and in possession of the controlling powers of governance, with a corresponding loss of powers by district boards of education, district superintendents, district teachers, and district citizens. Then another phase in the sequence of struggles over school governance will commence, as the state superintendent of schools, the state organizations of teachers, and the state groups of citizens strive to gain for themselves or sympathetic others a share in the possession and exercise of the powers centralized in the state board.

References

Chicago Board of Education. *Twenty-Fifth Annual Report of the Board of Education.* Chicago: Clark & Edwards, 1880.

Chicago Board of Education. *Forty-First Annual Report of the Board of Education.* Chicago: J. M. W. Jones & Co., 1895.

Chicago Board of Education. *Forty-Second Annual Report of the Board of Education.* Chicago: J. M. W. Jones & Co., 1896.

Chicago Educational Commission. *Report.* Chicago: Lakeside Press, 1899.

Chicago Tribune, April 24, 1893.

Committee of University Presidents. Report on the administration of the

Chicago Public Schools to Mayor Edward J. Kelly, June 17, 1946.
In Havighurst-McCaul project archives, University of Chicago.
Committee on Schools, Fire, Police, and Civil Service of the City Council
of the City of Chicago. *Recommendations for Reorganization of
the Public School System of the City of Chicago.* Chicago: Bar-
nard & Miller, 1916.
HAVIGHURST, R. J. "The Reorganization of Education in Metropolitan
Areas." *Phi Delta Kappan,* 1971, *52,* 354–358.
North Central Association of Colleges and Secondary Schools. "Action
taken in regard to the Chicago Public Schools, March 30, 1946."
In Havighurst-McCaul project archives, University of Chicago.
WHISTON, F. M. "Statement to Board and Teachers." *Agreement between
the Board of Education and Chicago Teachers Union, January
1, 1967 to December 31, 1967.* Chicago: Chicago Teachers Union,
1967.

CHAPTER 21

The Incandescence of Tradition

Cyril O. Houle

> *To understand our own motives and to use well the institutional tools lying within our reach, we must realize not only that leaders of American academic life have always sought to foster the common welfare but also that our forebears construed the dictates of public conscience in varied and somewhat divergent ways. If the ingredients of our tradition are not recognized for what they are in all their distinctiveness, the tradition itself, like a burned-out bulb in a youngster's hand, can do little good but much harm. Rightly understood, tradition is incandescent [Storr, 1956, p. 84].*

It was in the autumn of 1960 that the newly inaugurated president of West Dakota A. & M. University, Dr. John Starr, came to the conclusion that his institution would need to pay much more attention than before to serving the educational needs of the men and women who lived in the state's largest city, New Francisco.

This was a surprising decision, for Dr. Starr was a true-blue product of the land-grant-college system. In his twelfth year he had joined the 4-H Club; and his career had continued within the comfortable and wholesome tradition that he knew and loved. In acquiring his three degrees and moving smoothly and rapidly up the academic ladder, he had changed from one state university to another with no sense of strain or tension. He loved the land-grant system, and he never understood why some people said that it is inbred or that it devotes too large a share of its resources to agriculture and rural life.

And yet he found that things looked different when he got over to the office with the deep carpet and the big walnut desk. Sitting there one day, he reflected that three matters troubled him deeply. First, he had apparently taken over his new responsibilities at a time when the Cooperative Extension Service (which most people called "agricultural extension"), the chief vehicle for community service education, was undergoing a violent and cataclysmic internal struggle, which was raising such a dust that he could detect neither the lines of battle nor all the antagonists. Second, it appeared that other universities in the state thought they had as much right as the land-grant university to carry on extension activities; what was worse, they expected to get state and federal money for doing so. Third, it turned out that the institution over which he was now presiding had not one but many extension services, which already, in the aggregate, reached many more people than did the residential program on the campus.

Taking this last point first, Dr. Starr ticked off as many of the activities as he could readily recall: the Cooperative Extension Service itself; the General Extension Division, with its residential continuing education center, its off-campus and correspondence classes, and its extension centers dotted over the state; special extension bureaus in the colleges of education, engineering, and pharmacy; much informal work done independently by the other professional schools; an alumni educational program; and both radio and television stations. This was just the formal part; in addition, as Dr. Starr got out into the state, he found many members of his faculty out there too, engaging in various kinds of entrepreneurial consultative and lecturing services. He knew better than to try to restrict the individual enterprise of his professors, but it did seem to him that someone less busy than himself should coordinate the university's formal program. This conviction was deepened one day as he drove around and around the courthouse in a county-seat town unable to find a parking place for himself but noting that five other university cars had managed to do so.

This wealth of different services was further enriched by the fact that each of the other institutions of higher learning in West Dakota had its own programs and seemed to want to keep them. There was the state university, which a mid-nineteenth-century legislature had decreed should be separate from the land-grant college; what had then been put asunder, no man had ever been able to join together. There were the three regional institutions, which had rapidly moved, by grace of modern legislatures, from normal schools to teachers' colleges to state colleges and soon would be universities, at least in name. There was St. Catherine's, the large Catholic university, in the heart of New Francisco. There was New Francisco University itself, near the outskirts of that same city. Each of the seven was completely separate from the others, and that is the way the presidents wanted it, though the heads of the public institutions occasionally announced a deep feeling of brotherhood, particularly when hotheads in the legislature suggested creating a single governing board with a chancellor.

On their campuses, these seven institutions could stay apart from one another; but when they got out into the field, they entered into a common area of service. Moreover, they then encountered the new community colleges. The problem of coordination had not previously troubled West Dakota A. & M., since it alone had been able to offer most of its programs to the public without charge. This open-handed generosity had been made possible by the fact that, in the support of extension, the land-grant institution had long been the chosen instrument of the federal government, though it was not quite clear who did the choosing. This system was reinforced by the support of a far-seeing and intelligent group of farm leaders and perpetuated by a legislature so apportioned that the vote of each substantial and thoughtful resident of rural areas was equal to from five to ten of the votes of the irresponsible and flighty people of New Francisco.

But in the twenty years from 1940 to 1960, one of the greatest mass migrations of all time occurred as Americans left rural areas and moved to towns, cities, and suburbs. This movement was greater, for example, than the inpouring of migrants from abroad during the peak years of 1890 to 1910. Efforts were made to hush up this loss of the rural population, but finally the Supreme Court got wind of it—with unfortunate results. The state legislature and even the federal congress came to include many strange new people, never previously visible and often with odd names. It turned out that they had studied at all kinds of institutions, and, for the life of them, they could not see why the land-grant university should be a chosen instrument of governmental service. Why should their own colleges and universities—public or private, state, municipal or regional, secular or religious—not be allowed to serve the public also?

These institutions, Dr. Starr came to realize, had their own traditions of community service. American colleges and universities were moving out into their surrounding communities to use education as a way of curing human ills. Leaving behind, often rejecting, the established format of the classroom and improvising with scarce resources, educational pioneers were creating new ways to learn and to teach. Usually these ventures were highly individualistic. Each case was unique, each remedy immediate, each loss a catastrophe, each success a triumph.

In earlier ages, in a primitive, rural, agricultural country, the chief frontier for continuing education had been on the farms and in the villages and small towns. But by 1960, when Dr. Starr's tenure as president began, the major arena of service was the city. West Dakota had come late to an urbanized culture, but now New Francisco had become dominant in the life of the state and had all the promises and problems of other large concentrations of people. Woodrow Wilson had identified them a half century earlier, when he left the presidency of Princeton to assume the governorship of New Jersey:

> . . . *all the great urban problems, all the great problems of water supply and of drainage, all the problems which are created by congestion of population lie here right around us, where we are. Jersey has to solve the problem of the home and the problem of the city and the problem of transportation under conditions which put her character and sagacity to a greater test than the character and sagacity of any other equal population in the country is put. That is what is infinitely interesting about New Jersey. We have got the problems of the country in such a form that they are raised to their highest degree of difficulty and complexity . . . we in New Jersey have got to show the country how these problems are to be met and settled [Bebout and Grele, 1964, p. 111].*

Dr. Starr had recently driven across the industrial landscape of New Jersey and had a vivid picture of how far short of success its efforts to master the ills of urbanization had been. But he did not see how he could fail to accept the challenge of Wilson's words. His own university, like every other, was a center of knowledge and talent. It had achieved its power from the support given to it by a rural society, but all its hopes for the future depended upon the increasing strength of an urban society. Dr. Starr had early determined that every president needs to put his emphasis somewhere. He resolved to make the reconstruction of the university's community service and continuing education program the central emphasis of his early presidential years. And so in the 1960s West Dakota A. & M. embarked on a series of shifts of structure and emphasis that was to bring its program of service to adults (particularly those of New Francisco) into as rational a pattern as the conflicting hopes and demands of mortal people will allow.

The first task of Dr. Starr and his colleagues was to make an inventory of the services West Dakota A. & M. provided in the field. To their surprise, they discovered that virtually every part of the institution was involved in some fashion. (Dr. Starr urged similar surveys on his fellow presidents at their quarterly summit meeting; they decided uneasily that he must be up to something, and began getting together statistics of their own.) When the catalog of activities at A. & M. was looked at by the steering committee that Dr. Starr had appointed, a semantic problem arose. West Dakota A. & M. had said for years that its three functions were research, teaching, and service. What was meant by "service"? A vocal group developed the argument that the only proper functions of a university are teaching and research and that, in the field as on the campus, the university should do nothing that did not fall within these two categories. Anything else was suspect. Should a county agent cull a farmer's chickens or weigh his steers? Should an industrial consultant set up a company's books? The hypothetical—often lurid—examples of service and servicing continued; and the group won its point. The classic statement of the university's functions was reduced by one third.

The steering committee recommended a revised structure to coordinate the off-campus education that was now being handled unevenly by all parts of the institution. Some years were required to put this whole reorganization into effect, since it was necessary to wait for a few deaths and retirements. Even yet the plan is not perfect, nor are all the slots in the organization chart admirably filled.

The overall design may be briefly suggested. A vice-president for off-campus activities helps set general institutional policy, handles the major outside contacts of the university, and exercises general supervision over all of its community education. A dean of extension and his staff have direct administrative control over all facilities related to his function, such as the residential center for continuing education, the television and radio stations, the correspondence division, the field staff, and the other special units and personnel. To assist this dean in building programs, a staff member has been appointed in each school, college, or other major division of the university. In the larger units, he has the title of "assistant dean"; in the smaller units, he has a lesser title—if there is a lesser title than "assistant dean." This whole group works together, not always amiably, to administer present programs and to plan new ones.

The process has been aided by the fact that those who engage in community services and continuing education are encouraged to learn the basic principles underlying their work. To the old methods of apprenticeship and trial and error were added seminars, conferences, guided reading, and other forms of in-service education for all members of the extension staff. Many of them, going more swiftly and surely than their colleagues at the task of mastering their craft, secured graduate degrees in adult education and were encouraged and aided by the university to do so.

In the general reorganization, the major problems were presented by the Cooperative Extension Service, which was by far the largest unit of service to adults and which still had very potent allies in the farm lobby, the legislature, and congress. Its staff was profoundly uneasy about its future in an urbanized society. The dissent among the members of that staff was so strident and clamorous and the varying proposals so extreme that Dr. Starr at first thought he could never get consensus among the various proponents even if, as seemed unlikely, he could cut through the clouds of language to find out what they really wanted.

For example, some of the members of the extension staff had recently undergone strange changes in their viewpoints. In the past they had insisted, with an almost ritualistic incantation, that their work was based on sound scientific principles, that it grew inherently from the nature of agriculture itself. Now suddenly they were saying that what was important was the method of extension; its staff members knew how to work with people, how to develop community interest and support, and how to create dynamic learning situations. They could do this just as well in the city and the suburbs as in the country; furthermore, they could do it at once. Dr. Starr, a hard science man himself, wondered uneasily if the extension staff had become dangerously infected with sociology.

As time went on, however, the Cooperative Extension Service gradually learned how to live with the rest of the university—and a surprising thing happened to it. As soon as it stopped thinking about its glorious past, it turned out to have a glorious future. In a program of gradual change, it developed a diversified and flexible program, abandoned ancient rigidities and dogmas, found new audiences, discovered how to analyze and serve their needs, and in general became as different from the traditional Extension Service pattern as the present College of Agriculture is from the ancient model from which it evolved.

West Dakota was influenced in its urban extension program by certain national and state developments. Beginning in 1959, the Ford Foundation made grants "for experiments in applying the nation's university resources directly to the problems of American cities." By the time the program was concluded in 1966, a total of $4,500,000 had been provided for this purpose to eight universities and one community organization. While West Dakota was not adroit enough to secure one of the grants, it did profit from the experimentations conducted elsewhere and from the widespread discussion of them in books, journals, symposia, conference proceedings, and other places. Many ideas about how to proceed were tested: urban agents, urban teams, store-front centers, community organizations, problem clinics, urban specialists, planning centers, bureaus of community service, governmental reference centers, clearinghouses of information, policy seminars, demonstration projects, student volunteers, community-development officers, and special services to schools and other institutions (*Urban Extension,* 1966).

Though this profusion of devices and techniques seemed overwhelming, it was soon made insignificant by the actions of the federal government. For, from the President of the United States on down, everybody seemed to want to do something about the problems of urban America. New cabinet-level departments were created, and most existing departments got congressional authorization for programs designed to further their particular missions; the Department of Agriculture, for example, received major new funds to enable the extension division to work on nutritional problems in the inner city. Each of these new grants had its own special regulations, so that money flowed, showered, or trickled from Washington along many different channels.

The broadest and potentially the most significant program of support to community service and continuing education was that provided by Title I of the Higher Education Act of 1965. The language of this title was a bit confused, but it seemed to support the growth of extension to permit it to help solve social problems, particularly in urban areas. Despite the exacting and cumbersome requirements laid upon the states and territories that wished to secure Title I funds, the need for help was so great that forty-nine of the fifty-four had their plans approved within the first hundred days after the regulations were announced. The initial grant of funds was ten million dollars, but the federal government intended to increase that amount substantially in subsequent years. This hope was frustrated, as was so much else, by the Vietnam war; but by the start of the 1970s the program was moving forward strongly, though still on an austerity budget. In 1970–71, a total of 531 institutions of higher learning participated in 545 projects. West Dakota took full advantage of Title I and, like other states, managed to find two dollars of its own to add to every three dollars of federal support.

Within the state, the pattern of higher education changed drastically during the 1960s, with both good and bad consequences for the citizens of New Francisco. As expected, the state colleges became universities and broadened their own extension divisions, but only one of them was near enough to the city to offer it any services. St. Catherine's and New Francisco University had limited funds but used at least some of them in enlarging their evening college programs. The state university, amid much fanfare, opened a branch in the city so that its special needs could be met, but the achievement of this purpose was hampered by the dual desires of the faculty on the new campus to cut its ties with the mother institution and to shape its program in the image of Princeton. Community coleges proliferated, and most of them—particularly those in New Francisco—made determined efforts to serve the educational needs of adults.

In the last half of the decade, community service was joined by community action. Militancy, anger, and self-righteousness pervaded all the institutions of higher education in the state. Students and professors marched and demonstrated; academic senates took bold stands on current social issues; boards of trustees were vilified because they refused to support the views of their attackers; and everyone in authority was told that his ideas were no longer relevant, an adjective which turned out not to need a referent. Some good and some harm came from all this action, but no man can yet construct a balance sheet of its consequences.

While all these events were taking place, the colleges and universities of West Dakota were trying to learn how to collaborate with one another. At first, they went their separate ways, but, as federal money began to pour into the state, the absence of any mechanism to create and control a unified approach to community service became ever more apparent. President Starr became increasingly uneasy about the matter. A lot of funds were coming to A. & M., and he found ways to keep them well. But what about the money that, so unwisely, was going to the other institutions? As they moved out to serve essentially the same constituency, the adults of the state, would the various boards and administrators and faculty start squabbling? Would the legislature take up the matter? Would the difficulties finally lead to the dreadful culmination of an overall board and a chancellor?

Dr. Starr took a bold step. He asked for a special meeting with the presidents of all of the other colleges and universities in the state and, over the lunch table, reviewed for them the provisions of Title I, which call for the designation of a broadly based state agency to represent all higher educational institutions and all groups skilled in community improvement. He proposed that they jointly ask the governor to set up a special commission and to give it authority to allocate all federal funds for extension-type activities. The other presidents had had some fairly sober thoughts themselves about the way things might drift and finally agreed to the plan, though not until they had spent some time trying to outmaneuver one another on the composition of the commission. The plan was then taken to the governor and he gave it his support, after having his staff check it over thoroughly to be sure that there were no hidden pitfalls. He had had a lot of experience with college and university presidents.

The task of the commission was far from easy. Congress and the state legislature demand coordination and yet support a variety of conflicting arrangements, each of which must be followed to the letter. As time went on, however, the commission's fairness in allocating funds brought it increasing stature and skill in seeming to meet all of the detailed requirements while actually preserving freedom and flexibility. It was greatly aided by the fact that its executive secretary had spent five years in the Cooperative Extension Service as Assistant Director for Administration and therefore had had valuable experience in getting around regulations and in knowing how and where to bury bodies.

So much for structure. Dr. Starr realized that as long as people sat around talking about how to put lines on an organization chart, the net result would be one of jealous safeguarding of present interests. A forward thrust was needed. As he drove around the state and particularly around New Francisco, he saw plenty of problems worthy of attention. How could his own university work upon them as fruitfully as it had upon the needs of rural life in earlier days? More specifically, how could the faculty of the rest of the university be led to follow the example of the College of Agriculture and immerse themselves deeply in the task of serving as change agents? More broadly, how could all the institutions represented by the commission work collectively at the same task?

No pattern came readily to mind. Both the Ford Foundation projects and the federal programs had displayed a panorama of techniques, but no firm structure of service had coalesced. Perhaps it was still too early for one to appear. The agricultural leaders of the nation had worked steadily from about 1845 to develop an agricultural extension service, but it did not take firm shape until the early part of the twentieth century. Dr. Starr hoped that urban extension would not take as long a time as this to develop, but he knew of no way to achieve an established service other than to let it emerge from the crucible of experience.

He found a dynamic guiding principle, however, in a passage from Mary Jean Bowman's description of the development of the agricultural curriculum. "Here learning was a joint affair," she said; "the professor and the student worked it out together by trial and error. . . . If nothing to suit their purposes could be found in books, then it must be found by going back to the roots of things, by observing, experimenting, testing" (Bowman, 1962, p. 543). What those first professors did with their students on the campus, their successors did with the farmers in the field. It was because both professor and farmer went to "the roots of things, by observing, experimenting, testing," that the agricultural extension service helped change the nature of rural life in the United States and became a model for the world.

Was the university now beyond all that sort of thing? The faculty members seemed to be sitting securely on their respective disciplines. And yet, Dr. Starr wondered, was it not possible that many of the university's advanced specialists might find that if they worked with people out in the community, going to the very roots of their difficulties, the disciplines themselves might be refreshed by becoming more responsive to social needs?

With this question, there began that probing problem-solving approach which has since so revolutionized West Dakota's program by giving it a constant infusion of new thought. A growing interaction sprang up not only between field and campus but also between campus and campus as scholars found themselves working collaboratively with the community leaders of the state. It became increasingly clear, as McGeorge Bundy (1962) had said it would, that "the university, properly construed, is not merely a place of full-time effort by young students and old professors; it is also a home, for hours, or days, or weeks at a time, of all highly civilized men."

New adult educational programs must always be designed to

meet the specific needs of a student or students in a given social setting for an immediately applicable body of subject matter. Since the campus of West Dakota A. & M. is so beautifully situated out in the country, its faculty members felt awkward at first about moving into the city. The two metropolitan institutions did little to discourage this sense of awkwardness. But those faculty members are specialists in many subjects: in land-use planning, music, public health, and the fine arts; in marketing, criminology, public administration, and recreation; in the theater, gerontology, public health, and water pollution; in family life, welfare, management, engineering, and education; in industrial development, labor relations, world affairs, and transportation. And, of course, in the humanities. More than that, the members of the university's staff have special expertise in leadership training, group dynamics, the use of mass media, conference planning, community organization, counseling, and those intangible but important arts which have to do with locating and influencing the leaders of the power structure. This technical competence and social expertise were deeply needed by the people of the city. Presently, as faculty and city dwellers learned to work together, the old mistrust between them began to dissolve. And, as he watched the working out of these processes, Dr. Starr began to feel better about sociology.

Like many another farm boy, he had picked up a frightening impression of urban life during his 4-H Club days. It seemed a strange blend of squalor and magnificence—of Wabash Avenue under the elevated tracks and of beautiful boulevards along the lake front, of mean and nasty streets leading to the amphitheater and of splendid clubs and ballrooms, of sleepless nights huddled four in a room in a giant hotel, and of steak for breakfast, accompanied by the Purdue Glee Club. As Dr. Starr came to know the people of New Francisco, however, he began to realize how narrow his viewpoint had been. For he found that many city people live in pleasant neighborhoods and have a sense of community. He found that even in the slums people depend upon one another and some of them can be depended upon. He found that community leaders are genuinely and deeply concerned to leave the city a better place than they found it.

This feeling was greatly strengthened at a gathering one evening at the extension center in the heart of New Francisco. The advisory council of the center was meeting and asked him to attend. As he sat through the session, he heard the city dwellers express the same mixtures of wisdom and folly, of generosity and ill-concealed self-interest, and of long-range hopes and short-range fears which he had heard so often in the meetings of rural people. He saw, too, that the views of his own faculty members were respected as representing knowledge, not opinion. As a result, plans were formed that struck a balance amid all the divergent views and, because they were effective compromises based in part on the advice of experts, had a good chance of acceptance.

Human beings are pretty much the same everywhere, he thought as he drove home that evening. Man may sometimes be apathetic or do foolish things to his physical or social environment, but sooner or later he has the wisdom to try, through reason and knowledge, to reach his potential or to remedy his mistakes. Whether in the open fields or the crowded city, the university can use its own incandescent tradition as a means of helping through education and research to shape and perfect the human mind and spirit.

References

BEBOUT, J. E., AND GRELE, R. J. *Where Cities Meet: The Urbanization of New Jersey.* Princeton, N.J.: Van Nostrand, 1964.

BOWMAN, M. J. "The Land-Grant Colleges and Universities in Human Resource Development." *Journal of Economic History,* 1962, *12,* 543.

BUNDY, M. "A Report from an Academic Utopia." *Harper's,* 1962, 10–15.

KELLOGG, C. E., AND KNAPP, D. C. *The College of Agriculture.* New York: McGraw-Hill, 1966.

STORR, R. J. "The Public Conscience of the University." *Harvard Educational Review,* 1956, *26,* 84.

Urban Extension, A Report on Experimental Programs Assisted by the Ford Foundation. New York: Ford Foundation, 1966.

PART VI

Philosophical
Perspectives

⬧⬧⬧⬧⬧⬧⬧⬧⬧⬧⬧⬧⬧⬧⬧⬧

Philosophers, as members of an interpretive foundational discipline, shed light on the problems of educational practice. As such, they explore the following questions: What necessary reforms are needed to relate educational objectives to urban change, and upon what value systems should they be premised? How can the "phenomenological crisis" in urban education be resolved to accommodate the urban school's diverse ethnic populations? How can school practitioners understand their clientele without personally experiencing their particular cultural environment? To what extent would the application of the overlooked European concept of "Heimat" to American urban problems assist in the solution of some of our current educational concerns?

Weldon believes that the aims of the "comprehensive school" of a generation or two ago—to purify, balance, and unify society—are unsuitable to urban schools today. The problems of urban schools, he feels, can be met only with far-reaching reform. He finds Dewey's notion of evolutionary reassessment of goals and means more attractive than the revolutionary structured change described by Engels. The kinds of evolutionary changes now required are individualized learning, cultural pluralism, and emphasis on affective education.

Morris senses that educational theory and practice have been traditionally associated with the scientific and humanistic disciplines. But general academic conceptions cannot depict the true character of cultural specificity and individual uniqueness. This "phenomenological crisis" is most apparent in the city, with its diverse ethnic groups. He specifies provocative solutions that universities and particularly colleges of education can implement to bridge the dichotomy between the truths of objective scholarship and personal phenomenologies.

Schieser describes the principle of "Heimat," the notion of "home" or "homeland," which finds expression in language, culture, tradition, and beliefs. European education has long fostered this principle and extended it for the child from his home to his neighborhood, city, and country, and finally to the world. In the United States, despite recent changes in curriculum and instruction, more research, and greater infusion of funds into the educational enterprise, we have overlooked the principle of Heimat, and perhaps this is the root of our current difficulties.

CHAPTER 22

Metropolitan Transformation of Aims of Education

Ward Weldon

A generation or two ago most of us were growing up in what we have come to call "comprehensive" schools. Such a school was supposed to instruct us in all the important subject-matter areas. It was expected to serve both the college-bound minority of students and the larger group of those who expected to go to work immediately upon graduation. In most school districts, the comprehensive school was, in fact as well as in theory, an agent of community unification and shared experiences. All economic and social classes attended one school. This was especially true at the high school level, where one school building typically housed the community's only secondary school program. Even elementary schools served a wide variety of social and economic groups, and this intermixture and inter-communication of the various identifiable social segments was considered an important function of the school.

But even a generation ago, certain factual discrepancies had to be ignored if one tried to take seriously the ideal that the school should function as a comprehensive institution. One such discrepancy was the widespread racial segregation in schooling. The existence of separate school facilities for white, black, or brown children was accommodated to the ideal of a comprehensive school either by thinking of minority groups as separate communities or by ignoring them altogether. A second factual discrepancy was private schooling for the wealthy and for certain religious minority groups. In most communities, the number of students attending private schools was small. Where there was a large percentage, however (in communities with well-developed church-sponsored school systems), educators worried about divisive social effects of such a dual system of education. A third discrepancy was the fact that a small but growing number of cities had more than one high school. The existence of two or more high schools detracted from the comprehensive-school ideal, even when the course of study was the same in both schools; for schools located in different parts of the city soon became associated with the neighborhoods they served, and one usually came to be regarded as educationally superior to the other.

In spite of factual discrepancies, most educators believed Dewey's assertions that the school should unify, balance, and purify the society. In the comprehensive school, we felt, our society was discharging its democratic responsibility to educate all of its citizens so that they could communicate with persons from all walks of life. We felt that schools offered all segments of the society a way to get a good start in the race for dignity, power, status, and wealth.

The comprehensive school was a satisfying dream, which encouraged educators and laymen alike to work for commonalities, unities, and mechanisms of free intellectual and social interchange in their schools. But the dream is dead. We no longer think of the comprehensive school as a factually accurate description of reality. Some still hold it up as an ideal or as a myth, but a new dream is being born and the old one has largely lost its power of attraction. We are in a period of transition between ideals. The small-town comprehensive school is no longer the type of education for which we strive. The big-city diversified school is here.

Urban Schooling

I told a lady who teaches in a wealthy suburban district that I work in urban education. "Oh, well," she replied sympathetically, "somebody has to do it."

Her remark reveals a depressingly widespread attitude. Many seem to feel that urban education concerns itself with substandard and somehow unpleasant schools and is therefore a second-rate area of specialization within the education profession.

For this teacher and for many other people, "urban education" is a misused and therefore a confused and ambiguous phrase. Even though wealthy suburban schools are a part of urban education (when the city is defined socially and economically rather than on the basis of archaic political boundaries), the term is frequently misused to apply only to schooling that occurs in economically poor or ethnically segregated areas of the "inner city." Urban education is frequently misunderstood as an unsuccessful attempt to apply standardized and comprehensive educational programs to unwilling or unable students.

Under this misconception, "inner-city" schools are bad in the same way that individual students became bad in the comprehensive schools of the past. Since the comprehensive school allegedly offered all students the same opportunity, those who failed to take advantage of the opportunity were held to be either stupid or rebellious. The educators comfortably pointed out that they had done all that could be reasonably expected. A similar "It's their fault, not mine" excuse, growing out of the ideology of the comprehensive school, is directed toward inner-city schools today. This kind of attitude will not be fully corrected until there is a new ideology and new common understanding of the purpose of schooling.

The old question was: How can our comprehensive schools be used to unify and transform society? Although this older question is becoming hypothetical and merely academic, value patterns change slowly. Urban schools are still being condemned for their failure to be comprehensive. Soon, however, critics will be applying a different yardstick—a yardstick that measures what urban schools actually *do*, instead of what they do *not* do. A new schooling ideal is already developing. The new ideal focuses its attention on the strengths of the urban school. The new question is: How can the differentiated and multifaceted experiences available in urban schools fulfill our needs and desires?

Our values and ideals are finally beginning to take account of the fact that our schools are large-scale operations, with considerable differences existing from school to school and within schools. An increment that makes a school larger may have one of two quite different effects. It may be merely quantitative and lead to no sharp change in the functioning of the school; or it may force the school to become different in quality.

An example of the first type of change is the addition of one student to an elementary school with an enrollment of two hundred pupils. It is reasonable to suppose that there will be no apparent differences in the character of the school as a whole when it increases its enrollment by a single student. Let this process of quantitative change continue, however, and the situation becomes ripe for a change of the second type. If the elementary school should increase its size gradually to one thousand students, it will become a qualitatively different school. Some of the changes will be sudden, no matter how smooth and gradual is the climb in enrollments.

A school serving only about two hundred pupils in grades from kindergarten through sixth grade is likely to have only one self-contained classroom at each grade level. When the school enrollment reaches one thousand, there will be about five self-contained classrooms at each grade level. Sudden and thorough qualitative changes in the nature of the school experience will have occurred.

The change from one to two second-grade classrooms is one of the qualitative transformations that have occurred along the way. Second-grade teachers and second-grade pupils find their performance being compared to that occurring in other second-grade classrooms. Ability grouping is possible, and predictions by students as to who will be their teacher for the next year have become speculative rather than a foregone conclusion. When two self-contained classrooms are organized along ability-grouping lines, a tremendous difference comes into being almost immediately. Room assignment begins to indicate intellectual status and affects teacher and student performance expectations.

Changes in enrollment also bring about changes in methods of communication. A principal with a total staff of ten persons can keep himself informed of progress, problems, and concerns merely by conversing with his staff and by visiting classrooms. When there is a staff of fifty, new methods of communication and new forms of reporting are necessary. Another sudden change in the quality of schooling experience occurs when the hall-pass system is instituted. A school in which a student must get a pass to leave his assigned room and then go through interviews with a clerk and a counselor before being ushered into an office to see the principal is qualitatively different, from the student's point of view, from a school in which students regularly see their principal in classrooms and corridors and frequently have opportunities for informal conversation with him.

These changes in quality of the schooling experience are associated with the school's increasing enrollment. The changes in kind came suddenly, even though the numerical growth occurred gradually and evenly.

Transformations of Educational Ideals

The idea that gradual increments in quantity can lead to revolutionary changes in quality was put forward by Friedrich Engels. The increasing size of our cities and schools has contributed to a qualitative change in the purpose of schooling. The ideal of the comprehensive school is being replaced by one based on differentiation and individualization. Whereas Engels emphasized the sudden and explosive nature of changes in quality, Dewey argued that qualitative change can be smooth and continual.

For Dewey, as for Engels, gradual numerical change leads finally to qualitative transformation. The main difference between Dewey and Engels on this point is that Engels describes a largely deterministic process, in which human choice is incidental and unimportant, whereas Dewey recognizes the role of human choice in the making of changes in goals and values and suggests that these changes can occur naturally and continually. For Dewey, there need be no explosion unless people choose to behave unintelligently by ignoring the fact of change. Dewey's emphasis on education may properly be interpreted as his investigation of intelligence as it began to adjust itself to the special environment of the school.

There is another important difference between Dewey's description of change and the version given by Engels. For Engels, the quantitative, bit-by-bit change is swallowed up in the sudden qualitative change. For Dewey, there is a renewal mechanism or continuity device. The goal becomes a part of a continuing string of numerical changes interspersed with qualitative transformations and reorganizations.

Dewey's clearest example of the ends-means continuum (his notion that ends and means are qualitatively similar, with ends—after they are achieved—turning into means toward a further end) is that of the ship's pilot on the high seas. The port is his goal; but after the ship has traversed miles of quantitative change and finally is safely berthed, then the pilot realizes that the port is just a way station. A new goal arises—perhaps having a good time, perhaps unloading the cargo. In either case, the harbor is no longer a goal. It has become, in retrospect, the means to some further goal. If bad weather or faulty navigation should throw the ship off course and prevent the immediate achievement of the goal, the goal will not endure in its present form for any length of time. If it is not achieved within some reasonable period of time, a new objective (possibly one that will eventually convert itself to a means of reaching the old objective) must be selected.

The implication of Dewey's "ends-means continuum" for educators today is that educational objectives are necessarily temporary phenomena. They will eventually be transformed whether we succeed in accomplishing them or not. If the goal is achieved, new ones arise beyond it. If not, new goals arise between the educator's present circumstances and his former immediate objective.

Proponents of the idea that educational goals are fixed and permanent usually mention the symbol-processing skills of reading and mathematical computation as examples. In fact, even these goals are temporary ones, from the viewpoint of the individual learners and teachers involved. A given child either learns to read and then adjusts his goals to something beyond or fails to learn this skill and begins to focus on ways to get along in the world without reading. It is the generality of the goal "Teach Every Child to Read" that gives it the illusion of permanence.

The Urbane School

The same suburban schoolteacher who inadvertently expressed her condolences to me when she discovered that I am involved in *urban* education considers herself sophisticated and *urbane*. The difference in meaning of these two words reveals the nature of the value of transformation now occurring in education. As schools become too large and finally too diverse to express the comprehensive-school ideal, a new goal springs into prominence for those who are able to perceive the metropolitan transformation of education. Let us examine the three main characteristics of the new ideal: individualization of learning experiences in instruction and in curriculum development, cultural pluralism, and emphasis on affective education.

Individualized learning. Learning has become more personalized and individualized than it used to be. In the just-initiated era of the urbane school, the old notion that everybody must do his learning in a large and intercommunicating group is disappearing. This emphasis on group activity and group cohesion was important in the comprehensive-school era. Learning with others and learning the same things were necessary parts of the unifying and balancing social mission of the school. Now, technology has given us the means of individualizing instruction. Audio cassettes, video carrels, and computer-assisted learning consoles are one-person-at-a-time learning systems.

Even the more conventional printed materials are becoming individualized. It is an old-fashioned teacher who lectures for an hour and then tells all students to read the same chapter and do the same homework exercises before the next day's class. Learning centers, open classrooms, and self-pacing learning materials capture the spirit of these early days of the urbane-school era.

Instruction is the first educational process to be individualized. Curriculum development and evaluation are not far behind. No matter how thoroughly the presentation and intake of the subject matter is individualized, a school is comprehensive rather than urbane until it has a way to allow individuals to select the material to be covered and arrange it in the sequence which the learner finds appropriate. Programmed learning is individualistic in its styles of presentation, but it is still largely group-oriented and conformance-based in its curricular aspects. The transition to the urbane school will not be completed until curriculum development and course planning are as well developed as individualized instruction. Students in urbane schools will choose their own topics and devise their own programs of learning. There will always be a "core curriculum" of communication and learning skills, which students must acquire before they can strike out on their own; but these core studies will quickly lose their status as educational goals by becoming means to a multitude of further goals.

In a sense, the individualization of learning in the urbane school is an extension downward in grade level of our most advanced learning activities rather than a radical departure in format. We now teach most subjects in the hope that students will later continue this study on their own outside of school. The capstone of a school career at the present time is the independent study and research that go into a Ph.D. dissertation. When the era of the urbane school gets into full swing, seventh and eighth graders will be doing individualized learning in the Ph.D. style, and first graders will be carrying out individualized applications and extensions of their formal course work.

Cultural pluralism. Schools have already given up any substantial pretense of inducting students into the total society. Suburbia continues its liberal-arts, college-preparatory curriculum, but this course of study is now easily recognized as only one of many differing approaches. In racially integrated schools, ethnic studies programs are aimed at segments of the school's total population. The idea that schools should have similar curricula to give everyone the same start or the same chance is evaporating. Its replacement is the concept that different groups, like different individuals, should choose their own programs of learning and arrange them in ways of their own choosing. Perhaps the most powerful type of learning experience possible is the one in which students must choose what to learn and how to organize themselves to meet their learning goals.

Affective learning. Since the school is no longer Dewey's microcosm of the broader society, spending time in school is no longer thought to contribute to a unified and intercommunicating society. Because individuals and groups must develop their own curricula, expressing their own values and priorities, there is no longer an automatic mechanism for achieving understanding through the joint experiences of school participation. Special new techniques are required for dealing effectively and peaceably with those whose values, experiences, and perceptions are different from those of the majority.

Affective learning is difficult to describe in words. It must be experienced to be understood. Its theory is still under construction, but its obvious experiential base is the practice of recognizing and developing personal and value-laden factors in learning and communicating. The teaching of listening skills, sensitivity workshops, training in goal setting, conflict-management laboratories, and simulation games designed to allow direct or vicarious experiencing of the workings of groups different from one's own all fall under this general setting. Getting along with others, once thought to be the normal side effect of all types of school experience, is becoming a school subject matter in its own right.

Recommendation for Transition Period

The key to successful transition from one era of schooling to the next is an intelligent and well-applied theory of how educational objectives change. Our presently dominant model of educational planning is static rather than dynamic. This model takes the objectives as given and then proceeds to make arrangemetns for instruction and evaluation in terms of these objectives. This kind of educational planning was acceptable in the comprehensive-school era, when the goals of intercommunication, social balancing, and opportunity equalization were considered unchanging and universal. The recognition that urbane-school objectives are individualized and changing creates the need for a new way of looking at curriculum planning.

As a start toward the type of dynamic and individually flexible model of curriculum development that will be required during the era of the urbane school, we might invert the presently dominant model. That is, we might develop an inductive and cyclic conception to replace the deductive and linear one with which we have been working. As we do so, we must be careful to note the difference between a flexible structure and no structure at all. The fixed objectives of the comprehensive-school ideal must be replaced with individualized goals and values which readily become means to further goals. We cannot tolerate (either psychically or economically) an unproductive and confusing state of planlessness. Each learner can become his own curriculum planner. To provide the necessary tools and procedures to make this potential situation become an actual one is the task of educators during this metropolitan transformation of the nature of schooling.

CHAPTER 23

Phenomenology and Urban Teacher Education

Van Cleve Morris

⬯⬯⬯⬯⬯⬯⬯⬯⬯⬯⬯⬯⬯⬯

As the graffito has it, "Nostalgia is not what it used to be!" There was a time when we could lament the passing of the university's traditional role in society—the quiet retreat for reflective study—and really believe that this paradigm represented what we could or should try to work our way back to. Nowadays, our nostalgia takes another form. Our homesickness for the old days is an empty longing. The way back is blocked. The Precious Tradition in Western higher learning is really over. Not only has the university changed; the world has changed. And we all know it.

Those of us who work in urban universities sense that the change in the American university is somehow more profound and deep-running than any formal explanation so far advanced. Of course, we are incessantly asked to be *relevant* and to *respond* to urban problems. And much of contemporary social science literature attempts to show us how. But at a deeper level, we seem to be experiencing a shift in the strategy of higher education itself, in its encounter with modern American life. I refer to the shift in strategy governing the conduct of scholarship and inquiry—the heart, after all, of the university's business. It so happens that teacher education as a derivative discipline is caught in the squeeze resulting from this shift in strategy, because its traditional support disciplines seem to be falling away and new ones emerging. In the uncertain confusion, there are faint signs that the field of education may assume a new role in academic politics. The present paper attempts an examination of this reshuffling and suggests a possible outcome.

The problem has its roots in the fairly recent past. Since its emergence as a professional discipline about seventy-five years ago, teacher education has built its case on the argument that education is a science and that its concepts and analytical structures can be extrapolated generally from the social sciences of psychology and sociology and, more recently, from the physical science of biology. For these seventy-five years, its scientific base has gone unquestioned. Now, in urban teacher-education institutions especially, we are discovering that preparing teachers for ethnic subcultures and minority populations requires the teacher educator to become aware of idiosyncratic outlooks (what I call "phenomenologies") of various urban groups before he can educate the teacher. And these outlooks, precisely because they are idiosyncratic and culture-specific, cannot be assimilated to the pursuit of general laws. They are therefore countervailing to the development of a science of education. Hence, the teacher educator's scientific house of cards comes tumbling down; and he now finds himself with a kitful of psychological, sociological, and biological concepts which are no longer relevant to his work, not because they are not true, which they are, but because they are scientific and his professional task is not. He finds himself in what I here label the "phenomenological crisis," a shift in the strategies of epistemology by which teacher education is governed and directed.

I am using the term "phenomenology" in its technical connotation in epistemology. It stands for a particular stance of contemporary philosophy regarding the nature of knowledge. At the risk of oversimplification, the phenomenologist's argument can be put somewhat as follows: "Philosophers can never be sure that the world exists or that they, as human beings, exist. It would be difficult, however, to fault the claim that in our 'natural attitude' [Husserl's phrase] of encountering the world, something called consciousness occurs. But consciousness is always intentional; that is, it is always consciousness *of* something. Consider, then, these two terms: 'consciousness' and 'something.' Consciousness without intentionality—that is, without the 'somethings' —is the province of psychology. On the other hand, the 'somethings' without the presence of consciousness are the province of traditional metaphysics. What we are after is a reality lying somewhere between psychology and traditional metaphysics, somewhere between nonintentional consciousness and the world we are conscious of. We shall call this region *phenomena,* an admittedly elusive term derived from a Greek word meaning 'that which presents itself.' Hence, the best we can do is to say that phenomena are the primitive features of the world which present themselves to our consciousness" (Morris, 1967, p. 145). The awarenesses described in this paper represent a practical illustration of how this form of knowledge increasingly insinuates itself into academic life and particularly into the education of teachers for urban schools.

Let me spell out more specifically what I think is happening.

It is no secret to anybody in the teacher-education business that the establishment of education as a university discipline has been a steady struggle over the last three quarters of a century. From Thorndike in the early years, to John Dewey and William Kilpatrick in the twenties and thirties, through the progressive-education movement of the forties, through B. F. Skinner, Jerome Bruner, and Jean Piaget in the fifties and sixties, the study of education has slowly and painfully gained access to the pantheon of academic disciplines in the American university.

The interesting feature of this achievement is that we in teacher education have made our way into the sunlight largely by convincing our academic colleagues and the American people generally that education can be treated as a science and that human learning can be examined empirically, much the same way that physiologists study digestion or psychologists study maze running. It is true that we have carried on a continuing flirtation with so-called "individual differences" in American educational theory. But the fact is that the phenomenon of individual differences is fundamentally antiscience. Science, as an epistemology, is not interested in differences. It is interested in general tendencies, plottable regularities, and universal laws that embrace the group, the class, the subset or the genus. Science is generic prone, and it is altogether proper that it should be. For that is the great genius of science; namely, that it can lead us to understandings that cover not just an isolated instance but a whole set of instances taken together. These understandings help us manage our experience much better and provide the basis for science's primary advertisement for itself; namely, that it is a method of knowing which makes possible "the prediction and control" of events.

One of the sad poignancies of contemporary scholarship is that the logical consequence of this absolute requirement of scientific epistemology—the drive toward general laws—is conveniently ignored by those who cannot bring themselves to break with science but wish at the same time to resuscitate the individual person as the primary datum of their thinking. There is a contradiction here which they apparently do not see. Rogers (1964, p. 119), as the paradigm case, says that the new phenomenological psychology will "explore the private worlds of inner personal meanings in an effort to discover lawful and orderly relationships there"; but a few pages later he asserts that this new movement represents man *"choosing* himself, endeavoring . . . to *become* himself—not a puppet, not a slave, not a machine, but his own unique individual self" (p. 130). Even the unsophisticated student, innocent of the esoterics of phenomenological psychology, might be tempted to inquire how one squares "lawful and orderly relationships" with the "unique individual self." How can anything unique be understood through general laws? This highly educated myopia travels undetected through much of modern social psychology.

But to get back to the argument and summarize the initial point: Teacher education has made its way into the university faculty club on the basis of its claim that education is a science and can be studied about and taught to prospective teachers like any other science. Accordingly, we have built our teacher-education curricula on the foundations of (a) the scientific philosophies of pragmatism and experimentalism; (b) the social and behavioral sciences of psychology and sociology; and, more recently, (c) the physical science of biology.

The practical consequences of this in schools of education are well known. Since education is a science, the phenomenon of learning (and teaching) can be viewed as more or less homogeneous throughout experience, and an individual prepared in the skills of instruction can be expected to practice education wherever children are brought together for schooling. Thus, we have come to believe that we can prepare teachers much as we prepare doctors; that is, by instructing them in the general knowledge of their craft and equipping them with general skills that can be made to apply to a relatively constant set of variables in their prospective clients.

Urban Dilemma

What is the situation today? Teacher education, at least in the major universities, is inexorably becoming urban in focus. And an "urban focus" means that preparing teachers for specific subcultures or minority populations is one of the new missions of any teacher-training institution. We are finding out that subcultures in urban America are as sharply different from mainstream America as the Trobriand Islanders are from the Western Europeans. Not only that, but the outlooks and perspectives of these ethnic populations are not susceptible to the conventional canons of social science. You cannot take a series of Margaret Mead field trips into the black ghetto or the Spanish barrio, run exhaustive surveys on local conditions and attitudes, and write up your findings. It simply will not work. Science cannot invade, let alone understand, the culture-based outlooks and perceptions of America's urban minorities. And that is because these outlooks and culture-specific perceptions, these "phenomenologies," are simply not susceptible to scientific inquiry. They will not reveal themselves to the inquirer or the investigator who relies on the conventional canons of social and behavioral science. And that is because they represent a wholly new kind of knowledge, which the American university is attempting to understand.

We have a dramatic contemporary example of this: the so-called "black experience." Although blacks have known it for a long time, the remainder of society is now beginning to comprehend that the experience of being black in twentieth-century America, in and of itself, is a unique psychological dynamic to which only some individuals are privy. This dynamic, this transaction between the person and his environment, leaves a deposit of awareness which can never be fully communicated to the white man. And this awareness—although not really expressible and therefore shareable, sometimes not even among blacks themselves—is primary in the structure of a black man's knowledge. It is the ground from which all his experience is gathered in, and it therefore is necessary in understanding how a black man comes to know a world controlled by whites. At an unsophisticated level it is manifest in a black's perception of a policeman. He sees there, as few whites do, potential repression and brutality. This is his "truth." At a more sophisticated level, it is revealed in the black intellectual's demand for "black sociology" or "black psychology." The black experience tells you that social science, "phenomenologically" speaking, is either black or white and not the disinterested, objective, value-free "quest for truth" it has always been advertised to be.

But to bring this back to our focus on teacher education, here is the situation: When we wish to prepare an individual for teaching black children, it is no longer sufficient to prepare that individual in the general knowledge of pedagogy and the technical skills of classroom instruction. A whole new kind of knowledge is called for, a new awareness, a new perception, a new outlook, which lies somehow beyond the social scientist's tools of inquiry.

And let me pause right here for an extended footnote on what this new kind of knowledge is *not*. This strategic shift from scientific to phenomenological ways of knowing is not another tired allusion to C. P. Snow's two-culture theory. Greater stress on the humanities, in contrast to the sciences, would be only a gross response to our predicament. The humanities are cognition-oriented rather than awareness-oriented; more precisely, they are an attempt to render our feelings and awarenesses cognitive. Although the name by which we call them sounds as if they are more "human," the humanities are like the sciences in that they are, as mentioned earlier, "generic prone." The humanities—art, music, philosophy, history, literature, religion—seek the overall meaning of life; they stretch out in the direction of generic principles of the nature of man and the ultimate aim of the human endeavor. Phenomenological awareness has a much more modest, more immediately personal scope.

Nor is this merely another version of the well-known distinction between the cognitive and the affective zones of experience. Phenomenological awareness is not merely how one feels; nor is it the sum total of one's emotions, in whatever array or disarray they may be. On the contrary, one's phenomenology is the perceptual ground *out of which* one's feelings and emotions emerge and become manifest in daily experience.

Another example may be helpful. Every member of a minority group—blacks, Latins, Indians, Jews, women—encounters the WASP male with a basic, built-in suspicion and distrust. This suspicion is of course more pronounced in some than in others, depending on heritage or personal experience, but it is a constant in the perceptual outlook of every discriminated-against individual. Now, this primitive form of distrust is not what one would call part of the affective life. Rather, it is what one starts with in encountering his fellowman. It is the ground out of which feelings and emotions are fashioned. Like water to a fish, it is the very medium out of which an effective life is created. Anger, hostility, frustration, pride, brotherhood, love, hate—all these are constructed out of the life lived by an individual who peers out on his world from the starting position of suspicious wariness.

To sum up, what we are after is an understanding of a new form of knowledge; namely, the set of phenomenological awarenesses that each individual or each subculture brings to the human encounter. Social science, as we have seen, turns out to be an impotent epistemology. Nor will the humanities be of much help. Finally, we are not speaking merely of affect as against cognition. I think what I am trying to penetrate is an unnamed zone of knowing, which is somehow personal and private and idiosyncratic in character; it is a precognitive mode of awareness, which differs almost from individual to individual and which actually shapes and edits the significance of other knowledge—empirical or intuitive—later gathered in by the individual.

In an earlier time, we used to speak of something called "the sociology of knowledge." This concept had vague reference to the ways in which time and place have an effect on what is considered to be truth. What I am reaching for here is something we might dub "the *psychology* of knowledge." We are discovering that knowing is a very personal act and that there is a tacit, private component in every assertion that "Such and such is true." This thesis has been spelled out with great persuasion by Michael Polanyi in his book *Personal Knowledge* (1964). It has been extended, with her characteristic brilliance, by Marjorie Grene in *The Knower and the Known* (1966). Now the argument is coming home to haunt the American university, dedicated for so long to the impersonal, antiprivate, generic-prone quest for what Paul Goodman has called "objective consciousness."

As this phenomenological argument returns home to the university, it hits teacher education first, since the preparation of teachers stands in that precarious region between the social and behavioral sciences on the one hand and the real world of phenomenological reality on the other. We are thus caught between the classical requirements of the university—reason, disinterested criticism, and impersonal and opinion-free knowledge—and the as yet unmanageable requirements of idiosyncratic or at least subcultural phenomenology.

Phenomenology and Teacher Education

What is the contemporary college of education going to do about all this? For one thing, in the shaping of our discipline we must gradually turn away from heavy reliance on the conventional forms of social and behavioral science. There is, as we all know, a coordinate upheaval in these sciences right now; the political scientists, the sociologists, the anthropologists, the psychologists regularly make the headlines at their national conventions nowadays when they shout and rage at each other over how their discipline should be studied. It is possible that out of this collision of methodologies will emerge new tools of understanding, which can eventually be adopted by those of us in the study of education.

But beyond this long-range hope for a solution, there lie only the more immediate, pragmatic, managerial kinds of accommodations to the problem. One of them is the tactic of simply purchasing these elusive phenomenologies on the open market; that is, through the employment of what amounts to an "ethnic in residence." If you need the black perspective articulated in your work, you name more black professionals to your staff. If you need the Latin or American Indian or Oriental phenomenology, then you acquire a walking compendium of that phenomenology in the form of a Latin or an Indian or an Oriental scholar. Their role is explained to them: "We want no 'house niggers' or 'coconuts' here. Rather, we want you to educate the faculty in the phenomenologies you represent. Sit in our committee meetings and faculty meetings, and when you see either subtle ethnocentrism or pernicious institutional racism at work, point it out to us. Our own phenomenologies have never included these awarenesses, and we want to learn and grow in our comprehension of these perceptions."

More often than not, the ethnic response to this summons is unfriendly. "We will not," they say, "be used as institutional therapists or in-service educators of your faculty. The white man's racism is his problem, not ours. So go educate yourself, and leave us alone to get on with our work with our own people."

Although this rejoinder has a plausible ring to it and springs from motivations we could certainly anticipate, it is not an answer we can settle for. Admittedly, we in teacher education must now do lots of homework in what might be called "phenomenological literature." This includes not only the specifically philosophical modes of phenomenological analysis represented by the work of Polanyi and Grene, referred to above, but also the more psychological and sociological treatments to be found in Eldridge Cleaver's *Soul on Ice* (1968), Vine DeLoria's *Custer Died for Your Sins* (1969), and Kenneth B. Clark's *Dark Ghetto* (1965). Also, we need to study the forecasts implicit in such works as Charles Reich's *The Greening of America* (1970) and Theodore Roszak's *The Making of a Counter Culture* (1969). In these more popular arguments, we seek the emergence essentially of a new kind of knowledge; there is, so to speak, a crunching forward in the American consciousness of a new state of awareness concerning the meaning of the American experience. This new consciousness has no basis in science or art or religion or politics. It is just a new and fresh way of looking at things. It does not matter whether it has been triggered by an excessive bureaucratic technology, or racial injustice in urban areas, or the endless slaughter in Vietnam. What does matter is that this new consciousness is a way of encountering truth, and, as such, it is an imperative subject of study for the American university.

It is an understatement to say that the contemporary university is quite unprepared for this new epistemology. We have lived so long on a diet of objective truth and have been punished so persistently for allowing personal opinion and idiosyncratic outlook to creep into our investigations that we are understandably gun-shy of any appeal to drop our guard. Indeed, the passion for objectivity is its own phenomenology, a special form of fanaticism in the American mind; we have grown so accustomed to it that we can hardly see its virtually religious power over us. No medieval serf believed any more strongly in the overpowering hegemony of God than we do in the total hegemony of science.

The university is thus caught in the vise of change. If it wishes to continue to function in society as a generator of new knowledge and as a delivery system for that knowledge, then it must somehow come to terms with a zone of knowing which it has never been asked to explore. But to do so, it is required to repudiate some of its own traditions and principles. More especially, it is required to lay those traditions and principles open to public criticism. It must question its emotionally held dogma: objective, depersonalized truth.

Can the university take this courageous step? And can it accommodate the new social requirement to humanize its knowledge? There is an outside chance that it can, and assistance may arise from an unlikely quarter. Of all the specialties on the American campus, the field of education may provide the most probable vehicle for facilitating this transition. Education is the study of the bridge *between* truth and persons. Teaching and learning are phenomena of linkage. We do not study knowledge; nor do we study persons. Our task is to understand and to explain what happens when knowledge and the person are brought together. Our work is preeminently dependent upon the knowledge-generating departments; but it is also preeminently dependent upon the world of real persons beyond the university, young and old, in school and out, whose lives can be enlarged and enriched by learning.

We may be able to say something to the departments about how a person responds to their truth, how he assimilates it to his own life and makes it a part of him. But we may also be able to say something to boys and girls in our schools and men and women in our colleges about how knowledge and understanding are generated and how a personal response to that knowledge is not possible until serious attention is given to its objective substance.

Faculties in education may thus find themselves at the fulcrum of a new educational epoch. With one foot in objective scholarship and the other in the human encounter, they may become brokers for a new enlightenment in higher learning. It is a disquieting but flattering summons.

References

CLARK, K. B. *Dark Ghetto.* New York: Harper & Row, 1965.

CLEAVER, E. *Soul on Ice.* New York: McGraw-Hill, 1968.

DE LORIA, V. *Custer Died for Your Sins.* New York: Macmillan, 1969.

GRENE, M. *The Knower and the Known.* New York: Basic Books, 1966.

MORRIS, V. C. "Is There a Metaphysics of Education?" *Educational Theory,* 1967, *17,* 141–146.

POLANYI, M. *Personal Knowledge.* New York: Harper Torchbooks, 1964.

REICH, C. *The Greening of America.* New York: Random House, 1970.

ROGERS, C. "Toward a Science of a Person." In T. W. Wann (Ed.), *Behaviorism and Phenomenology.* Chicago: University of Illinois Press, 1964.

ROSZAK, T. *The Making of a Counter Culture.* Garden City: Doubleday, 1969.

WANN, T. W. (Ed.) *Behaviorism and Phenomenology.* Chicago: University of Illinois Press, 1964.

CHAPTER 24

The Principle of *Heimat* in European Urban Education

Hans A. Schieser

The theme of an "urban crisis" and "urban education" appears nowadays in so many discussions and publications that one may almost see it as the *leitmotiv* of contemporary education. The problem is not so new, however. The histories of philosophy and education suggest that the city has been a problem for man at all times. (Here we can use the word *problem* in its original Greek meaning: "something that is thrown at me.") It seems that our urban problems—crowded cities, crime and violence, ghettos and social tensions, ignorance and exploitation—were present in Babylon, Rome, and in the medieval cities. These lines from Sallust, for example, written about 1,900 years ago, might well have been written by a contemporary writer: "Ever since the city fell under the sway of a few powerful men . . . all influence, rank, and wealth have been in their hands. To us they have left danger, defeat, prosecutions, poverty. What have we left save only the breath of life?" Similar complaints appear in Hammurabi's *Codex* (c. 2100 B.C.) and in other recordings of antiquity. Along with their descriptions of the problems, the ancient writers also suggested possible solutions. Some pointed to the responsibility of parents and educators; others challenged the authorities of the cities to do something about the misery. In fact, both educators and political authorities have tried to remedy the problem—the educators with a variety of philosophies and curricula, and the politicians with programs and subsidies. In the meantime, however, things have grown worse. Perhaps all the approaches so far have not been "radical" enough; that is, they have not got at the real roots of the problems.

What are the roots of our "urban problems"? The answer to this question may lead as far back as the beginning of the city itself, when man chose to abandon the nomad life and settle together at safe and good places. With this decision, we have immediately the awareness of belonging together. Ortega y Gasset (1930) and Toynbee (1967) point to this philosophical dimension, which makes the close settlement into a corporate social life, a consciousness which has been handed over to all the following generations living in cities. We may not see much of this closeness left in the American city-dweller who chooses to live in the city for its opportunities and who never lives there long enough to develop the feeling of belonging, but it is still visible in Europe, where people are not only more stable than Americans but also are proud of belonging to a particular city. It is not the opportunity but the privilege that determines this awareness. In contrast to the peasant who struggles with nature's whims, the city-dweller from childhood has achieved some freedom from this task. Education, for example, has handed over to the young generations of the cities the collective experience of urban life. In other words, the people of the city have not been concerned exclusively with the tasks of survival and wrestling with the forces of nature but also with the building of a culture, a structure of a world that transcends nature, while the peasants outside have been tied down to the earth and to the whims and forces of nature, which occupy them for all their lives.

Looking at contemporary situations in our American cities we see the set-back into preurban times: man struggles for survival even in the cities and the main concern of our schools seems to become more and more to enable the young to survive. We find hardly any awareness of belonging together and belonging to a city among our young generation. Crime and violence are symptoms of a rootlessness and alienation not unlike those of the barbarian hordes that invaded the early cities.

It is true that the same problems appear now in some of the European cities as well. To be exact, they have existed at all times, but educators and politicians have recognized much more where the roots are than we seem to do. In the eighteenth century, Rousseau (1762) pointed out that the "unnatural life" in the cities leads man into corruption. He proposed a return to nature, away from the cities, which he saw as the "graves of mankind, as men are not meant to live in ant hills, piled up one above the other!" His Emile was to be educated so that he felt at home in nature. Pestalozzi, picking up this idea, was more realistic as to a "natural life." He held it impossible to return; the city was meant to be man's home and must be made into such a home. His concept of *Heimat* gave direction to European education and made it truly urban in terms of considering urban problems at its roots.

Pestalozzi saw that all the tensions and crime in the cities come from rootless people who are denied or deprived of the basic human need to have a place where one belongs. The German concept of *Heimat* denotes this "place," which we must, however, conceive in a much wider meaning than a "home" or "homeland." It is not limited to the geographical givens but comprises the whole spectrum of human existence: nature and culture, work and leisure, language and traditions, the concrete and the transcendent. When Pestalozzi proposed that education be based on this basic need of man, he saw the masses of people flocking into cities to seek the opportunities of work and freedom. Their aim was not to work only—they had to work under the yoke of their feudal lords before—but to have freedom. They wanted to live their own lives, have families and decent places to live. The schools were meant to gear their objectives to these needs, and we can still see this idea underlying most of European education at both the elementary and the secondary levels: "The main objective of education is to educate youth in the love of the people and the homeland (*Heimat,*) toward moral and political responsibility, vocational and social accountability, and a democratic attitude" (*Verfassung von Baden-Württemberg,* 1953, Article 12.1).

The arguments that such an emphasis on the *Heimat* may lead to "provincialism" or even nationalism seem to be justified by the presence of these symptoms in most European countries. However, there is not much of an alternative in education. Erik Erikson, a psychologist, points to the necessity of having an "ideology" in order to

find identity. This ideology is nothing else than the pattern of concen-
tric circles on which education is based; the child's first world—the
home—expands into the larger horizons of a city, a country, and eventually the whole world, while, at the same time, the *Heimat* remains
a firm point of reference. However critical a person may become of the
native culture, he always identifies himself with basic ideas and values
formed in his early childhood.

The school cannot ignore this fact in its attempts to lead a child
into the world. We see this aspect again in the European schools and
their curriculum: "It is the purpose of the schools to lead the children
from the free and playful encounter of things to a purposeful attitude
toward work. The school arouses and develops the children's potential
by interaction with the objects of their everyday environment and by
their manifold observations of the spatial and spiritual *Heimat*"
(*Bildungsplan für die Volksschulen Baden-Württembergs*, 1958, Pre-
amble). For many children, this "everyday environment" is the city.
The school is part of this world, and the teachers are responsible for
making it into something that is not alien to the child. When many of
our children look at the school with hostility and when so many of
them drop out of school or vandalize the buildings and classrooms,
their behavior is only a symptom of their alienation. Broken windows
and open hatred of the schools are rare in European cities.

It is true that European cities generally are not large and still
retain the unity that originally characterized cities: people live and
work in them; the downtown districts are not deserted after working
hours; and the residential areas are not places of emptiness and bore-
dom, as they often are in suburbia. The schools thus belong to the
neighborhood, and children can walk to school instead of being bused
in from far away. (Only recently have socialist governments in Western
European states consolidated some of these neighborhood schools. This
collectivization has very often gone over the heads of protesting parents
and educators who insisted that the school belongs in the neighborhood.)

It is remarkable to see even Soviet education being geared to
the principle of *Heimat*. The success of Anton Semionovich Makarenko's efforts to integrate gangs of juvenile delinquents into society
through his workers' colonies seems to prove that even in a totalitarian
setting urban education cannot ignore the fundamental needs of man.
The philosophy of the Soviet educator is essentially the same as Don
Bosco's, who offered a "home" and the "spirituality of a Christian
community" to the young delinquents and orphans of Italy in the last
century. His schools and Boys Towns all over the Western world have

served as models for a successful urban education. (It is hard to understand why Father Flanagan's Boys Town in the United States has found so little imitation, especially as it seems to be no less successful than all the Boys Towns elsewhere in the world.)

The most interesting attempt to solve the urban problems through education is the Pestalozzi Children's Village Trogen in Switzerland. Youngsters from all over the world are educated in this "town," as they are brought from the troubled cities of war-ridden countries. Each nationality has a house where the mother language and original culture of the children's *Heimat* characterize the atmosphere. All children attend the central school, however, where German is the official language (Trogen lies in the German-speaking part of Switzerland), but French and Italian, the other languages of the country, are learned. The curriculum is not much different from that of any other school, but the whole setting aims at the development of the awareness of belonging which "automatically" prevents the attitudes and the behavior that cause trouble in our cities.

Recent developments in the metropolitan areas of the continent seem to be leading to the same problems that America has encountered in the last hundred years. In Western Germany, for example, masses of foreign workers have come to the cities to find work and make money, but not to live there. Wherever urban authorities succeed in "integrating" these guest workers, as the Germans call them, there is less tension and none of the typical symptoms of rootlessness, like delinquency and violence. On the other side, there is trouble as soon as these foreign workers are crammed together in makeshift living quarters and so-called ghettos. Here, one can see most clearly how urban problems arise from the roots of alienation and frustration. Whenever people move into a city from outside, they are faced with the given facts of an established structure. How much they grow into this structure and make it their own eventually determines their behavior and attitudes. Just as a child who enters the world inexperienced and helpless, the adults need help in this stage of being newcomers.

Here it does not help for schools to provide classes in civics and other political enlightenment. Concrete knowledge of how to live in a city, of how to make use of the facilities, of rights and duties is the first-aid measure schools must offer. This knowledge is, in fact, part of the regular curriculum of all European elementary schools. In most countries there are also classes for adults in the "people's high schools," which originated in Denmark when social problems were most intense. (Nicolay Frederik Severin Grundtvig, the founder of the people's

high school, may be regarded as the "Pestalozzi of adult education.")
The influence of these institutions upon the solution of urban problems
cannot be overestimated. They have provided a continuing education
for thousands and thus made them employable in the cities, and they
have sped up the integration of newcomers into the urban world.

In our attempts to solve the problems that trouble our cities,
we may have spent too much time on peripheral factors. American
cities are unique in that they were founded not so much by people who
wanted to live together as by those who sought opportunities. While
the early cities were characterized by a unity of life and work, the
frontier cities of America were everything but such a unity. We cannot
return to the beginning and get a new start, but we have to get at the
foundations of urban existence: the will and ability to live together.
The latter can be acquired through learning and experience, but the
former comes by decision of the individual. Unless people will to live
together in peace and work together in their cities, all educational efforts
are in vain. The experience of the cities in Europe may teach us that
people will so decide when they find themselves at home in their cities.
Education in the families and in the schools can and does contribute
to this end.

References

*Bildungsplan für die Volksschulen Baden-Württembergs (Official Cur-
riculum for Elementary Schools)*. Stuttgart: Kultusministerium,
1958.

GRUNDTVIG, N. F. S. *Udvalgte Skrifter (Works)*. Kopenhagen, 1904–1910.
10 vols.

MAKARENKO, A. S. *Werke*. (German edition). Berlin: Volkseigener Verlag, 1956–1962. 8 vols.

ORTEGA Y GASSET, J. *La Rebelión de las Massas*. Madrid, 1930.

PESTALOZZI, J. H. "The Evening Hour of a Hermit." In R. Ulich (Ed.),
Three Thousand Years of Educational Wisdom. Cambridge,
Mass.: Harvard University Press, 1965.

ROUSSEAU, J. J. *Émile*. Amsterdam: Jean Néaulme, 1762.

SALLUST, C. C. *De Coniuratione Catilinae*.

SHEPPARD, L. C. *Don Bosco*. Westminster, Md.: Newman Press, 1957.

TOYNBEE, A. (Ed.) *Cities of Destiny*. New York: McGraw-Hill, 1967.

Verfassung von Baden-Württemberg (Constitution). Stuttgart: Klett
Verlag, 1953.

PART **VII**

Concluding
Perspectives

I n this final section, Robert J.
Havighurst, the urban educational scholar, capsulizes and assesses the
present-day crisis in urban education. His review of current literature
on the subject shows that much is helpful but not necessarily valid or
reliable. He acknowledges that schools have apparently failed to bring
about equality of educational opportunity, but he notes that this failure is not synonymous with equality of educational achievement. He
analyzes factors that bring about achievement and focuses upon the
diverse clientele which the schools must serve. He suggests procedures
that can help to minimize conflict and achieve an equitable, viable,
flexible, and variegated urban educational system.

We live in an age in which rapid and complex changes are a
certainty. Professor Havighurst believes that the urban educational
scene, though grim, is not hopeless, since our crucial problems can be
resolved. The experimentation and experiences of the past decade
make it possible to take massive forward measures to improve urban

schooling. Human variability and potentiality can be maximized to effect needed educational reform.

Next to excellence is the appreciation of it. In this spirit, the editors have included a biographical profile of the man in whose honor the present volume has been written and whose pursuit of excellence for educational concerns has been exemplified in the areas of research, service, and leadership.

CHAPTER 25

Crisis in Urban Education

Robert J. Havighurst

𓆩𓆪𓆩𓆪 𓆩𓆪𓆩𓆪 𓆩𓆪𓆩𓆪 𓆩𓆪𓆩𓆪 𓆩𓆪𓆩𓆪 𓆩𓆪

$\mathbf{W}$hen we look at what has happened in big-city education since 1965, we see two contrasting pictures —both accurate. On the one hand, we see a set of massive, bureaucratic school systems responding ineffectually to the pressures of rapid social change in our cities. They are being criticized analytically by social scientists, venomously by anarchists, frantically by desperate parents, coldly by teachers' unions, and passionately by young educators. On the other hand, we see a growing number of research and development efforts, creative and solidly supported by systematic evaluation, which are building the base for an educational program that promises within the next decade substantially to eliminate the widespread educational retardation of children and youth in the big cities.

The educational problem of the big cities is more complicated today than it was ten years ago, partly because the cities are worse off. At the same time, the situation is more favorable to a successful solution than it was ten years ago. The educational situation is more

This chapter is adapted from a keynote address presented at the DePaul University colloquium, *Crisis in Urban Education,* held in Chicago on November 13, 1970.

complicated because the disadvantaged minority groups have demanded a voice in decision making; the teachers' organizations have demanded a voice in determining educational policy and practice; and the professional educators and the educational "establishment" have been placed on the defensive. The educational situation is more favorable because there is public concern, money for attacks on the problem, and some five years of recent active and imaginative experimentation with possible solutions.

Inner-city school problems are one large part of the "crisis of the cities," which is our domestic plague of the 1970s. This problem has very nearly demoralized some public school systems. The major sources of dissatisfaction with the schools are two quite different ones.

First, there is the low school achievement of many children of poor families—white, black, Spanish surname, American Indian, Appalachian. These children have streamed into the schools of the big cities, as their parents have moved to the big cities since 1950 in search of better incomes and better living arrangements. These same groups of children had equally low school achievement, or even lower, before they came to the big cities, but they were not so visible in rural areas. Now, crowded into slum schools and making up as much as 30 to 50 per cent of the enrollment of big-city school systems, these groups produce a small but troublesome number of hostile students, on the one hand, and apathetic students, on the other hand, to make the task of teaching in these schools especially difficult. And the parents of these students, as well as the parents of the average students in these schools, are disgruntled and critical of the schools.

Second, there is the claim that the schools are making middle-class youth into sheeplike supporters of the status quo in the American society, instead of intelligent, critical individuals who will improve the society and create their own individual life styles. This claim is made by a number of people with basic philosophies variously called "romantic," "anarchic," or "individualist"—the dissenters and gadflies always found in a society that permits or encourages free speech. Their criticism is repeated by a small but vocal minority of middle-class students and parents.

Different as these criticisms are, they share a common target—the public school system. One group of critics blame the schools for not bringing all socioeconomic and ethnic groups to the same average level of school achievement. The other group of critics blame the schools for making students too much alike—too similar in their attitudes and values and their acceptance of the status quo.

This tendency to blame the schools when young people disappoint their parents or some social critics can lead to such serious consequences that it requires careful analysis by people who want to understand what the schools can and should do in our society.

In a democratic society, which prides itself upon offering equal opportunity to all children, it is a disappointment when the children of low-income families, as a group, achieve below the level of the rest of the children. Even though the children of low-income families get as many days of school as middle-class children, in classes the same size, and with teachers of the same level of training and experience, a thoughtful person is likely to say that there is some inequality of opportunity unless there is equality of school achievement. Thus, a number of critics are now saying that *equality of opportunity* is present only when there is *equality of achievement* among various groups in the society; and they add that the school system should be held responsible for securing equality of school achievement.

However, we know enough about school achievement to be able to say with certainty that such achievement depends on four factors: (1) *The person himself*—his innate biological equipment for learning plus his aspirations and expectations for himself. Since individuals show a normal distribution of learning ability, within a definable social group we expect wide individual differences. But we expect the averages of various groups to be equal. That is, we generally assume that there is no genetic difference in learning ability between social and ethnic groups, though this proposition has not been fully proved. However, the person's expectations of himself, and his values and attitudes, partially determine his school achievement. (2) *The family*. Research of the past decade has shown that experience within the family contributes to the child's mental, social, and moral development. (3) *The neighborhood and community*. The neighborhood tends to determine the playmates of the child and the kinds of adults he meets outside of his family. The local community provides churches, libraries, museums, theaters, clubs. The community, extending out to the city and the region, may have customs and prejudices and laws which determine the jobs he may expect, the financial assistance he may get, and the adult roles he may aspire to. If the society has social classes or tribes or clans, these are considered a part of the community. (4) *The school system*. Whether the children of a group do well or poorly in school, the cause of their performance lies in some combination of all four factors. Thus, one child may do very well in academic performance because his family, church, local community, and self-concept all work on his behalf although he has a mediocre school, while another child in a very good school may do poorly because the other factors are poor.

With these considerations in mind, it is evident that the schools cannot usefully be blamed or credited with the level of academic achievement of the children of a community unless the quality of the other factors is taken into account. Nevertheless, the school can partially compensate for low quality or inadequacy of the other factors and must be used by society for this purpose if the society hopes to achieve equality of opportunity. We do not know how far this compensation can go. We believe certain forms of compensatory schooling can be very valuable for economically or socially disadvantaged children.

As educators concerned with making the school system contribute as much as possible, we need to study and understand these other factors, to study their interaction with the school system, to experiment with ways of making the school factor more influential. At the same time, we can usefully point to the noncontribution made by the researchers and the critics who tell us that the schools are failing in their function if any social group of children performs below the national average. Unless the schools can make up completely for the disadvantages of such children caused by family poverty, family disorganization, neighborhood blight, and community isolation, we must expect some groups to achieve on the average below the national average. Therefore, it appears to be an extreme position for a serious student of education to argue that a school system should be expected to make up completely for the other disadvantages.

Yet this is what several of the contemporary "revisionist" critics of public education appear to be saying. For example, Greer (1972, p. 3) says: "Every school child and certainly every education major learns the same heart-warming story about the history of our public schools. The public school system, it is generally claimed, built American democracy. It took the backward poor, the ragged, ill-prepared ethnic minorities who crowded into the cities, educated and Americanized them, and molded them into the homogeneous productive middle class that is America's strength and pride. But that story is simply not true."

I think this a most naive statement about what education students and teachers are taught concerning education. In a little book published in 1944 (Warner, Havighurst, and Loeb, 1944), I and others pointed out that children of low-income families do poorly in school and suggested that school people were not sufficiently aware of their biases and prejudices toward such children.

In his book, Greer goes on to argue that the great increase of high school enrollments after about 1920 did not contribute to the occupational and material achievement of pupils. "The assumption that extended schooling promotes greater academic achievement or social mobility is, however, entirely fallacious. School performance seems consistently dependent upon the socioeconomic position of the pupil's family. For example, of high school graduates who rank in the top fifth in ability among their classmates, those whose parents are in the top socioeconomic status quartile are five times more likely to enter graduate or professional schools than those of comparable ability whose parents fall in the bottom quartile" (p. 109). We can leave it to the historians of education to argue with Greer and other revisionists as to whether the historians have been adequately aware of the facts concerning the school achievement of children of poor families and of ethnic and racial minorities. Sociologists of education have known these facts and published them quite fully throughout this century.

Some children of poor and immigrant and black families have made full use of the schools to get ahead and become upwardly mobile. School performance is correlated with family socioeconomic status with a correlation coefficient only of the order of 0.4, which means that a good many pupils of low socioeconomic status do quite well in school. For them, schooling does promote social mobility. Nevertheless, the schools have not performed the very difficult task of bringing the average of all ethnic-minority and lower-class children up to the national average. It is too much to expect. Whether the schools have done as much as could reasonably be expected is a question over which people will argue endlessly. But the schools should attempt to do as much as they possibly can.

A useful proposition about the relation of achievement in society to school achievement goes something like this: All achievement in American society depends on the four factors described above; the school systems should be operated to assist children of all social and ethnic groups and especially to help children of socially and economically disadvantaged groups to compensate for their disadvantages stemming from the other three factors.

Schools have done this to some extent for black students during the past three decades. There has been an enormous rise in the social and economic status of Negroes as a group since 1940, resulting from change in community attitudes and opportunities as well as from education. Racial discrimination in the labor market has been reduced, many middle-class occupations have been opened more freely to blacks, and civil rights laws have been passed. In this changing situation, the educational system has become increasingly relevant to social mobility for Negroes and has provided the skills and knowledge that many young blacks are now using to achieve middle-class status.

With a reasonably balanced and objective view of what the school system can contribute to the all-round education of American youth, it becomes possible to look critically at urban education today and to see ways in which the schools can do their part of the job more effectively. One thing we can do, as urban educators, is to recognize the existence and the validity of a number of interest groups which compete for the attention of the school system:

Inner-city parents. Knowing that their children are not doing well in school, inner-city parents are asking for more and better schooling. Some of them also ask for help in getting their children ready and eager to perform well in school.

Ethnic groups. Blacks, Puerto Ricans, Mexican Americans, American Indians, Appalachian whites, and other groups, all disadvantaged by poverty, are organizing and demanding influence or power in their local schools.

Established working-class groups. In every big city there are sections of the city populated by working-class groups who have achieved a stable, relatively high-level standard of living, anchored in home ownership. Most of them came from earlier waves of immigration—Irish, Scandinavians, Poles, Italians. For these "hard-hat" groups, the local neighborhood school is a precious possession. They find their way of life threatened by the push of the more recent ethnic groups into their residential areas and by the pressure of the school administration to achieve racial integration in the neighborhood school.

Upper-middle-class parents. This influential group of parents tends to split into two subgroups. One of the subgroups wants high academic standards to prepare children well for the competition of entrance to selective colleges. The other subgroup wants a curriculum and extracurricular activities to encourage and help children to become active participants in movements for social justice or for contemporary art and music.

Students—hostile or alienated. Especially in the high schools, there are groups of students, brought together by a common interest or a common complaint, who put pressure on the faculty for such things as new courses in ethnic studies; assemblies to honor ethnic-group heroes; more teachers of certain ethnic groups; the right to hair styles and clothing styles of their choice; the right to publish student papers free of censorship.

Teachers' organizations. The teachers' organizations have naturally asked not only for higher salaries but also for influence and power over decisions about the assignment and transfer of teachers, about the curriculum, and about working conditions. As they see parent groups organizing to exert power, they seek a countervailing power, to be used if they think it necessary.

Administrators and supervisors. The bureaucracy that operates a school system is interested in making it run smoothly and efficiently. Though not averse to innovation, it has a considerable amount of inertia that resists change.

These interest groups have a right to be heard. Their wishes and demands are generally legitimate, though often in conflict with the wishes of other groups. The decision makers—the people in power in the educational system—have to keep the system responsive to the interest groups. They must avoid the opposite evils of, on the one hand, rigid authoritarian policy and, on the other, a kind of paralysis which is unable to make decisions or to respond to practical issues. The successful system is a flexible, variegated system which maximizes the options in an atmosphere of experimentation with objective evaluation. This system is open to change based on evaluated experience. And it gives each interest group as much freedom of action as possible without interfering with the rights and the freedom of other groups.

There are some ways to maximize the options and to obtain and maintain flexibility. There are also some ways to reduce the options and reduce flexibility.

In general, it appears that the desirable flexibility is *not* gained in a big-city educational system by cutting up the school district into semiautonomous smaller districts. Such a procedure inhibits the achievement of goals that depend on cooperation of the parts of a complex urban-metropolitan system. In addition, flexibility is *not* obtained by assigning students or teachers to schools, or to courses or programs within a school, by rules that permit no exceptions. While some grouping of students by ability is desirable, it need not be completely arbitrary. Bussing to achieve racial integration in a school is often desirable, but there probably should be an option which permits every student to attend the school nearest his home if he wishes to do so. Finally, flexibility is *not* obtained by hiring outside agencies to operate a school program and paying fees based on test scores of the students. Such a practice is almost certain to result in the imposition of a system aimed at achieving specific goals and ignoring other essential goals of a school. It should be possible to employ outside agencies to demonstrate the effectiveness of their methods without forcing them or the schools into a limiting pattern of objectives and methods.

How *is* flexibility obtained? The following five general procedures promise to keep the options open and to provide a vigorous program of internal improvement in large city public school systems.

First, *establish a sytem of local community participation in school affairs in disadvantaged local communities.* There has been an aggressive drive for greater participation and influence of poor and disadvantaged people in public education for the last seven years. This is sometimes called *decentralization,* though *local community influence* is a more accurate term for it.

> *We shall need a truly radical conception of decentralization, for what is involved in creating means by which principals and faculties can obtain from their communities, far more regularly than they now do, both their signals and their rewards.*
>
> *One way to bring this about would be to establish in every school a group of parents and other citizens to work with the principal and teachers . . . [to] advise the school staff on educational priorities and objectives, on curriculum development, and on the types of services most likely to aid the students. It could submit to the local board at least annually its appraisal of the school's success in meeting the problems the community considers important [Fischer, 1968, p. 16].*

School principals are now considering seriously and constructively how they can work with local school advisory boards in a number of cities. One of them, Herschel Rader, is a member of the Chicago Caucus of Inner-City Principals. He has written an article in which he proposes that each inner-city school have an advisory school-community council, with members named by the PTA, other parent groups, and local community groups. This proposal has been adopted and put into force in substantially the following form:

> *Every principal of an elementary school, middle school, and high school shall be instructed to notify his superior within two weeks of the names of the members of the school-community council for his school.*
>
> *At its first meeting, one week following the principal's notification to his superior, the council shall elect officers, including an executive committee of nine persons, no more than four nor less than three of which may be board of education employees. One member shall be the principal, another the delegate of the teachers' organization. [Members other than board of education employees] will be reimbursed for their time at some uniform rate.*

*A sum of money shall be allotted to the council to be spent
for the development, operation, and supervision of educational
programs as the council sees fit, provided no law, board rule, or
legal agreement (e.g., a union contract) is violated. This sum
is to be known as the Council Program Fund.*

*Cooperative arrangements may be worked out between
the councils of different schools or between the councils of elementary, middle, and high schools, concerning programs which
overlap in scope. Ad hoc joint committees may develop into
standing joint committees representing several councils which
would develop programs of mutual benefit. A council might even
be organized to include three or four school committees to use the
combined resources of all in developing programs for the combined unit.*

*The central administration shall retain control over the
certification and appointment of teachers and administrative
personnel and over the certification of nonprofessional personnel.
The local councils shall have the right to appoint nonprofessional
personnel from the centrally maintained pool. A continuing study
shall be conducted by the central administration of the feasibility
of transferring to local councils the power to appoint professional
personnel and civil service personnel (janitors and engineers)
from centrally maintained pools.*

*The central administration's auditing department shall
develop appropriate forms upon which all transactions of local
councils may be recorded and shall conduct periodic in-service
training sessions for financial officers of the councils.*

*The central administration shall retain control over all
capital outlays, but the local council shall have the power to
originate requests for capital expenditures to be included in the
annual line-item budget [Rader, 1969, pp. 194–201].*

Second, *establish within the school programs and methods that
pupils can understand and use for their own purposes.* The essential
element is the pupil's perception of the connection between what he
does in the classroom or in his schoolwork and a result that he wants.
When this condition is met, the pupil's ego can come into action to
guide his effort and reward his success. According to this view, the
pupil must accept the notion that he has hard work to do which will
require effort on his part in order to achieve the goal that he sees
clearly.

Programmed learning, when used skillfully, is an example. The
pupil accepts an assignment to learn a particular lesson or set of facts,
and he is informed immediately of every successful step he takes toward

this goal. Another example is the Mastery Program, which Benjamin Bloom has helped to work out in schools in Puerto Rico and is now ready for general use. The work assignments are divided into relatively small units, with frequent tests for mastery. The pupil works for the mastery of his assignment and keeps on working until he has demonstrated mastery. No matter how slow he is, compared with the rest of his class, he achieves mastery before going on to the next assignment. Bloom has found that the slow pupils move along much more rapidly than he had expected. Not only do pupils learn more effectively; they also come to enjoy learning: "The clearest evidence of affective outcomes is the reported interest the student develops in the subject he has mastered. He begins to like the subject and to desire more of it. To do well in a subject opens up further avenues for exploration of the subject. Conversely, to do poorly in a subject closes an area for further study. The student desires some control over his environment, and mastery of a subject gives him some feeling of control over a part of his environment. Interest in a subject is both a result of mastery of the subject [and] a cause of mastery" (Bloom, 1968, p. 4; see also Bloom, Hastings, and Madaus, 1970).

The successful innovative programs for students of high school age also contain this element of motivation toward a clearly understood goal. For example, the store-front academies that provide for high school dropouts a chance to prepare for the G.E.D. test, which will give them the equivalent of a high school diploma, probably are successful because they work with young people who have become convinced that they need more education and can see clearly the connection between their study in the store-front academy and the achievement of this goal. The Upward Bound and High Potential programs for disadvantaged high school and college youth, where they are successful, seem to combine the element of motivation with a clearly outlined program of study for a summer or a semester.

Third, *maintain a preschool program for disadvantaged children, followed by a primary school program built upon it*. This procedure has now been tried and proved successful in eight or ten different school systems. Disadvantaged children who have had one or two full years of preschool work have gained at least ten IQ points, have moved into the first grade ready to learn to read, and have maintained this level of learning ability to the third grade. These experimental programs need another year or two of continued evaluation, but it can now be said responsibly that several alternative preschool programs are available as models for city school systems to adopt and adapt. At the same time, no big-city system has yet put a really effective preschool program into effect. The country-wide evaluation of Head Start programs (made by Westinghouse Learning Corporation and Ohio University in the spring of 1969) showed that those programs on the average were not effective in helping children carry the gains made in Head Start on into the primary school grades. Thus, the big-city systems have this task yet to accomplish. They have federal government money available for substantial support of the program, and they have several successful experimental models to follow.

Fourth, *develop appropriate systems of rewards for school achievement by children of various subcultures.* The job of educating socially disadvantaged children will be done much better when educators understand more fully the nature of *rewards,* particularly their function in human learning, and apply this knowledge directly to their work with children and parents of socially disadvantaged children (Havighurst, 1970).

In the years since 1960, a number of psychologists have studied the nature of rewards in human learning. Among others, Zigler, Rotter, Katz, and Crandall have widened the field of research and have stimulated others to work in this field. What these people have in common is the following proposition: Human learning is influenced by a variety of rewards, which are themselves arranged in a culturally based *reward-punishment* system—a system that the individual learns. Reward systems might vary with social class or with ethnic subculture; and, in any social or cultural group, a child learns his reward system mainly in the family but also in the school and the peer group and the wider community.

On the basis of recent research on learning, there appear to be four major types of reward-punishment. The earliest, in terms of operation in human learning, is satisfaction or deprivation of physiological appetites—the physiological need for food and for pain avoidance. In this same category belong other material rewards, which arise later in physiological development, either through the maturation of the organism or through experience—such rewards as release of sexual tensions, toys and play materials, money, and perhaps power over other people. Next in order of appearance comes approval-disapproval from other persons, beginning with praise and reproof and expressions of affection and esteem from parents, and extending to approval-disapproval from others in the family, from adults such as teachers, and from age mates. Next comes the self-rewarding and self-punishing action of the child's superego, or conscience. This is extremely important, from the point of view of educational development, because it means that the child who has reached this level can become capable of pushing ahead with his own education without being stimulated and directed by his parents or his teachers or his peers. Finally comes the rewarding and punishing action of the ego, the executive function of the personality. This is more difficult to conceptualize as a source of reward or punishment. It is essential as a means of *anticipation* of future reward or punishment, success or failure, which will result as a consequence of an action performed now, in the present.

The following six propositions have received some research testing: (1) Different subcultures carry their children along this evolutionary path at different rates and in different ways. (2) There are differences between ethnic subcultures among disadvantaged groups in the reward systems they teach their children. (3) In general, external rewards (material as well as intangible) have positive values for disadvantaged or failing children. (4) An effective reward system in a complex changing society must be based on a strong ego. (5) A strongly developed ego gives a sense of personal control and personal responsibility for important developments in one's life. (6) People, by the time they reach adolescence, learn to operate at all the several levels of reward; and the level at which they operate varies with the action area.

With this partially confirmed theory about the education of disadvantaged groups, we can say that teachers will teach more effectively if they use a great deal of praise and numerous material rewards with disadvantaged children and if they put such order and consistency into the school setting that every child can see how to gain rewards for himself by making systematic efforts to learn in school.

Fifth, *develop a central school administration which relates the school system to other school and governmental systems in the metropolitan area.* What is most needed in big-city school districts is quite different from the administrative decentralization that has become a shibboleth in some circles. Admittedly, there are useful forms of administrative decentralization—specifically, those that delegate some decision-making power to regional or district superintendents who operate under a central administration and a single board of education. Thus, Chicago has three regional superintendents who have a good deal of autonomy under the central administration. However, the great need is for a single metropolitan-area authority, which finances the schools of the entire metropolitan area equitably and brings the various local school systems together for area-wide planning and research into area-wide problems.

The social and physical renewal of the cities should proceed with the fullest participation by the school system. The renewal of the cities should be a metropolitan-area operation, since the central city and the suburbs are in continual interaction, and anything that happens to the central city affects the suburbs and vice versa (see Havighurst and Levine, 1970).

In this discussion we have attempted to be realistic and positive. The educational situation in the big cities is grim—no doubt about it. But we have studied it and experimented with it for the better part of a decade, and we are now ready to take massive positive measures to improve it. These positive measures must be based on careful study and on scientific evaluation. We cannot solve the problems of urban education without searching out the truth and acting rationally on the basis of the truth. Numbers of people are trying to substitute emotion for reason in their sincere efforts to improve education. One can see the drive for "authenticity," "doing your thing," taking precedence in some people over the effort to find the truth and act rationally upon it.

Basic to the argument of this paper is the proposition that the educational system of the big cities is reasonably healthy and can respond effectively to the challenge of this complex urban situation. Strenuous efforts are necessary within this system, and men and women of devotion and drive are needed to make these efforts.

There are many different interest groups concerned about urban education—ethnic groups, economic groups, student groups, teachers' organizations, school administrators—and most of them have goals and desires which are valid in a democratic society. Yet their present proposals and demands seem often to be conflicting or impracticable. The perplexed and harried school administrator and school board find it impossible to fit these conflicting and often expensive proposals into a single, simple and rational program. In this situation we propose that the decision makers create more *options*— for pupils, parents, teachers, and administrators—within a metropolitan system that has a coherent set of educational goals and a structure that encourages cooperation among the parts, but permits wide latitude.

Given this kind of 'live and let live" policy, we believe that the decade of the 1970s will provide experience on the basis of which many disagreements of today will be resolved and a more coherent and generally satisfactory school program will emerge.

References

BLOOM, B. S. "Learning for Mastery." *Administrator's Notebook,* April 1968, *16*(8), 1–4.

BLOOM, B. S., HASTINGS, J. T., AND MADAUS, G. (Eds.) *Formative and Summative Evaluation of Student Learning.* New York: McGraw-Hill, 1970.

FISCHER, J. H. "Fischer on Decentralization." *Education News,* August 5, 1968, 16.

GREER, C. *The Great School Legend: A Revisionist Interpretation of American Public Education.* New York: Basic Books, 1972.

HAVIGHURST, R. J. "Minority Sub-Cultures and the Law of Effect." *American Psychologist,* 1970, *25,* 313–322.

HAVIGHURST, R. J., AND LEVINE, D. U. *Education in Metropolitan Areas.* (2nd ed.) Boston: Allyn and Bacon, 1970.

RADER, H. "Shared Control: An Interim Agreement." *Illinois Schools Journal,* Autumn 1969, *49,* 194–201.

WARNER, W. L., HAVIGHURST, R. J., AND LOEB, M. B. *Who Shall Be Educated?* New York: Harper and Row, 1944.

CHAPTER 26

Robert J. Havighurst: Pursuit of Excellence

Andrew T. Kopan

The educational career of Robert J. Havighurst was clearly influenced by the ideals of basic service and hard work that pervaded his home and family life. The son of a Methodist minister and a "very intelligent mother," Havighurst was born June 5, 1900, in DePere, Wisconsin, the oldest of five children. His father, a professor of history at Lawrence College in Appleton, Wisconsin, later left college teaching to become a Methodist minister. His mother was a graduate of Lawrence College in music. His paternal grandfather, Rudolph Havighörst, immigrated from Germany in 1849 and became an influential minister in the German Methodist Church.

Robert Havighurst attended public schools in Wisconsin and Illinois, and graduated from high school at Decatur, Illinois, in 1917. He attended Ohio Wesleyan University, earning his B.A. in chemistry in 1921. Immediately afterward, he entered Ohio State University as a graduate student and obtained his Ph.D. in physical chemistry in 1924. From 1924 to 1926, he pursued postdoctoral studies at Harvard University on a National Research Council fellowship.

Fortunately for the field of education, during 1926 a turn took place in Havighurst's career. While in Europe for a year of reflective study of European culture, he spent four months at the university town of Göttingen, Germany, and began to read widely in the areas of history and literature; his reading served as a catalyst for him to switch from atom and physical science research to college teaching.

At Miami University, Oxford, Ohio, where he was an assistant professor of chemistry from 1927 to 1928, he developed an interest in the history of science and was awarded a fellowship by the Carnegie Institute of Washington, D.C., to work with Professor George Sarton at Harvard. Just as he was ready to commence with this new work, he encountered Alexander Meiklejohn, Director of the new Experimental College at the University of Wisconsin, who asked Havighurst to join his staff as a physical scientist. Meiklejohn's influence led him eventually into experimental and progressive education.

During his sojourn at Wisconsin (as an assistant professor of physics from 1928 to 1932), Havighurst married Edythe McNeely, an instructor in physical education at Hunter College, and subsequently had five children, three girls and two boys.

In 1932–1934, Havighurst was back at Ohio State as an associate professor of science education. During 1934 he joined the staff of the General Education Board, one of the Rockefeller Foundations, as assistant director for general education. His expertise in science education enabled him to study high schools and colleges throughout the country. In 1937 he was appointed director for general education and supervised this part of the foundation's program. He also became responsible for administering the program of support for research in the field of child and adolescent development. This role led him into the literature of the field, and it was through the influence of Lawrence K. Frank that his interest in educational concerns grew both in depth and scope.

At the end of 1940, Havighurst left the General Education Board to become professor of education at the University of Chicago and executive secretary of the university's Committee on Human Development. Later, from 1949 to 1954, he served as chairman of this committee. His work at Chicago brought him into close contact with Daniel Prescott (head of the Center for Child Development, which operated under the joint auspices of the American Council on Education and the University of Chicago) and with W. Lloyd Warner (professor of sociology and anthropology and a member of the Committee on Human Development). Both of these men exercised an important influence on Havighurst's work and led him, along with Allison Davis and others, to commence a series of research studies in the field. Studies were conducted on child development in the community of Prairie City (Jonesville), and an extensive study of American Indian children was undertaken in collaboration with the U.S. Office of Education. Havighurst usually took the role of the psychologist, while the other researchers took the lead in the sociological and anthropological fields. These studies resulted in the publication of several books, written collectively with colleagues during the decade 1944–1954: *Who Shall Be Educated?* with Warner and Loeb (1944); *Father of the Man,* with Davis (1947); *Adolescent Character and Personality,* with Taba (1949); *Social History of a War-Boom Community,* with Morgan (1949); and *American Indian and White Children,* with Neugarten (1954). In addition, Havighurst and his colleagues co-authored two books on the process of aging: *Personal Adjustment in Old Age* (1949) and *The Meaning of Work and Retirement* (1954).

The concept of developmental tasks of children and adolescents as a means of understanding and applying human development to education was conceived and presented in a booklet entitled *Developmental Tasks and Education* (1949). Havighurst later expanded this idea in his book *Human Development and Education* (1953), one of his major and best-known contributions to education.

Toward the end of the 1940s Havighurst turned to international and comparative education. In the summer of 1947 he became a staff member of the first UNESCO seminar on education, held near Paris. The following year he worked intensively in Germany as an officer of the Rockefeller Foundation in charge of the social and educational rehabilitation of central Europe. In 1953 he spent a year as a Fulbright professor of education at the University of New Zealand in Christchurch, where he taught and conducted research on child development, subsequently publishing a book, *Children and Society in New Zealand.* He also spent two months studying the educational scene in Australia and South Africa.

These pursuits led him to Brazil between 1956 and 1958 on a UNESCO appointment as codirector of the Brazilian Government Center for Educational Research. He prepared a set of readings on society and education in Latin America for use in Latin American normal schools as well as in training South Americans for educational research.

In December 1959, in collaboration with the U.S. Department

of State, Professor Havighurst directed a University of Chicago seminar on higher education in the Americas. In 1961 Havighurst began a six-month assignment in South America—three months at the University of Buenos Aires, where he taught a research seminar on the sociology of adolescence; and three months in Brazil, where he worked in a teacher-preparation project under the auspices of the Brazilian Ministry of Education. Again the following year, he was a Fulbright visiting professor at the University of Buenos Aires and at the Brazilian Government Center for Educational Research at Rio de Janeiro and Sâo Paulo. During the fall of 1962 he served on a UNESCO appointment at the University of Sâo Paulo. While there, he visited the depressed areas of Brazil, advising staff on the project of Education in Favela. This project, which dealt with slum schools in Rio de Janeiro, was similar to the Great Cities School Improvement project supported by the Ford Foundation in the United States.

As evidenced by his work in South America, the 1950s saw a shift in Havighurst's interest from psychological toward sociological perspectives. In 1951, in a medium-sized United States city, Havighurst established a ten-year Community Youth Development Project. His role in this project was that of sociologist; his colleagues were psychologists. The first book reporting this project was published in 1961 under the title *Growing Up in River City*. During 1957, in cooperation with Bernice L. Neugarten, he published an important textbook, *Society and Education* (3rd edition, 1967), which marked his transition into the field of sociology of education. This shift of concern was evident in his Kappa Delta Pi lecture "American Higher Education in the 1960s." He had become interested also in the problems of juvenile delinquency, in the education of the gifted (in 1957 writing a book with Robert F. DeHaan, *Educating Gifted Children*), and in the organization of public schools to meet problems of social change in the central cities and the outlying suburbs of metropolitan areas.

The realization that many urban problems in education are premised on the existence of minority subcultures in American society prompted Professor Havighurst to write numerous journal articles, monographs, and books dealing with facets of education and subcultures. The latest has been his recently completed *Summary Report and Recommendations of the National Study of American Indian Education,* a three-year study financed by the U.S. Office of Education, which tested two thousand Indians—ages ranging from eight to twenty years, representing thirty-nine school systems. Psychological questionnaires were utilized to measure the Indian youths' self-esteem and their attitudes toward the future, their respective schools, their own ethnicity, and the white culture.

The early 1960s found Havighurst firmly grounded in the problems of urban education. Concerned with the oncoming crisis in urban education, he shifted his research and attention into seeking possible solutions to problems confronting large urban school systems. In 1960 he organized and taught the first course in urban education at the University of Chicago. In 1963 he was called upon by the Chicago Board of Education to make an appraisal of the problems confronting that city's schools. The survey, completed in 1964 and published under the title *The Public Schools of Chicago,* created much community interest.

In January of 1965, Havighurst joined the faculty of the University of Missouri at Kansas City, and served as Director of a new Center for the Study of Metropolitan Problems in Education. The center conducted intensive research on educational opportunities and problems of the nation's metropolitan areas. Similarly, a study of education and society in the Chicago metropolitan area was launched in 1965. Entitled "Interaction between Education and Society in Chicago" the project is being researched under the direction of Havighurst in collaboration with Robert L. McCaul of the University of Chicago. It attempts to bring the two disciplines of history and sociology to bear on a study of the impact of social forces upon education in the Chicago metropolitan area since 1925. The findings of this extensive research project are expected to be published soon.

During the academic year 1967–1968, Havighurst occupied the new John H. Mosler Chair in Urban Education at Fordham University in New York City. On the basis of his extensive research, he wrote *Education in Metropolitan Areas,* published by the National Society for the Study of Education in 1968. A revised edition, with Daniel Levine, appeared in 1970. In it they describe the evolution of the contemporary metropolitan social structure.

A major work in the study of big-city education is his *Profile of the Large City High School* (1970) and his *Four Hundred Losers: A Study of Delinquent Boys* (with Winton M. Ahlstrom, 1971). His work on the multifaceted issues in urban education has made him one of the outstanding authorities in this field. Indicative of his diverse interests in the extensive manifestations of educational problems, he published in 1965 *The Educational Mission of the Church* and in 1968 *Comparative Perspectives on Education;* in 1969 he published *Adjustment to Retirement: A Cross National Study* and *Brazilian Secondary Education and Socio-Economic Development.*

His numerous involvements did not curtail him from being active in the following roles: planning consultant to the Interprofessional Research Commission on Pupil Personnel Services; member of the editorial and production committee of the National Education Association's Project on Instruction; vice-president of the Citizens School Committee of Chicago; member of the board of the National Society for the Study of Education; and chairman of the Committee on Policy for Research and Training of the Gerontological Society, representing the society at congressional hearings on the proposed new Institute on Child Health and Human Development. In addition, he serves as a member of the editorial advisory committee for the *Phi Delta Kappan* as well as on the Phi Delta Kappan Commission on Work-Study Education.

One project has never been enough to engage the whole of his energies. He undertook the study of metropolitanism and urban educational problems at the same time he was surveying the fields of human development, social class and ethnic subcultures, comparative education, gerontology, and juvenile delinquency. His work in these areas has become a model for educational research, resulting in an invaluable collection of educational studies.

A notable quality of Havighurst has been the zest and happiness he has always brought to his work. At a time when scholarship—especially in education—is excessively solemn and painfully impersonal and statistical, he has radiated his own sense of excitement, delight in the richness of the intellectual life, and a resounding "Yes" to all the demands and challenges of educational problems that man can pursue.

Another underlying quality in Havighurst's writings, closely connected with his sensation of excitement, is a sense of compassion and urgency. To Havighurst, people are human beings with feelings and aspirations, not merely statistical data in surveys. They are poor people reaching for higher education, blocked by poverty or prejudice, or by an unyielding lock-step system; "culturally deprived" people seeking their place in the sun; people thwarted by the social-class structure in America; and youngsters who have gone wrong because of societal conditions beyond their control. This humane quality in his work is always tempered by his basic belief that people must exert themselves in a positive manner so that the ills of society can be resolved.

A third quality of his work is his innate habit of induction—beginning with the particular and moving toward the general, rather than taking refuge in generalities. With Havighurst it is the individual experiences that count and that, in the end, illuminate the experience of the race. This concern leads to general applications to educational problems.

His ability to look into the future and to anticipate emerging critical issues in education has marveled many of his colleagues. Frequently he has been one of the first to address himself to approaching critical problems. Such foresight has not hampered his ability to adjust his position at any time in the light of new research. When queried about this trait of flexibility, he responded that he has notably increased his belief in the importance of *rational institutions* in a complex changing society. As a result, he has become less interested in the child-centered or student-centered educational program of the progressives (he was an ardent "progressive educationalist" from 1930 to 1940). He does not, however, see this shift as a shift toward conservativism, since he does favor "radical change" in educational institutions and in socioeconomic policies in society.

In surveying the past productive thirty years, Havighurst identifies the following improvement and major failure in American education. With reference to improvement, of paramount importance has been the bringing of a large percentage of children and youth between the ages of three and twenty-three years into educational institutions. This had to be done, for better or worse, according to Havighurst. The major failure, for him, has been the inability to develop a constructive and satisfying program of education in the broad sense (including work and community service) for the least successful 30 per cent of adolescents in the academic school. This, he tells us with his usual foresight, will be the main *problem* in the decade 1970–1980.

Professor Havighurst envisions urban education in the 1970s as an essential element in the remaking of the American city by bringing together the central city and suburban community. At the same time, he cautions us, urban education must become humanized and turn more to the arts (dramatics, music, and graphic arts) and to the humanities for the curriculum of the elementary and secondary school.

However, top priority in rethinking theory and practice in urban education must be given to the concept that urban education needs must be planned and administered with the metropolitan area as the basic unit for financing, for teacher recruitment and assignment, though this may not be necessary for the administration of all schools in the area. This, he feels, will help alleviate many of the educational problems currently being experienced by large urban systems.

Professor Havighurst is grateful for the many colleagues who have been "extremely important" to him, as evidenced by the fact that many of his publications were written jointly. Among these are the

following: W. Lloyd Warner, Allison Davis, Daniel Prescott, Hilda
Taba, Bernice Neugarten, Ernest W. Burgess, Ralph Tyler, Robert
Peck, Robert DeHaan, Paul Bowman, Robert McCaul, Daniel Le-
vine, Elizabeth Allen Murray, Guy Manaster, and his wife, Edythe
Havighurst.

This *festschrift* volume of essays written by colleagues and
former students appropriately honors Professor Havighurst for his
"pursuit of excellence" and exemplary leadership. May it take its
modest place on the shelf beside Robert J. Havighurst's own writings
on education.

Name Index

325

Subject Index